American Dietetic Association

Easy
Gluten-Free

American Dietetic Association

Easy
Gluten-Free

Expert Nutrition Advice with
More Than 100 Recipes

Tricia Thompson, M.S., R.D.

Marlisa Brown, M.S., R.D., C.D.E., C.D.N.

WILEY

John Wiley & Sons, Inc.

Published by John Wiley & Sons, Inc., Hoboken, New Jersey
Published simultaneously in Canada

The information contained in this book is not intended to serve as a replacement for professional medical advice. Any use of the information in this book is at the reader's discretion. The author and the publisher specifically disclaim any and all liability arising directly or indirectly from the use or application of any information contained in this book. A health care professional should be consulted regarding your specific situation.

For general information about our other products and services, please contact our Customer Care Department within the United States at (800) 762-2974, outside the United States at (317) 572-3993 or fax (317) 572-4002.

Wiley also publishes its books in a variety of electronic formats. Some content that appears in print may not be available in electronic books. For more information about Wiley products, visit our web site at www.wiley.com.

Library of Congress Cataloging-in-Publication Data:

Thompson, Tricia.
    American Dietetic Association easy gluten-free : expert nutrition advice with more than 100 recipes / Tricia Thompson, Marlisa Brown.
        p. cm.
    Includes bibliographical references and index.
    ISBN 978-0-470-47609-3 (pbk.); ISBN 978-0-470-64398-1 (ebk);
    ISBN 978-0-470-64399-8 (ebk); ISBN 978-0-470-63500-1 (ebk)
    1. Gluten-free diet.   2. Gluten-free diet—Recipes.   I. Brown, Marlisa.
II. American Dietetic Association.   III. Title.   IV. Title: Easy gluten-free : expert advice on nutrition with more than 100 recipes.
    RM237.86.T55   2010
    641.5'638—dc22

                                                                        2010013925

Printed in the United States of America

10 9 8 7 6 5 4 3 2 1

For my dietitian colleagues who work so tirelessly on behalf of people with celiac disease and for all my fellow travelers on this gluten-free path. Here's to good health! —Trish

For those who have paved the road toward better understanding of celiac disease, for my grandparents, Charles and Rose Brown, who taught by example the importance of helping others, and for my mother and father, Anna and Stuart Brown, for their love—Marlisa

Contents

Foreword

by Shauna James Ahern

When I was first diagnosed with celiac sprue in 2005, my gastroenter-ologist spent four minutes explaining the gluten-free diet and how my life would have to change. I was then handed pamphlets containing old information. All vinegars besides malt vinegar are naturally gluten-free, but the literature informed me I should avoid anything with distilled vinegar. Bye-bye to mayonnaise and ketchup. Bakers running stalls at the Saturday farmers' markets assured me that their spelt breads were "low gluten," and therefore wouldn't leave my intestines in knots. They were wrong.

Determined to understand the disease that had been ruling my life for decades, I read every page on the Internet that contained the word "celiac." Back then, there weren't that many since awareness of the autoimmune disorder was still murky at best. I read postings on forums that warned of a life of deprivation and others that promised that breads made with white rice flour and nutritional yeast really didn't taste that bad. Hundreds of people longed for lists of candies they could suck on without worrying if they were safe. Many of the postings I read consisted of complaints and frowning emoticons. I made my way through it, but I didn't like the misinformation and the lack of positive attitude I kept finding.

I started my own Web site to write what I wished I could read: recipes for good food, detailed stories, and correct information about what gluten is and how to avoid it. My entire life has changed since I started writing "Gluten-Free Girl," and all for the better, so I don't regret it.

However, if I had just been able to read *American Dietetic Association Easy Gluten-Free* when I was first diagnosed, I might not have started my own Web site.

This comprehensive and friendly guide for those who are learning how to live gluten-free is filled with great information. For years nutrition consultants Tricia Thompson and Marlisa Brown have been helping other people to understand their diets and how food affects their health. Their passion for making life easier and richer for those who must avoid gluten shines through in this book.

The book begins with useful advice about finding gluten-free ingredients, reading labels to make sure you are safe, and how to avoid cross-contamination. Thompson and Brown have plenty of words of wisdom about foods that feed us nutritiously, as well as deliciously. They introduce readers to good gluten-free grains and how to cook them. They even have tips for how to live gluten-free on a budget.

Mostly, the book is packed with interesting gluten-free recipes such as Spiced Quinoa Cereal, Citrus Millet Muffins, Scallop and Arugula Salad, Dates Stuffed with Brie and Almonds, Smashed Cauliflower with Parmesan Amaranth, Flank Steak with Homemade Teriyaki Sauce, and Chocolate Buckwheat Crepes with Raspberry Ricotta Filling. I don't know about you, but I'm hungry.

American Dietetic Association Easy Gluten-Free shows that anyone living gluten-free can live a vibrant life, filled with flavor, with ease. It may have been hard for me to find good information and compelling recipes when I was first diagnosed, but if you are holding this book in your hands, your path will be much easier.

Preface

We wrote this cookbook to demonstrate just how easy it is to cook delicious, healthy gluten-free foods. The gluten-free recipes in this book focus on the types of foods that are important for all of us to eat, regardless of whether we must follow a gluten-free diet: whole grains, legumes, fruits, vegetables, fish, poultry, lean meat, and low-fat dairy.

We are both registered dietitians with decades of experience between us. We have dedicated our lives to helping individuals, especially those who must eat gluten-free, maintain healthy diets. We are very aware of the nutritional challenges unique to gluten-free diets. Gluten-free diets can be high in fat and low in carbohydrates, as well as low in other nutrients such as fiber, iron, and folate.

It is understandable that gluten-free diets may be somewhat unbalanced, especially at first. When you are newly diagnosed with celiac disease, dermatitis herpetiformis, or non-celiac gluten sensitivity, your top priority is simply to make sure the food you buy and prepare is free of gluten. Most likely, you are not thinking too much about nutrition. We will show you just how easy it is to choose gluten-free foods that are also healthy for you and the rest of your family.

With a little planning, gluten-free diets can be exceedingly healthy. One reason they sometimes aren't very nutritious has to do with the grains that are frequently used in gluten-free baking mixes, breads, breakfast cereals, and pasta. Many of these products rely on refined, unenriched rice and corn flour, as well as starches such as tapioca, potato, corn, and rice. Unfortunately, these refined flours and starches provide little in the way of nutrition.

If you follow a gluten-free diet, you are exposed to very nutritious grains that most people have never heard about, never mind eaten, such as amaranth, buckwheat, quinoa, sorghum, millet, teff, and wild rice. This cookbook will show you how easy it is to incorporate them into your meals.

How to Use This Book

This book provides not only recipes but also advice on following a gluten-free diet. Chapter 1 includes extensive information on label reading to help ensure that the foods you buy are free of gluten. Chapter 2 focuses on essential nutrients you need for a healthy diet. Chapter 3 explains gluten-free whole grains and demystifies the less common ones—identifying what they are and where to buy them, and explaining how to use them.

The recipes are grouped in traditional categories: breakfast, breads, soups and salads, starters, sides, main courses, and sweet somethings. Each section is also divided into quick and easy gluten-free and creative gluten-free recipes.

Following a gluten-free diet can be a rich and satisfying lifestyle. There are so many new tastes and textures to try. On many fronts, but especially in regard to food, there has never been a better time to be diagnosed with celiac disease, dermatitis herpetiformis, or non-celiac gluten sensitivity. Gone are the days when rice cakes were one of the few available gluten-free "breads." You now have so many gluten-free flours, grains, mixes, and convenience foods to choose from that you may have difficulty deciding what to eat next.

We truly hope you enjoy this cookbook as much as we've enjoyed writing it. Here's to delicious and nutritious gluten-free cooking (and eating)!

About the Authors

Tricia Thompson, M.S., R.D., is a nutrition consultant, researcher, author, and speaker specializing in celiac disease and the gluten-free diet. She is the author of a variety of books on the gluten-free diet, including *The Gluten-Free Nutrition Guide* and *The Complete Idiot's Guide to Gluten-Free Eating*, as well as the American Dietetic Association's booklet "Celiac Disease Nutrition Guide." She is also the author of the chapter titled "The Nutritional Quality of Gluten-Free Foods" in the book *Gluten-Free Food Science and Technology*. Tricia is a contributing author to *The American Dietetic Association's Nutrition Care Manual* and is a workgroup member of the association's Evidence Analysis Library project on celiac disease.

Tricia writes a weekly column for Diet.com titled "Living Gluten-Free" (www.diet.com/dietblogs/read_blog_expert.php?uid=926693) and a quarterly column for registered dietitians about celiac disease in *Medical Nutrition Matters*. She has also written numerous articles for both scientific and popular readers, including those that have appeared in *Gluten-Free Living* magazine, the *Journal of the American Dietetic Association*, the *Journal of Human Nutrition and Dietetics*, and the *New England Journal of Medicine*. Tricia has a master's degree in nutrition from Tufts University in Boston, Massachusetts, and a bachelor's degree in English literature from Middlebury College in Vermont.

For more information about following a gluten-free diet, visit Tricia's Web site at www.glutenfreedietitian.com.

Marlisa Brown, M.S., R.D., C.D.E., C.D.N., is a registered dietitian, a certified diabetes educator, a chef, an author, and an international speaker. As president of Total Wellness Inc., for more than fifteen years Marlisa has worked as a nutritional consultant specializing in diabetes education, celiac disease, gastrointestinal disorders, cardiovascular disease, sports nutrition, culinary programs, and corporate wellness.

She is the author of *Gluten-Free, Hassle Free: A Simple, Sane Dietitian-Approved Program for Eating Your Way Back to Health* and has also contributed to many dietary programs and books, including Richard Simmons's FoodMover program and cookbooks, Jorge Cruise's 3-Hour Diet, Leslie Sansone's Walk Away the Pounds, Kathy Smith's Project: YOU! DM 2, and Aspen's Women's Sports Medicine and Rehabilitation.

She is also the creator of www.glutenfreeeasy.com, a comprehensive celiac Web site.

With more than thirty years of culinary experience, she has been featured on more than fifty cooking shows for the American Heart Association on international cooking. Marlisa is a past president of the New York State Dietetic Association and has been the recipient of the following awards: the American Dietetic Association's Emerging Dietetic Leader, the Long Island Dietetic Association's Dietitian of the Year, *LI Press*'s 2008/2009/2010 Best of Long Island, and CW Post's Community Service Award, and is currently listed on CW Post's Web site as an outstanding alumna.

Marlisa has bachelor's and master's degrees from CW Post Long Island University, and she has also studied at the Culinary Institute of America.

Professional Reviewers
Madeline (Lynn) Cicero, M.S., R.D.
Morristown, New Jersey

Nancy Patin Falini, M.A., R.D., L.D.N.
West Chester, Pennsylvania

Dee Sandquist, M.S., R.D., L.D.
Fairfield, Iowa

Mary K. Sharrett, M.S., R.D., L.D., C.N.S.D.
Nationwide Children's Hospital
Columbus, Ohio

Consumer Reviewers

Lisa Joyce Goes
New Lenox, Illinois

Mary Lassila
Chicago, Illinois

Acknowledgments

I owe a tremendous debt of gratitude to the American Dietetic Association for its efforts over the years to make available first-rate information on celiac disease and the gluten-free diet to both consumers and dietitians. Thank you to Laura Pelehach, the manager of acquisitions and development at ADA, for asking me to write this book. Thank you to Marlisa Brown, who agreed to be part of this project and developed all of the recipes. Thank you also to the peer and consumer reviewers of this book, Lynn Cicero, Nancy Patin Falini, Mary K. Sharrett, Dee Sandquist, Lisa Joyce Goes, and Mary Lassila. Your thoughtful comments helped make this book better. Huge hugs to my husband, Dave, and son, Marcus, who continue to put up with my constant talk about all things celiac!

—Tricia

I would like to extend my special thanks to all of those people who helped make this book possible: To my husband, Russell, for his endless tastings; Catherine Brittan, M.S., R.D., L.D., for her help with the recipe testing and nutritional work, and my agent, Stephany Evans, for her continued support. Thank you all.

—Marlisa

Part One

Eating Gluten-Free

If you have celiac disease or non-celiac gluten sensitivity, food may be an emotional issue for you. It's normal to develop a love-hate relationship with food when much of what is available in the standard American diet makes you ill. These gluten-containing dishes may smell and taste delicious if you eat them, but before long they are wreaking havoc with your health and digestive system. You may envy people around you who can enjoy mouthwatering pastas, hearty breads, savory pizza, waffles and pancakes, holiday cookies, rich chocolate cake, crisp crackers, and all of the wheat-based goodies so abundant in the Western diet.

Now you can leave behind your sense of deprivation from following a gluten-free diet. You can have all of the foods that you crave—or, rather, a non-gluten version of them. This book will show you how.

The first three chapters of the book contain all of the information you'll need to cook safely and healthfully on a gluten-free diet. There are tips on reading labels, eating nutritiously, and using gluten-free whole grains. You'll learn what these grains are, how to cook them, and how to easily incorporate them into your meals.

1

I Have to Eat Gluten-Free. Now What?

If you bought this book, it is likely that you, a family member, or a friend has celiac disease, dermatitis herpetiformis, or non-celiac gluten sensitivity. You may not be familiar with all three of these conditions, so here is a quick overview.

Celiac disease is a genetically based autoimmune disease. If you have it, you cannot eat a type of protein (called gluten) that is found in the grains wheat, barley, and rye. If you do, the protein in these grains triggers an immune system response that causes damage to the lining of the small intestine.

Specifically, the lining of the small intestine contains hairlike projections called villi that help you digest food and absorb its nutrients. In untreated celiac disease, the villi become shortened or completely flattened, which prevents food from being properly absorbed. Malabsorption of food may cause a variety of gastrointestinal symptoms—for example, diarrhea, gas, and stomach pain—as well as conditions such as bone disease and anemia. Currently, the only available treatment for celiac disease is a lifelong gluten-free diet.

Dermatitis herpetiformis is a type of celiac disease that involves the skin. If you have dermatitis herpetiformis, you most likely experienced damage to the lining of your small intestine before you were diagnosed and treated. In addition, you develop a severely itchy skin rash when you eat gluten. As with celiac disease, the treatment for dermatitis herpetiformis includes lifelong adherence to a gluten-free diet.

Non-celiac gluten sensitivity is currently thought to be an immune system response to gluten. It is not considered an autoimmune disease like celiac disease, however, or a food allergy such as a wheat allergy. Nonetheless, eating gluten may result in some of the same symptoms that are experienced by a person with celiac disease. As with celiac disease, the current treatment for non-celiac gluten sensitivity is a gluten-free diet.

For a more complete discussion about the differences between celiac disease and non-celiac gluten sensitivity, please see www.diet.com/ dietblogs/read_blog.php?title=Celiac+Disease+vs.+Gluten+ Sensitivity&blid=11838.

Even if you "know" you have a problem with gluten, do yourself a favor and get tested for celiac disease *before* starting a gluten-free diet. If you start eating gluten-free before being tested, your test results may not be accurate. The first step is getting a simple blood test that can be ordered by your physician.

How Do I Know What Foods I Can Eat?

Following a gluten-free diet may seem overwhelming and confusing at first, but, rest assured, you won't feel this way for long—we promise! In this chapter, you will learn which foods and ingredients are gluten-free and which are not. In the past, finding gluten-free foods was a fairly daunting and time-consuming task. Thanks in large part to the Food and Drug Administration's Food Allergen Labeling and Consumer Protection Act (FALCPA) and proposed new rules regarding the labeling of foods as gluten-free, it has become far less stressful to determine whether a particular food or ingredient is gluten-free. You will learn how to read food labels later in this chapter.

When cooking gluten-free, you must avoid using all varieties and most forms of the grains wheat, barley, and rye, as well as cross-bred varieties of these grains, such as triticale (a cross between wheat and rye), and ingredients made from these grains.

You may come across information, even from health-food store employees, indicating that certain varieties of wheat, such as spelt, are safe for people with celiac disease to eat. This is not true. You must avoid all varieties of wheat, including (but not limited to) durum wheat (which is used to make semolina), common wheat, einkorn wheat, emmer wheat, kamut, and spelt wheat. They all are closely related; they contain gluten and amino acid sequences that are harmful to people with celiac disease.

Although oats themselves do not contain gluten, they must not be eaten unless they are labeled "gluten-free." Oats without the label may contain small amounts of wheat, barley, or rye picked up from the fields where they were grown, the railcars in which they were transported, or the manufacturing plant where they were processed. Note: If you would like to add oats to your gluten-free diet, the American Dietetic Association recommends that this be done under the supervision of your physician or registered dietitian.

The good news is, gluten-free doesn't mean grain-free. When you prepare gluten-free meals, you have a wide variety of tasty gluten-free grains to choose from, many of which will be discussed in this book. These include rice, corn, gluten-free oats, millet, teff, sorghum, wild rice, buckwheat, amaranth, and quinoa. These grains are full of all kinds of wonderful nutrients, such as fiber, iron, and B vitamins. Although you may not be familiar with all of the grains now, by the time you finish reading this book you will have learned how to shop for them, prepare them, and incorporate at least some (and hopefully all) of them into your meals.

Reading Food Labels

When you start following a gluten-free diet, one of the first habits you should form is reading food labels, every time you shop. With very few exceptions, when determining whether a food is made with gluten-containing ingredients you are looking for five words on the food label: wheat, barley, rye, oats (unless gluten-free), and malt (unless the label says otherwise malt is made from barley). In general, if you see any of these words on a food label, the food is not gluten-free.

In addition to these five ingredients, you will need to look out for a few other ingredients, such as modified food starch and dextrin, that may be made from starch or starch hydrolysates (starches that have been partially broken down). It is possible that these ingredients contain gluten because wheat may have been used as the source of starch, and trace amounts of protein may remain in the starch. Nonetheless, if wheat protein is present in either of these ingredients, the word "wheat" will be included on the label of any packaged food regulated by the Food and Drug Administration (FDA). If you see the words "modified food starch" or "dextrin" in an ingredients list of an FDA-regulated food, and neither the ingredients list nor the "Contains" statement includes the word "wheat," then that food does not contain wheat protein. If, however, you see "modified food starch" or "dextrin" on the label of a food product regulated by the United States Department of Agriculture (USDA) and the source of the ingredient is not named, these ingredients may contain protein from wheat.

Both FDA- and USDA-regulated foods may also contain brewer's yeast. Brewer's yeast that is used in food as a flavoring may be a by-product of the beer-brewing process and, as such, may be contaminated with malt and grain. At this time, it is recommended that you avoid food products that contain brewer's yeast. See the next two sections for a more thorough explanation of FDA- and USDA-regulated foods.

Note: Although the ingredients maltodextrin, glucose syrup, and caramel color may also be derived from wheat starch hydrolysates, these ingredients are unlikely to contain significant (or any) amounts of gluten protein. In fact, because wheat starch–based maltodextrin and wheat starch–based glucose syrup contain such small amounts of protein, they have been permanently exempted from allergen labeling in the European Union.

FDA-Regulated Foods

The Food Allergen Labeling and Consumer Protection Act (FALCPA), which took effect on January 1, 2006, has taken much of the stress out of determining whether a particular food or ingredient is free from gluten-containing ingredients. Under this act, if ingredients in a packaged food regulated by the FDA contain wheat protein, then the word "wheat" must be included on the food label, either in the ingredients list or in a separate "Contains" statement. This statement is usually found immediately after the ingredients list.

In addition to wheat, FALCPA applies to seven other major allergens, namely, milk, eggs, fish, crustacean shellfish, tree nuts, peanuts, and soybeans. The FDA regulates all foods with the exception of meat products, poultry products, and egg products. If you are reading the label of a food product regulated by the FDA and do not see the word "wheat," you can be assured that the ingredients in the food do not inherently contain wheat protein.

USDA-Regulated Foods

The United States Department of Agriculture regulates meat products, poultry products, and egg products (meaning any dried, frozen, or liquid eggs, with or without added ingredients), which includes any mixed food products that contain more than 3 percent raw meat, at least 2 percent cooked meat, or at least 2 percent cooked poultry. Products regulated by the USDA that may contain gluten include lunch meats, hot dogs, canned meats, and prepackaged seasoned "fresh" chicken products. As of this writing, the USDA did not have a mandatory allergen rule in place, although it may develop one in the future. Nonetheless, the USDA strongly encourages manufacturers to voluntarily label the eight major allergens as described in FALCPA. Even though allergen labeling is voluntary, the USDA believes it has widespread compliance among its manufacturers. Chances are good that if you do not see the word "wheat" on a USDA-regulated product, none of the ingredients that are used to make the product contain wheat protein.

The USDA does require all ingredients in a USDA-regulated food product to be listed on the food label by their "common or usual name." Unfortunately, the common or usual name of an ingredient does not always indicate the source of the ingredient. Examples of common or usual names that can mystify a consumer include "dextrin" and "modified food starch." You may come across these ingredients in any number of products, such as lunch meats, canned chicken products, hot dogs, and sausages. There also are several common or usual names for wheat-based flour that may be used on a food label, including semolina, farina, durum flour, enriched flour, graham flour, white flour, and plain flour.

Perhaps voluntary labeling is not quite good enough for you, and you would rather be absolutely certain that a USDA-regulated product is free of ingredients that contain wheat protein. If you see "modified food starch" or "dextrin" on the label of a product that otherwise appears to be free of gluten-containing ingredients, contact the manufacturer and ask about the source of its modified food starch or dextrin. Chances are good that the source will be corn.

For an in-depth interview with the USDA on its policies related to allergen labeling, please see www.diet.com/dietblogs/read_blog.php?title=Labeling+of+USDA-Regulated+Foods&blid=17330&sh=1.

Should I Be Concerned about Caramel Color?

In both FDA- and USDA-regulated products, caramel may be made from malt (in addition to starch hydrolysates). You probably shouldn't worry too much about this ingredient, though. Caramel is usually made from corn starch, and even if it is made from malt, it probably won't contain much, if any, gluten protein because it is so highly processed.

For more information on caramel color, see www.diet.com/dietblogs/read_blog.php?title=Caramel+Color&blid=17069.

Do I Need to Watch for Natural Flavors?

In FDA-regulated food products, natural flavor could be derived from barley or rye (a natural flavoring could also be made from wheat, but if it does contain protein from wheat, this will be declared on the food label). If the flavoring is barley-based, it most likely is called some form of malt in the ingredients list. If the flavoring is made from rye, it is probably listed as "rye flavoring" in the ingredients. In addition, rye flavoring tends to be used in products that you wouldn't be eating anyway, such as bread. If natural flavor is the only suspect ingredient in an FDA-regulated food product, the food is in all likelihood fine for you to eat.

In USDA-regulated foods, ingredients that contain protein cannot be included under "natural flavor" but instead must be listed by their common or usual name on the food label. In other words, if you see "natural flavor" in the ingredients list of a USDA-regulated product, it does not contain undeclared protein, such as from wheat, barley, or rye.

How about Ingredients That May Contain Barley?

A few ingredients, such as brown rice syrup and smoke flavoring, may occasionally contain barley protein. Some brown rice syrups may use a form of barley, such as barley enzymes, during processing. It is unclear whether these enzymes might contain small amounts of barley gluten. If you are concerned about this ingredient, please choose only rice syrups and products containing rice syrup that are labeled gluten-free. Some (but certainly not all or even most) dry smoke flavorings use malted barley flour as a carrier for the smoke flavor. If this flavoring is used in a poultry or meat product and it contains barley protein, barley will be listed in the ingredients by its common or usual name. It will not be "hidden" under the term "smoke flavoring." If this ingredient is used in an FDA-regulated food, such as salsa, sub-ingredients may or may not be included. If you are concerned about this ingredient, please contact the manufacturer and ask whether the smoke flavoring used in its product contains barley.

For more information on barley enzymes, see www.diet.com/dietblogs/read_blog.php?title=Barley+Enzymes+In+Gluten-Free+Products&blid=15895.

The Bottom Line on Reading Food Labels

When reading the labels of FDA-regulated foods (which will be on most of the food you purchase), you are looking primarily for wheat, barley, rye, oats (unless it's labeled gluten-free), and malt. At this time, you should also watch out for brewer's yeast.

On the labels of USDA-regulated foods—that is, meat products, poultry products, and egg products—you mainly need to check for wheat, barley, rye, oats (unless it's labeled gluten-free), malt, dextrin (unless a gluten-free source is named), and modified food starch (unless a gluten-free source is specified). At this time, you also need to be alert for brewer's yeast. Finally, familiarize yourself with words that mean "wheat" if they are used on the label of a USDA-regulated food; some examples include "durum flour," "enriched flour," "farina," "graham flour," "plain flour," "semolina," and "white flour."

Reading Alcohol Labels

The labeling of wines, distilled spirits, and malt beverages falls under the jurisdiction of the Alcohol and Tobacco Tax Trade Bureau (TTB). This agency is currently in the process of developing rules similar to FALCPA for the mandatory labeling of major food allergens used in the production of alcoholic beverages. These rules will apply to fining agents (which are used in wine making to remove substances that may cause wine to look cloudy) and to processing agents as well. Currently, producers of wines, distilled spirits, and malt beverages may voluntarily choose to declare the presence of the eight major allergens, including wheat, on product labels as described in FALCPA.

Certain types of alcohol are off limits to people with celiac disease. These include malt beverages, such as beer, porter, stout, and pilsner, which by definition contain malted barley with hops. Although most beers are considered malt beverages, gluten-free beers are not, because they are made using a substitute for malted barley. As a result, gluten-free beers are regulated by the FDA and not by the TTB.

Wine and pure distilled spirits, such as vodka, whisky, gin, brandy, rum, and tequila, are considered gluten-free. Certain classes of wines and distilled spirits may contain added colorings and flavorings. Brandy, rum, tequila, and whisky may be colored with caramel. Cordials and liqueurs may have flavorings and colorings added after distillation. Depending on the type of alcohol, colorings and flavorings may or may not have to be declared on the alcohol label. You probably shouldn't concern yourself with either caramel color or flavoring, though. As stated previously, caramel may be made from wheat starch hydrolysates or barley malt but is most likely made from corn. Even if caramel is made from wheat or barley, it is unlikely to contain much, if any, gluten. A flavoring agent used in a cordial or liqueur probably won't be derived from wheat, barley, or rye. If you have any concerns, contact the manufacturer.

For more information on the allergen labeling of alcoholic beverages, see http://edocket.access.gpo.gov/2006/pdf/06-6467.pdf.

What Is Gluten-Free Labeling?

As of this writing, the FDA had not yet released its final rule on the definition of "gluten-free" for the purposes of food labeling. When this rule is released it will be the first time the United States has had a government definition of the term "gluten-free." Unlike allergen labeling, this rule will most likely apply to foods regulated by both the FDA and the USDA. At this time, the USDA does not plan to make its own rules for gluten-free labeling and instead plans to adopt the FDA's ruling. Some facets of the rule may change when it is finalized, but under the FDA's current proposal, a "gluten-free" food label will mean:

1. The food does not contain a prohibited grain, namely, wheat (which includes all varieties, such as common wheat, durum wheat, einkorn wheat, emmer wheat, kamut, and spelt wheat), barley, rye, or cross-bred varieties of these grains, such as triticale.
2. The food does not contain an ingredient made from a prohibited grain that has not been processed to remove gluten. Examples include hydrolyzed wheat protein, wheat bran, wheat germ, barley malt extract or flavoring, and malt vinegar. In other words, hydrolyzed wheat protein is derived from wheat, and the processing of this ingredient has not resulted in gluten being removed.
3. The food does not contain an ingredient made from a prohibited grain that has been processed to remove gluten but whose use in the food results in the food containing 20 or more parts per million of gluten. Ingredients that may be used in a product labeled gluten-free (depending upon how much gluten they contain) include modified food starch and wheat starch. In other words, wheat starch is derived from wheat and the processing of this ingredient has resulted in much of the gluten being removed. Yet the gluten content of wheat starch varies greatly. For wheat starch

to be used in a product labeled gluten-free, the final food product must not contain 20 or more parts per million of gluten.

4. The food contains less than 20 parts per million of gluten.

Now I Really Have a Lot of Questions!

The proposed definition of "gluten-free" for labeling purposes may raise additional questions in your mind, some of which we hope to address here. (The answers we've provided are based on the proposed rule and may therefore change once the rule is finalized.)

Do all foods that happen to be gluten-free need to have a "gluten-free" label?
No. The labeling of a food product as gluten-free is voluntary. If a food does not carry a gluten-free label, it does not mean the food contains gluten. In fact, foods that are inherently gluten-free, such as plain milk and honey, cannot include a gluten-free claim on the food label unless it is made clear that all milk (or honey) is gluten-free. For example, the label could say, "Milk, a gluten-free food" or "All milk is gluten-free."

Can oats carry a "gluten-free" label?
Yes. Although oats are considered naturally gluten-free, they are frequently contaminated with wheat, barley, or rye. For this reason, oats may be labeled gluten-free if they contain less than 20 parts per million of gluten. Unlike for other naturally gluten-free foods, however, packagers of oats cannot state on their label that "All oats are gluten-free" or that "Oats are a gluten-free food."

What does "20 parts per million of gluten" mean?
This is a proportional measure of how many milligrams of gluten are in a kilogram of food. There are 1 million milligrams in a kilogram, so 20 parts per million of gluten means that 20 milligrams out of 1 million milligrams of food contain gluten. In other words, if you had a giant bag of M&Ms that was supposed to contain 1 million red candies, but out of that 1 million candies, 20 were blue instead of red,

you could say that your bag of red M&Ms was contaminated with 20 parts per million of blue M&Ms.

Why did the FDA choose 20 parts per million as the cut-off point for gluten-free labeling?
At the time the proposal was written, 20 parts per million was the level at which the Food and Drug Administration believed gluten could be reliably and consistently detected using currently available tests.

Is 20 parts per million of gluten a safe amount?
Although it is best to strive to consume as little gluten as possible, 20 parts per million is considered a very small amount. Recent studies on the daily amount of gluten that can be safely consumed by a person with celiac disease indicate that 10 milligrams of gluten is a safe amount. If you were to eat a 1-ounce serving of a bread product containing 20 parts per million of gluten, you would take in about 0.57 milligrams of gluten. At this ratio, you would have to eat 17½ 1-ounce slices of bread (or the equivalent) to reach a total intake of 10 milligrams of gluten.

Why doesn't "gluten-free" mean zero gluten?
It is currently impossible to test a food down to zero gluten, so a zero gluten level would be unenforceable. Also, manufacturers would be unlikely to guarantee that their products contain zero gluten because even in the most controlled environment, the possibility of some contamination exists as a food makes its way from the field where it is grown to the plant where it is processed.

If a food is labeled "gluten-free," does this apply to gluten that may be in a product due to cross-contamination?
Yes, if a food is labeled "gluten free," the product contains less than 20 parts per million of gluten, regardless of whether the gluten is found in the ingredients or is in the food unintentionally through cross-contact. This differs from the FALCPA's guidelines, which address only ingredients and do not apply to substances that may be in a product unintentionally due to cross-contact. In other words, if you pick up a

container of oatmeal, the only listed ingredient is rolled oats. If the product is labeled gluten-free, you know that this particular brand of oats contains less than 20 parts per million of gluten from contamination with wheat, barley, or rye. If you pick up another container of oats that is not labeled gluten-free, you have no way of knowing how much wheat, barley, or rye may be in the product unintentionally through cross-contact.

How do manufacturers of gluten-free foods ensure that their products contain less than 20 parts per million of gluten?

There are several steps manufacturers may take to produce gluten-free foods. These steps include using a dedicated gluten-free facility, room, or line or following standards of good manufacturing practice; having an allergen control program; testing of "raw" ingredients for gluten; in-house testing of their finished products; and periodically sending samples of the final food products to third-party laboratories for gluten testing. If you want more information regarding specific steps a food company is taking to ensure that its gluten-free products contain less than 20 parts per million of gluten, contact the company and ask to speak with a quality assurance representative.

Why are wheat starch and modified food starch considered ingredients that have been processed to remove gluten?

The processing of these ingredients removes most protein, leaving primarily carbohydrates. Yet some amount of protein does remain in the starch. Not all wheat starch is processed the same, and, depending on quality, various wheat starches will vary in the amount of gluten they contain. If wheat starch or wheat-based modified food starch is used as an ingredient in a gluten-free food, the final food product (as sold to the consumer) must contain less than 20 parts per million of gluten. If you come across a product that contains wheat starch, and the food is not labeled gluten-free, do not eat this product. If a food product contains modified food starch and the label includes the word "wheat" and the product is not marked gluten-free, do not eat this food. On the other hand, if a food label includes the word "wheat" and the product is labeled "gluten-free," the product contains less than 20 parts per million of gluten.

Must all ingredients used in a food product that's labeled gluten-free contain less than 20 parts per million of gluten?

No, the "less than 20 parts per million of gluten" threshold refers to the finished food product and not to individual ingredients.

Can any ingredients be used in a food product that is labeled gluten-free as long as the final food product contains less than 20 parts per million of gluten?

No, based on the FDA's proposed definition of "gluten-free," certain ingredients cannot be used in products labeled gluten-free. These ingredients include the grains wheat, barley, rye, and their cross-bred varieties. In addition, ingredients derived from these grains that have not been processed to remove gluten, such as hydrolyzed wheat protein and barley malt extract, may not be used in a food product labeled "gluten-free," regardless of how much gluten the final food product contains (even if the product contains less than 20 parts per million of gluten).

Might a food be labeled "gluten-free" and also contain wheat protein?

Yes. Under FALCPA, if any wheat protein is present in an ingredient, the word "wheat" must be included on the food label. Yet the amount of wheat protein in the product may be so low that the product may still be considered gluten-free under the proposed FDA rule. If you want to avoid gluten-free foods that contain wheat protein, just look for the word "wheat" in the ingredients list and the "Contains" statement of a gluten-free food. If you don't see the word "wheat," ingredients in the gluten-free food do not contain wheat protein.

What about voluntary allergen advisory statements on food labels?

Another statement you may see on food labels is voluntary allergen advisory labeling related to the manufacturing process. Examples include "made in a facility that also manufactures products containing soy and gluten" and "produced in a facility that uses wheat, milk, soy, almonds, pecans, and hazelnuts." Keep in mind that this statement is voluntary, and, unlike gluten-free labeling, which also is voluntary, there are currently no federal guidelines (proposed or otherwise) pertaining to the use of allergen advisory statements on food labels. Manufacturers who include this information on their labels are providing you with more information than is required by law. Just because you don't see precautionary statements on other foods doesn't mean that they, too, are not manufactured in similar environments. Also, if you see this statement on a product, this does not necessarily mean it is contaminated. If this type of wording appears on a product that's labeled gluten-free, remember that under the proposed rule the food by definition must contain less than 20 parts per million of gluten, regardless of the manufacturing process.

Both gluten-free labeling and allergen advisory statements are voluntary. If, however, a manufacturer chooses to label food products gluten-free, there are federal guidelines that must be followed once the rule is finalized. No such guidelines exist for allergen advisory statements. Also, remember that allergen advisory statements are different from the Food Allergen Labeling and Consumer Protection Act.

It is important to understand that all manufacturers should follow current good manufacturing practices. This means they should take steps to reduce or eliminate the chance of an allergen unintentionally finding its way into a food that does not contain that allergen as an ingredient. Steps that manufacturers may take include thorough cleaning of equipment between product runs and timed product turnovers—meaning that the first batch of a product, which is most likely to contain residual material from the last product, is not packaged for the consumer.

On food labels, you may also notice statements such as, "Made in a dedicated nut- and gluten-free bakery." If given the choice, most people who must follow a gluten-free diet would probably choose to eat foods that were manufactured in dedicated facilities or at least on production lines dedicated to gluten-free foods. Yet this is not possible for many mainstream foods or even for some specially manufactured gluten-free foods. If you would like to learn more about how particular foods are manufactured, check the company Web site or contact a quality assurance representative and talk with him or her about the company's allergen control program.

How Do I Avoid Cross-Contamination in the Kitchen and at the Table?

When you or someone in your household is following a gluten-free diet, it's important to prevent the contamination of gluten-free foods with gluten-containing ones. When contamination occurs, it is generally referred to as cross-contamination or cross-contact. If you are old enough, you remember a certain advertisement for Reese's Peanut Butter Cups. This ad illustrates cross-contact and why it's something you definitely want to avoid with gluten (although, in the case of the commercial, it was a happy accident and not something to be feared). In the ad, two people are sitting side by side. One is munching on a chocolate bar, while the other is eating peanut butter. They both end up accusing the other of getting "peanut butter on my chocolate" and "chocolate in my peanut butter." You probably get the point!

Concern over cross-contact does not necessarily mean that everyone in your family needs to follow a gluten-free diet, but all family members must take seriously the need to prevent cross-contact. The following recommendations should help you reduce the potential for cross-contact in your home:

- Designate certain cupboards or sections of your pantry as gluten-free. Have you ever noticed the flour and crumbs that accumulate in your cupboards? You want to keep separate all gluten-containing and gluten-free foods that make crumbs or "dust" to avoid cross-contamination. This includes flours, grains, mixes, pastas, breads, cookies, crackers, and so on. If you don't have the space in your kitchen to do this, designate certain shelves, preferably higher shelves, as gluten-free so that gluten-containing crumbs cannot fall down onto the gluten-free shelf.
- Insist on a "no-double-dipping" rule for shared foods that are spread on bread products. This includes butter, peanut butter, mayonnaise, mustard, jelly, and so on. It's amazing how many gluten-containing bread crumbs can end up in jelly or on butter when this rule is not used.
- Always use separate serving utensils for gluten-free and gluten-containing foods or, alternatively, serve the gluten-free food first.

For example, if you have only one ice cream scoop, serve the gluten-free ice cream first.

- Make sure that serving utensils stay where they are supposed to. You don't want the spoon that's used to dish up gluten-containing macaroni and cheese to also serve up the gluten-free maple-glazed carrots. And remind family members not to use their personal utensils as serving utensils. This is a common courtesy, after all.

- Cook completely gluten-free meals whenever possible. This is the easiest way to prevent cross-contact. It's especially important when you are having guests who might not understand the importance of not mixing up serving utensils. For occasions when this is not feasible, plate the food yourself in the kitchen. Try to avoid serving home-style at the table.

- If your meal involves both gluten-containing and gluten-free components, either prepare the gluten-free portion first or use separate kitchen tools for the gluten-free food. For example, if you are making a pasta dish, and not everyone in your family is a fan of gluten-free pasta, you might find yourself cooking two types of noodles. Ideally, it's best to have two sets of pasta tongs and two strainers; however, this might not be practical in your household. At a minimum, you must make sure to stir the different pastas with separate utensils. If you have only one strainer and one set of tongs, it is imperative that you strain the gluten-free pasta first and use the tongs to serve the gluten-free pasta first.

- Don't bake gluten-free and gluten-containing foods at the same time. If you have to bake both types of food on the same day, prepare the gluten-free foods first. There is too great a potential for leftover wheat flour to find its way into your gluten-free baked goods. It is far better for the gluten-free flours to make their way into the wheat flour.

- Invest in a toaster oven, if possible. It is much easier to clean than a toaster. If you do have a toaster, purchase some toaster bags for your gluten-free breads, or, if you can, buy two toasters and designate one as gluten-free. You can order toaster bags from www.celinalfoods.com. They are also convenient to use at work, at school, and while traveling. By using toaster bags, you will prevent errant wheat-bread crumbs from finding their way onto the gluten-free bread.

- When microwaving, always place food on its own separate plate or on top of a paper towel. If you use splatter covers, designate one for gluten-free food or make sure it is thoroughly cleaned between uses. Also, be sure to keep the entire microwave oven clean. You don't want crumbs from prior meals to contaminate the gluten-free food.

2

How Can I Make Sure My Meals Pack a Nutritional Punch?

A gluten-free diet can be very healthy, if you make the right food choices and are aware of the nutritional quality of the foods you buy. Otherwise, you may end up with a diet that is low in several nutrients.

Studies conducted on the nutritional adequacy of a gluten-free diet have found that it may be high in fat and low in carbohydrates, fiber, iron, folate, niacin, thiamine, riboflavin, calcium, B12, phosphorus, and zinc. One reason for this is that many processed gluten-free foods have a low nutrient density; in other words, the food contains very few nutrients for its calorie content. For example, a 100-calorie portion of brown rice is far more dense in nutrients than 100 calories' worth of rice starch. Unfortunately, many specially formulated gluten-free breads, pastas, breakfast cereals, and baking mixes are made with refined, unenriched grains and starches, such as white rice and corn starch. These products contain very few vitamins and minerals.

Gluten-free diets may also have low levels of fiber, because products made from refined grains and starches contain very little fiber.

There are several reasons why a gluten-free diet may be high in fat and low in carbohydrates. To improve the taste and texture of gluten-free foods, some manufacturers add fat—substantially more than is found in a comparable wheat-based product. In general, people with celiac disease may eat fewer grain foods and therefore a smaller amount of carbohydrates than the average person. In place of carbohydrate-rich foods, they may substitute foods that are high in fat or protein.

Some people think that anyone who follows a gluten-free diet is on a low-carbohydrate weight-loss plan, much like the Atkins diet. This is not true. A gluten-free diet is a medically prescribed food plan. People shouldn't follow it to lose weight or to eat fewer carbohydrates. Although individuals with celiac disease may eat fewer carbohydrates than the average person does, this isn't because gluten-free carbohydrate foods are not available. Rather, people who are newly diagnosed with celiac disease may simply be unaware of the plethora of gluten-free choices they have. They may also need time to get used to the new tastes and textures of gluten-free grains and products.

In the following pages, we will look at five food groups: grains, milk and milk alternatives, meat and beans, fruits, and vegetables. You will learn to make the right food choices, so that the meals you serve yourself and your family pack a nutritional punch.

Choose Wholesome Grains

Of all of the food groups, grains are most affected by the gluten-free diet. Most mainstream grain products—breads, pastas, breakfast cereals, and baking mixes—are wheat-based or are made with a gluten-containing ingredient, such as malt. Fortunately, plenty of specialty manufacturers make gluten-free grain foods. Yet it's important for you to understand that their nutritional quality varies greatly, depending on whether they are made from whole grains, enriched or fortified refined grains, or refined grains that haven't been enriched.

A whole grain contains all three parts of the grain seed: the nutrient- and fiber-rich germ and bran and the carbohydrate-rich endosperm. A refined grain has had the germ and the bran removed and contains only the endosperm. According to the Whole Grains Council, when the germ and the bran are removed from grain, 25 percent of the protein and seventeen important nutrients are lost. When a refined grain is enriched, some of these nutrients are added back, namely the

B vitamins thiamine, riboflavin, niacin, and folic acid, as well as the mineral iron. When a food such as a breakfast cereal is fortified, nutrients are added that may or may not have been found in the original food product.

Try to consume at least three 1-ounce equivalents of whole-grain foods daily. In general, at least half of our grain servings should be whole grain. The remaining servings should be either whole grain or enriched refined grains—none of our grain food servings should be unenriched refined grains. If you want a nutritious gluten-free diet, it's important to follow this recommendation. Grains provide the B vitamins thiamine, riboflavin, niacin, and folate; the minerals zinc and iron; and fiber, all of which may be lacking in gluten-free diets.

Many naturally gluten-free whole grains are available, such as brown rice, whole corn, gluten-free oats, millet, teff, sorghum, wild rice, buckwheat, amaranth, and quinoa. There is not, however, an abundance of either whole or enriched gluten-free breads, pastas, breakfast cereals, or baking mixes on the market. Nonetheless, from a nutritional standpoint, it is well worth your effort to seek out products that are made with either whole grains or enriched grains.

To increase your consumption of gluten-free whole and enriched grains, try these tips:

1. Make the recipes in this cookbook! Gluten-free whole grains are widely used in our recipes.
2. Serve gluten-free whole grains as hot cereals, as side dishes, or added to soups and chili. Cook kasha, teff, sorghum, and gluten-free oats as hot breakfast cereals. Brown rice, wild rice, and quinoa make delicious side dishes. Amaranth and buckwheat groats are great additions to soups, stews, and chili.
3. Bake from scratch using gluten-free whole grains. It is just as easy to add brown rice flour as it is white rice flour to a baking recipe.
4. If you buy processed gluten-free breads, pastas, breakfast cereals, and baking mixes, choose products that are whole grain or enriched/fortified. When reading the food label, look for products that list a gluten-free whole grain (for example, whole corn, brown rice, teff) as the first ingredient. Also, look for the whole

grain stamp from the Whole Grains Council on product labels. If a product is enriched or fortified, the vitamins and the minerals will be included in the ingredients list. Suppliers of gluten-free whole grains include Bob's Red Mill, the Teff Company, and the Quinoa Corporation. Some manufacturers of enriched or fortified gluten-free foods are Gluten-Free Creations Bakery; Enjoy Life Foods; Perky's; Ener-G Foods; Schar, USA; Maplegrove Gluten-Free Foods; and General Mills. For a more complete list of manufacturers, see the Resources section.

Ensure Adequate Calcium and Vitamin D Intake

Fortunately, the majority of milk (including lactose-free milk) and milk-based products, such as yogurt and cheese, contain no traces of gluten. Many (but not all) milk alternatives, such as soy- and grain-based milks, are also free of gluten-containing ingredients.

Try to drink three cups of fat-free or low-fat milk (or the equivalent) daily. For a nutritious gluten-free diet, it's important to follow this recommendation. Milk is a primary source of calcium and vitamin D in American diets. People with celiac disease should choose fat-free or low-fat milk products, to compensate for the other foods they eat on a gluten-free diet that might have a high fat content.

Although the Dietary Reference Intake (DRI) amount for vitamin D has not been changed (at least, at the time this book went to press), the National Osteoporosis Association recently revised its recommendations regarding vitamin D. It now says that adults under age fifty should get 10 to 20 mcg (400 to 800 IU) of vitamin D each day; adults who are fifty and older should get 20 to 25 mcg (800 to 1,000 IU) daily. In addition, the American Academy of Pediatrics (AAP) recently issued new guidelines for vitamin D intake. The AAP now recommends that all children consume 10 mcg (400 IU) of vitamin D each day. This is double the amount of the current DRI (5 mcg, 200 IU).

People who follow a gluten-free diet may consume inadequate amounts of calcium. If you or a family member is lactose-intolerant, as many people with celiac disease are (at least temporarily, until the intestine heals), you should still meet these recommendations. Lactose-free milk is generally gluten-free. Hard, aged cheeses have very low lactose content and are usually well tolerated, as are yogurt and kefir (cultured milk) with active live cultures.

If you don't drink milk or eat dairy products because you follow an ovo-vegetarian or vegan diet (or if you simply choose not to eat dairy foods), you still need to consume three 1-cup equivalents of milk alternatives daily. One cup of calcium-fortified gluten-free soy milk, one cup of calcium-fortified orange juice, and varying amounts of calcium-processed tofu (check the labels) contain about the same amount of calcium as a cup of milk (approximately 300 milligrams). One cup of cooked collard greens, cooked spinach, or cooked rhubarb has around 300 milligrams of calcium.

To ensure that you and your family drink your daily quotas of milk or the equivalent (and minimize your fat intake), along with getting adequate calcium and vitamin D, try the following:

1. In general, purchase low-fat (1 percent) or nonfat milk most of the time. Please note, however, that according to the American Academy of Pediatrics, children younger than two years of age should consume full-fat dairy products. If you don't like to drink plain milk, then make milk-based soups, such as corn and potato soup; hot chocolate (just add cocoa or carob powder and a little sugar to the milk and heat it); and milk-based desserts, such as vanilla pudding. You can do all of the above with gluten-free soy, nut, potato, or grain-based "milk" —just make sure they are calcium- and vitamin D–fortified.

2. Purchase nonfat gluten-free yogurt and kefir most of the time. Yogurt mixed with gluten-free cold cereal makes a wonderful breakfast, as does a gluten-free waffle topped with yogurt and diced fresh fruit. Kefir poured over gluten-free cold cereal is also tasty.

3. For non-milk drinkers, make sure that any soy-, nut-, potato-, or grain-based "milk" is gluten-free and fortified with calcium and vitamin D. Read the ingredients list for the words "calcium" and "vitamin D2" or "vitamin D3." Check the Nutrition Facts label to see how much calcium and vitamin D a serving contains. Their amounts will be presented as a percentage of the Daily Value (DV).

The Daily Value for calcium is 1,000 milligrams. To determine the amount of calcium in milligrams from the Daily Value percentage, first convert the percentage to a decimal (for example, 30 percent becomes 0.30) and multiply by 1,000. For example, using the previous numbers, 30 percent DV for calcium is equal to .30×1,000 milligrams or 300 milligrams of calcium. The Daily Value for vitamin D is 400 international units. To determine the number of international units from the Daily Value percentage, first convert the percentage to a decimal and multiply by 400.

4. Make sure that tofu is calcium processed—it really does make a big difference in calcium content. If you are new to tofu, try it in stir-fries or grilled on the barbecue. You can even crumble it up and use it as a substitute for ricotta cheese in lasagna. You can also replace half of your ground beef or ground poultry with tofu in a recipe—put both ingredients in a food processor and blend them together. Prepare your ground ingredient combination as you normally would if you were using the meat or the poultry alone. (Thanks to one of our reviewers for this last tip!)

5. If you have a family of orange juice drinkers, buy varieties that are fortified with calcium and, ideally, with vitamin D, too. In the summer, freeze orange juice in Popsicle molds for the kids.

6. Include foods that are naturally rich in calcium, such as cooked greens (spinach, collard, turnip, and kale), cooked soybeans, and cooked broccoli, in your family meals. Serve chicken or fish over the cooked greens. Cooked soybeans (which are also called edamame), with a little coarse salt added, are delicious as a snack or an appetizer.

7. Eat more fish, especially fattier fish, such as salmon, which is a natural source of vitamin D.

Choose Lean Protein Foods

Plain red meat, poultry, fish, legumes (dried beans, peas, and lentils), nuts, seeds, and eggs are inherently free of gluten. When these foods are seasoned or sauced, however, the chances increase that they may include gluten-containing ingredients. It's best to buy these foods in their natural form anyway. If you are like most Americans, you probably eat enough protein foods. Even if you follow a vegetarian or a vegan diet, you probably get adequate protein, according to the American Dietetic Association (although some women on a vegan diet may have borderline protein intakes). What you may not be doing is eating the right types of protein.

When you select meat and poultry, make your choices lean. According to the United States Department of Agriculture, lean beef cuts include round steaks and roasts, top loin, top sirloin, chuck shoulder, and arm roasts. Examples of lean pork choices are loin, tenderloin, and center loin. Lean poultry choices include boneless, skinless chicken breasts and turkey cutlets.

Most of the fat in your diet should come from foods that are rich in polyunsaturated and monounsaturated fats, such as fish and nuts. There are three groups of fatty acids—saturated, polyunsaturated, and monounsaturated—and fats are classified as one or the other, based on the predominant fatty acid they contain. Beef, pork, chicken, and eggs contain primarily saturated fat, whereas fish, nuts, and seeds contain mostly polyunsaturated and monounsaturated fatty acids. Beans are low in fat, with the exception of peanuts and soybeans (which contain primarily polyunsaturated and monounsaturated fatty acids).

The type of fat you eat affects your chances of developing heart disease. Diets high in saturated fat are associated with increased levels of low density lipoprotein (LDL) cholesterol. A high level of LDL cholesterol in the blood usually accompanies an increased risk of heart disease. Diets that contain primarily polyunsaturated and monounsaturated fats are associated with low levels of LDL cholesterol in the blood.

To ensure that the protein foods you prepare for yourself and your family are lean and contain mostly polyunsaturated and monounsaturated fats, try these tips:

1. Make at least two dinners each week that are free of animal protein. Base your meal around beans or tofu instead. Make vegetarian chili, a hearty bean soup, or black bean tacos.

2. Have fish at least once or twice a week. Good choices include wild salmon, trout, cod, and tilapia. Bake or broil the fish with a little salt, garlic, onion, and lemon—delicious!

3. Keep to a bare minimum the amount of fatty and processed meats you eat, such as bacon, sausage, regular hamburger, and salami.

4. Eat beef and pork if you want to, just not too much. Pick lower-fat cuts, such as round steaks and roasts, top loin, top sirloin, chuck shoulder, and arm roasts for beef, and choose loin, tenderloin, and center loin for pork. Serve beef and pork sliced over cooked greens, rice, or quinoa, or in a salad or a stir-fry, so that the meat is merely part of a dish and not the main attraction.

5. When you eat chicken, skip the skin—this is where most of the fat is found.

6. Incorporate nuts and seeds into your meals and recipes. Add them to salads, stir-fries, rice dishes, breakfast cereals, and baked goods.

7. Use nut butters, such as cashew and almond, as a topping on waffles and pancakes.

A note about oils: Another way to make sure your diet contains mainly monounsaturated or polyunsaturated fats, instead of saturated fats, is to use oils instead of solid fats in your cooking and baking, as well as at the table. Choose vegetable oils such as olive and canola as much as possible, and limit your use of butter, stick margarine, and shortening.

Eat Your Daily Fruit Quota

All fresh fruit is free of gluten, and almost all dried, frozen, and canned fruit is as well. Sometimes, however, fruit is frozen or canned in a sweet sauce that includes a gluten-containing ingredient, so check labels carefully. Also, dried fruit, especially dates, may be dusted with oat flour to prevent sticking. This oat flour is unlikely to be gluten-free. If oat flour is added to a dried fruit, it will be included in the ingredients list on the label.

If you consume 2,000 calories a day, try to eat 2 cups of fruit (4 servings) daily. If you require more or less than 2,000 calories, adjust your fruit consumption accordingly. Also try to eat a variety of fruits each day and choose fiber-rich fruits most often, such as raspberries, blackberries, dates, pears, blueberries, strawberries, and apples. Along with its many other nutrients, fruit is a good source of dietary fiber, iron, and folate, which are often lacking in gluten-free diets. Fruit is also a good source of vitamin C, which helps the body absorb iron. In addition, fruit is low in fat—one nutrient that people following a gluten-free diet may consume in high amounts.

There really is no excuse for not eating enough fruit (unless, of course, you have a medical reason to restrict your fruit intake). What could be easier to eat and more healthful than a piece of fruit? It is low in fat, low in calories, fiber-packed, nutrient-rich, one of nature's best "multivitamins," 100 percent natural, and conveniently packaged, often in single-serving sizes.

The following suggestions will help you incorporate more fruit into your meals:

1. Make it a habit to start your day with fruit. Add dried or chopped fresh fruit to your breakfast cereal or yogurt. Top your gluten-free waffle or toast with fresh or frozen berries or a mashed banana.
2. Use fruit in your lunch menus. Add grapes, apples, or pears to tuna or chicken salad. Add strawberry or orange slices to salads. Top peanut, almond, or cashew butter sandwiches with sliced fresh fruit, instead of jelly.
3. You can eat fruit for dinner, too. Add dried fruit, such as raisins or cranberries, to rice or quinoa. Add fresh chopped fruit to your salads. Sauté starchy fruits like plantains and bananas, and serve them with chicken or fish.
4. Make your own snack mix, using dried fruit—raisins, cranberries, papaya—and chopped dark chocolate pieces.
5. Keep bananas on hand at work or school for a quick pick-me-up.
6. Carry dates in your purse—they make a great snack, especially when paired with almonds.

7. Use fruit in your baked goods. Raisins, dried cranberries, and chopped dried papaya work well in cookies. Add mashed bananas, applesauce, and fresh berries, such as blueberries and cranberries, to breads and muffins.
8. Don't forget fruit for dessert. What could be better than a baked apple sprinkled with cinnamon in the winter or strawberries topped with fresh whipped cream in the summer?
9. One suggestion (given to us by a reviewer of this book) that may help you remember to eat enough fruit each day is to display four pieces of fruit on your window sill or desk, and make sure to eat them all before the day's end.

Choose a Rainbow of Vegetables

All fresh vegetables are naturally free of gluten. Many frozen and canned vegetables are as well, but they may be prepared with seasonings and/or sauces that have gluten-containing ingredients, so check the labels carefully. Frozen potato products may be made with gluten, so read the labels of these, too. Legumes (dried beans, peas, and lentils), such as black beans, kidney beans, and soybeans, are members of the vegetable group but are also included in the meat and beans group because of their high protein content. All dried beans and most canned beans are free of gluten-containing ingredients, but sauces and added seasonings may include gluten. Soybean products, such as tofu, do not contain gluten if they are plain. Seasoned varieties may be made with gluten-containing ingredients.

If you consume 2,000 calories a day, try to eat 2½ cups (or five servings) of vegetables daily. If you require more or less than 2,000 calories, adjust your vegetable consumption accordingly. Also try to eat a variety of vegetables from the five vegetable subgroups each week. These subgroups are dark green (broccoli, leafy greens, lettuces), orange (carrots, sweet potatoes, pumpkin), dried beans (black beans, kidney beans, lentils), starchy vegetables (corn, potatoes, peas), and other vegetables (zucchini, tomatoes, asparagus).

As with fruit, it really is important to eat enough vegetables. They contain a wide assortment of nutrients, such as fiber, folate, zinc, iron, and calcium, depending on the specific vegetable. All of these nutrients may be lacking in gluten-free diets. Vegetables are also low in fat and are a good source of vitamin C, which helps the body absorb iron. For maximum nutrition, use your fresh vegetables within a few days of purchase.

Here are some easy ways to eat more vegetables every day:

1. When you bake gluten-free breakfast muffins, add shredded carrots, shredded zucchini, or defrosted frozen corn kernels to the recipe.
2. Add vegetables to omelets.
3. Add sliced tomatoes, cucumbers, zucchini, green or red peppers, and leafy greens to gluten-free sandwiches.
4. Make up a batch of basil or spinach pesto. Spread it on bread, wraps, and crackers; serve it with chicken or fish; or mix it with pasta.
5. Add fresh or frozen greens to your red pasta sauces. Thawed frozen spinach works particularly well and is a tasty way to eat your greens.
6. Instead of French fries, serve sweet potato fries. Slice up some sweet potatoes, and toss them with olive oil and salt. Bake them at 350 degrees until they're crispy.
7. Make it a habit to serve a green salad every night with dinner.
8. Add vegetables to rice or quinoa dishes. For ease and maximum nutrition, cook the vegetables in the same pot as the rice or the quinoa.
9. Add beans to pasta dishes, soups, chili, tacos, and salads.
10. Keep some frozen vegetables on hand that everyone likes, such as corn and peas, for the nights when you don't have fresh vegetables in the house.

Tips for Eating Gluten-Free on a Budget

Let's face it, "gluten-free" can be expensive (especially if you buy costly flour blends and prepackaged foods), but there are ways you can reduce the cost of your gluten-free food and meals. Here are some suggestions:

1. Eat more beans. Dried beans (and even canned beans) are an inexpensive and delicious source of protein. There are many

types of beans and just as many ways to eat them. Mashed chickpeas mixed with a little garlic powder, salt (to taste), and olive oil make a great filling for corn tortilla roll-ups. Chickpeas also work well added to pesto sauce and served over pasta or rice. Add kidney or black beans to a rice bowl—just mix in tomatoes, onion, olives, defrosted frozen corn kernels, and whatever else you like. This dish is so tasty you don't even need a dressing.

2. Serve meat, chicken, and fish as just one ingredient in a meal, instead of as the main focus. That way, the amount can be stretched into at least two meals. For example, instead of serving whole chicken breasts for dinner, dice the chicken and serve it one night as filling for chicken tacos and the next as part of a chicken and vegetable stir-fry.

3. Buy fruits and vegetables in season. Some fruits, such as berries, can be purchased in season and frozen for later use.

4. When fruits and vegetables are not in season, buy frozen varieties instead. Plain frozen fruits and vegetables without added sugar, salt, or sauces are considered just as nutritious as fresh fruits and vegetables, because manufacturers usually freeze produce shortly after it is harvested, when the nutrient content is highest.

5. Eat food as close to its natural state as possible—food in its natural state is generally cheaper than processed food.

6. Buy gluten-free whole grains such as brown rice and quinoa, instead of prepared foods made with these grains.

7. Cut back on processed, ready-made, gluten-free snack foods. Pop your own popcorn or make your own tortilla chips and cookies, instead of purchasing premade varieties.

8. Buy gluten-free specialty foods in bulk. Amazon sells many gluten-free food items in bulk at a fairly substantial discount.

Note: Although it may be cheaper to buy gluten-free grains or flours from bulk bins, this is something you should avoid. There is a major risk of cross-contamination from gluten-containing grains—those scoops don't always stay where they are supposed to!

9. Shop around for the best prices on specialty gluten-free foods. In general, gluten-free foods at a supermarket cost less than the same

foods at a natural foods store. Large superstores like Costco, Stop-n-Shop, Wegmans, and Wal-Mart are carrying an increasing variety of gluten-free foods.

10. When ordering gluten-free foods, try to avoid shipping costs. Although you generally have to buy gluten-free foods in bulk through Amazon, shipping is free. Shipping is also free if you order a certain dollar amount through www.glutenfreeplaza .com; other manufacturers offer free shipping for minimum orders, too.

11. If you don't like to buy gluten-free food in bulk because you lack storage space or for some other reason, form a "buying club" where a number of people order food through the same account. This way, you can still take advantage of free shipping. You could organize such a club through your local support group.

12. Make use of coupons that are increasingly being offered online by manufacturers.

13. Check to see whether your local support group has a food assistance program. At the time of this book's writing, the Palm Beach County Celiac Disease Support Group has started the Gluten-Free Food Assistance Program (GFFAP) for qualifying individuals and families. It is hoped that other local support groups will follow the lead of PBC.

14. An organization called Angel Food Ministries provides food baskets to individuals at a reduced cost. At the time of this writing, the group had an allergen-free basket—all food was supposedly free of gluten. For more information, visit the organization's Web site at angelfoodministries.com.

15. Visit the Web site www.befreeforme.com. This site offers coupons for gluten-free food products, as well as product samples. You have to sign up, but it's free to do so.

16. Don't throw away your bread or cookie "mistakes." You can use savory breads and sandwich-style breads to make breadcrumbs. You can even freeze them until they're needed for other recipes. Use sweet breads to make bread pudding or as the "cake" layer in a trifle. Cookies can be crumbled to make a pie shell or as a topping for yogurt.

Easy Meals with Minimal Preparation

There will undoubtedly be days when you want or need to make a meal quickly, with minimal fuss. Although this is a cookbook, you don't need to cook every day to eat nutritious meals. Plenty of healthy (relatively speaking) convenience foods are gluten-free. Here are just a few of the many options available. Please note that not every product made by all of the listed manufacturers is gluten-free. Read labels carefully!

Quick Breakfast Ideas

- Bars: Nothing is quicker and easier than a breakfast bar. There are so many gluten-free varieties to choose from, such as Larabars (www.larabar.com), Andi Bars (www.autismndi.com), and Kind Fruit & Nut bars (www.kindsnacks.com). Add a glass of low-fat or nonfat milk (or nondairy "milk"), and you're good to go.
- Ready-made frozen waffles, pancakes, and French toast: All you have to do is heat these up and add some maple syrup and fruit. Varieties to try include Van's (www.vansfoods.com), Ian's (www.iansnaturalfoods.com), and Nature's Path (www.naturespath.com). Add a glass of calcium-fortified orange juice to round out your meal.
- A bowl of cereal: As long as the cereal is whole grain or fortified, it is fine—avoid the gluten-free types that are refined and unenriched, though. Many fortified Chex cereals are now gluten-free, including the rice, corn, and honey-nut varieties (www.generalmills.com). Don't shy away from hot cereal when you are in a hurry—quick oats really do cook fast (www.onlyoats.com). Top your cereal with sliced fresh or dried fruit and low-fat or nonfat milk (or nondairy "milk").

Fast Lunch Solutions

- Sandwich: Corn tortillas (www.missionfoods.com) or teff wraps (www.latortillafactory.com) make great "bread." Fill them with nut butter and jelly or gluten-free cold cuts (www.boarshead.com) and sliced vegetables. Add some fresh or dried fruit to complete your meal.

- Soup and crackers: Remember Cup of Soup? If your memories are fond ones, try the gluten-free noodle bowls made by Thai Kitchen (www.thaikitchen.com) and Simply Asia (www.simplyasia.com). Noodle bowls are even an option at work if your place of employment has a microwave oven. If you aren't a fan of noodle bowls, try Kettle Cuisine's (www.kettlecuisine.com) line of gluten-free soups. For extra crunch and nutrition, add some wholesome gluten-free crackers (www.marysgonecrackers.com, www.skinnycrisps.com) and sliced vegetables, such as diced carrots and bell peppers.
- Hearty salad: Nothing makes an easier lunch than salad, especially if you use a bag of prewashed greens. Add a can of rinsed beans—kidney, black, or chickpeas—sliced avocado, and orange slices. Toss them with some gluten-free salad dressing, and you are all set. Many salad dressings that are available in your local grocery store aren't made with gluten-containing ingredients, such as varieties of Newman's Own (www.newmansown.com/foodQA.aspx), Wishbone (www.wish-bone.com/Contact-Us-FAQs.aspx), and Kraft (www.kraftfoods.com/kf/healthyliving/articles/foodallergiessensitivities/glutenfreefoods.aspx).

Low-Prep Dinner Suggestions
- Beans and legs: Bake some chicken legs, heat up a can of gluten-free baked beans, and boil a few ears of corn, and you have dinner for your family. Many brands of baked beans are free of gluten-containing ingredients, including varieties of B&M (www.bgfoods.com/int_glutenfree.asp),which are widely available in grocery stores.
- Spaghetti: When you don't have time to make your own, many jarred spaghetti sauces are gluten-free, such as varieties from Classico (www.classico.com/flavors/faqs.aspx), available in most grocery stores, and Amy's (www.amys.com/products/category_view.php?prod_category=13), sold in natural food stores. Add some fresh vegetables to the sauce, and cook everything together; good choices are onion, diced green and red bell peppers, and zucchini—whatever you have on hand. Top your

pasta dish with a little grated Parmesan. Choose pasta made with whole grains, such as those by Ancient Harvest (www.quinoa .net), Lundberg Farms (www.lundberg.com), Tinkyada (www .tinkyada.com), and Orgran (www.orgran.com), all of which are generally available in natural food stores.

- Frozen entrees: When all you want to do is pop something into the microwave, you have many brands of gluten-free frozen entrees to choose from. Believe it or not, gluten-free frozen entrees are increasingly available in grocery stores (not only in natural food stores). Brands to try include Gluten-Free Café (www .myglutenfreecafe.com), Amy's Kitchen (www.amyskitchen.com), and, if you have kids, Ian's (www.iansnaturalfoods.com).

The specific products listed here are just a sample of the wide variety of gluten-free foods available to you. A new service to help you find gluten-free grocery items is www.zeer.com (Tricia is a member of Zeer's medical advisory board). You can search for any gluten-free product, such as gluten-free pizza, gluten-free fish sticks, and gluten-free soups. You have to sign up for membership to use the site—the most basic membership level is free.

3

What Are the Gluten-Free Grains?

There is an abundance of healthy and tasty naturally gluten-free grains available on the market: brown rice, whole corn, oats, millet, teff, sorghum, wild rice, buckwheat, amaranth, and quinoa. Some of these grains—for example, rice, corn, and oats—are staples in American diets. Others, such as teff, millet, and sorghum, remain relatively unknown. Thanks in part to more people adhering to a gluten-free diet, many of these grains are increasing in popularity. In the following pages, we will discuss each grain in detail and provide the information you need to easily incorporate them into your meals.

A Wee Bit of Science: Plant Taxonomy

Although rice, corn, oats, millet, teff, wild rice, buckwheat, amaranth, and quinoa have been considered safe to include in a gluten-free diet for many years, you may still come across outdated information that questions the use of some of them, especially amaranth, quinoa, and buckwheat. To help you understand why these grains are safe for you to eat, we'll explain a little about plant taxonomy—a classification system for plants. This classification system is frequently arranged as follows, with each division representing fewer and fewer plants. As you travel down the classification system, the plants within each division become more closely related.

Kingdom: The Kingdom name for all plants is "Plants."

Class: Rice, corn, oats, millet, teff, sorghum, wild rice, buckwheat, amaranth, and quinoa belong to the class of plants known as "Flowering Plants."

Subclass: Rice, corn, oats, millet, teff, sorghum, and wild rice belong to the subclass of flowering plants known as "Monocots." Buckwheat, amaranth, and quinoa belong to the subclass of flowering plants known as "Dicots." Dicots are not grains.

Family: All true grains, including gluten-free and gluten-containing grains, belong to the family of monocots known as "Grasses."

Subfamily: Millet, sorghum, and corn belong to the subfamily "Panicoideae." Oats, teff, rice, and wild rice (as well as wheat, barley, and rye) belong to the subfamily "Festucoideae."

Tribe: The gluten-containing grains wheat, barley, and rye belong to the same tribe. Oats, teff, rice, and wild rice each belong to a separate tribe.

The grains that are problematic in celiac disease—wheat, barley, and rye—are very closely related; all belong to the same tribe, "Hordeae." The "safe" grains oats, teff, rice, wild rice, and finger millet, although part of the same subfamily as wheat, barley, and rye, belong to different tribes. The "safe" grains millet, sorghum, maize (corn), and Job's-tears are even more distantly related and belong to a different subfamily from these other grains. (Note: While Job's-tears is a naturally gluten-free grain, at the present time it has limited availability and use in the United States and for that reason is not discussed in detail in this book.)

Millet, sorghum, corn, oats, teff, rice, wild rice, rye, barley, and oats all belong to the grass or "Gramineae" family and are true grains. Buckwheat, quinoa, and amaranth are not grasses and therefore are not true cereal grains. Yet they are often called "pseudocereals" because their seeds are used in a manner similar to true cereal grains. These pseudocereals are not closely related to wheat.

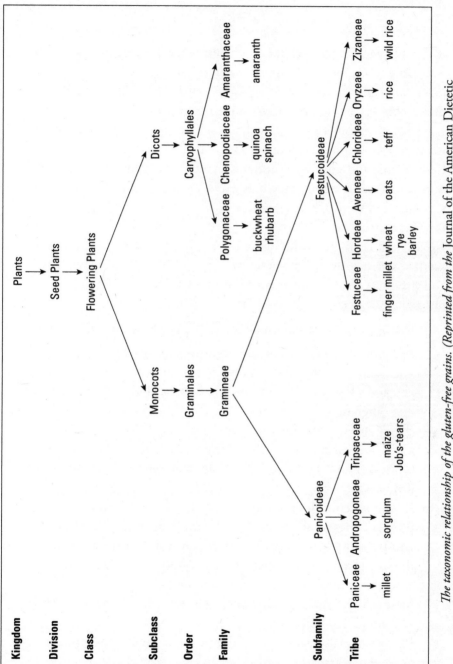

The taxonomic relationship of the gluten-free grains. (Reprinted from the Journal of the American Dietetic Association 100, Tricia Thompson, "Questionable foods and the gluten-free diet: Survey of current recommendations," 463–465 (2000), with permission from Elsevier.)

Brown Rice and Whole Corn: The Familiar Grains

Rice and corn are the two most frequently used grains in the gluten-free diet and undoubtedly appear often in your meals. Many specially formulated gluten-free breads, pastas, breakfast cereals, and baking mixes contain white rice flour, milled corn flour, rice starch, corn starch, or a combination of these flours and starches. The only problem with this scenario is that these are refined forms of rice and corn. Refined rice and corn and products made from them have very little nutritional value, unless they happen to be enriched or fortified with vitamins and minerals. As mentioned in the previous chapter, this is rarely the case.

Rice and corn are healthy gluten-free grains, but most of the time you should use the whole-grain versions—brown rice, whole corn, and products made from them. The following tips will help you do just that:

1. If you have never eaten brown rice, try it! It is nuttier, chewier, and more flavorful than white rice. If you'd like to ease into things, start with a 50:50 mixture of white and brown rice. We promise, you and your family (even your children) really won't notice much of a difference.
2. If you and your family think you don't like brown rice, do yourselves a favor and make the Creamy Dreamy Brown Rice and Quinoa Pudding (page 198). You will forever be hooked on brown rice.
3. If you use corn flour and cornmeal, make sure the products you purchase are whole grain. On the ingredients list, look for the words "whole cornmeal" or "whole corn flour." If you don't see the word "whole," the product is not whole grain. If you can't find whole cornmeal or corn flour in your local grocery or natural foods store, you can order them online from Arrowhead Mills and Bob's Red Mill.
4. If you normally bake with white rice flour, switch to brown rice flour or at least substitute half of the white for brown. You

should be able to purchase brown rice flour wherever you buy white rice flour. If not, you can order it from any number of mail-order companies, including Bob's Red Mill. The ingredients list will read "whole grain brown rice" or simply "brown rice."

5. Use brown rice flour to make the recipes for Carrot Raisin Pineapple Muffins (page 82) or Sweet Potato Rolls (page 84).

6. Make it a habit to read the ingredients lists of the gluten-free breads, pastas, breakfast cereals, and baking mixes that you purchase. If you buy a lot of corn- and rice-based products, that's fine, but you'll want to choose products made from brown rice and whole corn. Read the ingredients list and look for "brown rice flour" or "whole corn flour" or "whole cornmeal" as the first ingredient. Products that are made with brown rice flour include Bob's Red Mill brand Creamy Brown Rice Farina, Barbara's brand Brown Rice Crisps, and Tinkyada brand brown rice pastas.

Oats: The Familiar Grain You Can Eat Again

If you have celiac disease, you are undoubtedly familiar with oats, although you probably haven't eaten them since going gluten-free. For many years, it was believed that oats should not be included in gluten-free diets. In the United States, it is now the general consensus that most people with celiac disease can tolerate moderate amounts of gluten-free oats. A moderate amount is considered approximately 50 grams of dry oats a day. To determine the cup equivalent of 50 grams for the oats you purchase, check the label. A gram amount followed by a cup equivalent is generally provided. If you would like to add oats to your gluten-free diet, the American Dietetic Association recommends that this be done under the supervision of your physician or registered dietitian. (Note: A small percentage of individuals cannot tolerate oats at all; they may have an immune response to a protein in oats called avenin.)

Oats do not contain gluten; however, they are likely to become contaminated with gluten from wheat or barley or, to a lesser extent, rye while being harvested, transported, or processed. Perhaps the two crops were grown in rotation or in adjacent fields or they were transported by the same trucks or railcars and/or were processed in the same mills. For these reasons, it is very strongly recommended that you consume only oats that are labeled gluten-free. Under proposed FDA gluten-free labeling rules, if an oat product bears a gluten-free label, it contains less than 20 parts per million of gluten. The companies that currently process or supply gluten-free oat products include Gluten-Free Oats, Cream Hill Estates, Only Oats, Gifts of Nature, and Bob's Red Mill.

Most forms of gluten-free oats that you buy, such as steel-cut oats, rolled oats, quick oats, and oat flour, are whole grain. Oats are a good source of fiber, iron, zinc, and thiamine. If, together with your physician and registered dietitian, you decide to incorporate oats into your meals, start with small amounts because of their high fiber content. A half cup of dry rolled oats contains 4 grams of dietary fiber. If you experience gastrointestinal symptoms after eating oats, it may indicate that you are one of the few who cannot tolerate them. On the other hand, perhaps you are merely having symptoms caused by the increased fiber in your diet. Talk with your doctor or registered dietitian if you experience any symptoms.

Here are some suggestions to help you ease oats back into your meals:

1. Have oatmeal for breakfast again. With a little maple syrup or brown sugar, what better way is there to start the day? Serve the oatmeal with milk or gluten-free soy, rice, nut, or potato "milk" for added nutrition.
2. Remember no-bake cookies? These cookies combine quick oats (you can also use regular), cocoa powder, peanut butter (or any nut butter), sugar and a few other ingredients to make an absolutely delicious cookie. If you don't have a recipe, do an Internet search for "no-bake cookies." Tons of recipes will come up.
3. Make oatmeal cookies again—just be sure to adapt the recipe so that it's gluten-free.
4. Make homemade granola. Use it as a breakfast cereal, a snack, or a topping for yogurt.

5. Make a fruit crisp. It is as simple as placing a few sliced apples in a baking dish topped with a little butter, rolled oats, brown sugar, and cinnamon, and baking it until the apples are tender.

6. Add rolled oats to your baking recipes—for example, in muffins and bread—for more texture.

7. Make the sweet and satisfying Oatmeal Pear Spice Muffins (page 88) or Peanut Butter Oatmeal Granola Bars (page 70).

8. If you need additional ideas for baking with oats and oat flour, Gluten-Free Oats and Cream Hill Estates include recipes that use oats on their Web sites.

9. Try some of the tasty products that are made with gluten-free oats, such as Tracey's Treats Oat Bread Mix and Jessica's Natural Foods granolas. It is important to stress, however, that most food products that contain oats do not use a gluten-free variety. Unless the product made with oats states on the label that it is gluten free, do not eat it.

Millet, Teff, Sorghum, and Wild Rice: The Unfamiliar Grains

You may not be very familiar with the grains millet, teff, sorghum, and wild rice. Only fairly recently have these grains been incorporated into gluten-free diets. Although they are not yet household names in the United States, they are staple grains in many parts of the world. Rest assured that these grains are healthy, are easy to cook, and, most important, taste good!

To familiarize yourself with each grain, cook up a small batch and taste it. Think about the dishes you already make that would benefit from the added flavor and texture of these grains. Basically, you can use them in any dish that you would normally make with rice, such as rice medleys, salads, stuffed vegetables (peppers, eggplant, and tomatoes), soups, chili, and hot breakfast cereals.

Nutritional information for each grain has been taken from the U.S. Department of Agriculture's National Nutrient Database for Standard Reference, Release 22 (2009), and the Nutrient Data Laboratory Home Page, http://www.ars.usda.gov/ba/bhnrc/ndl.

Magnificent Millet

Millet is a staple grain in many areas of the world, including parts of Africa and Asia. It is grown in the United States and is available as millet flour, millet grits, and hulled millet. Millet is light yellow in color and tastes similar to cornmeal. The flour is fine and powdery, and the grits are similar to a coarse cornmeal. This grain is a rich source of fiber, thiamine, niacin, and folate.

Hulled millet works well as a hot cereal or in combination with other grains. Add it to your rice dishes or bean salads, or serve on its own as a side dish. You can also cook millet grits as a hot cereal. Millet flour can be used in a variety of baked goods, such as cornbreads, muffins, and cookies.

According to the Whole Grains Council, you should cook hulled millet at a ratio of 1 cup of millet to 2½ cups of fluid for approximately 25 to 35 minutes. For millet grits, Bob's Red Mill recommends cooking them at a ratio of one part grits to three parts water for approximately 10 to 15 minutes.

Millet flour, millet grits, and hulled millet may be available in natural foods stores, or you can mail-order them from Bob's Red Mill and Arrowhead Mills. Use millet to make the Multigrain Bread (page 86), Lentil and Millet Soup (page 102), or Sesame and Millet–Crusted Tuna and Pineapple Kabobs (page 182). For additional gluten-free recipes using hulled millet, millet grits, and millet flour, see the Web site of Bob's Red Mill.

Nutritional information

Amount: ¼ cup (50 grams) raw millet grain
Calories: 189
Fat: 2.1 grams
Carbohydrates: 36.4 grams
Protein: 5.5 grams
Dietary fiber: 4.2 grams
Thiamine: 0.21 milligrams
Riboflavin: 0.15 milligrams
Niacin: 2.36 milligrams
Folate: 42 dietary folate equivalents

Calcium: 4 milligrams
Iron: 1.5 milligrams

Tasty Teff

Teff is an indispensable grain in Ethiopia, where it is used to make a spongy flatbread called injera. It is grown in the United States in Idaho and is available as a grain and a flour. Depending on the variety, teff is tannish-brown or reddish-brown in color. Teff grains are tiny and have a mild nutty flavor. The flour is very fine and powdery. This grain is a rich source of fiber, iron, and thiamine.

Teff grain works well as a hot breakfast cereal or in combination with other grains as a side dish. According to the Teff Company, teff grain cooks in approximately 15 to 20 minutes at a ratio of one part teff to three parts liquid. Teff flour works well in baked goods, such as breads, muffins, pancakes, pie crusts, and cookies.

Teff grain and flour may be available in natural food stores or mail-ordered from the Teff Company and Bob's Red Mill. Try using teff in the recipes for Teff Flatbread (page 74), Strawberry Pie in Teff Crust (page 202), or Hot Mixed-Grain Cereal with Berries (page 62). For additional gluten-free recipes using teff grain and flour, see the Web sites of the Teff Company and Bob's Red Mill.

Nutritional information

Amount: ¼ cup (48 grams) uncooked teff grain
Calories: 177
Fat: 1.2 grams
Carbohydrates: 35.3 grams
Protein: 6.4 grams
Dietary fiber: 3.9 grams
Thiamine: 0.19 milligrams
Riboflavin: 0.13 milligrams
Niacin: 1.62 milligrams
Folate: not available
Calcium: 87 milligrams
Iron: 3.68 milligrams

Scrumptious Sorghum

Sorghum is one of the world's leading food crops and a staple grain in many countries, including parts of Africa and Asia. An increasing amount of sorghum is being grown in the United States for food and is available as a grain and a flour. Sorghum grain is tannish-white in color and looks like a small berry. This grain is a rich source of fiber and iron.

Sorghum grain works well as a hot cereal or in combination with other grains as a side dish. It may also be popped like corn! According to the Whole Grains Council, sorghum cooks in approximately 25 to 40 minutes at a ratio of 1 cup of grain to 4 cups of liquid. Sorghum grain should be soaked overnight before cooking. Sorghum flour works particularly well in baked goods, such as breads and cakes.

Sorghum grain and flour may be available in natural foods stores or can be mail-ordered from Twin Valley Mills, Authentic Foods, Bob's Red Mill, and Shiloh Farms. Sorghum is featured in the recipes for Sorghum with Garlic and Flax Bread (page 85) and Mediterranean Chicken with Sorghum, Feta, and Tomato (page 183). For additional gluten-free recipes using sorghum flour, see the Web sites of Twin Valley Mills and Bob's Red Mill.

Nutritional information

Amount: ¼ cup (48 grams) sorghum grain
Calories: 163
Fat: 1.6 grams
Carbohydrates: 35.8 grams
Protein: 5.4 grams
Dietary fiber: 3.0 grams
Thiamine: 0.11 milligrams
Riboflavin: 0.07 milligrams
Niacin: 1.41 milligrams
Folate: not available
Calcium: 13 milligrams
Iron: 2.11 milligrams

Wholesome Wild Rice

Wild rice is native to North America and is grown in Minnesota, Wisconsin, Oregon, and California. Despite its name, it is not "true" rice, although it is used like rice. Wild rice is available as a grain and a flour. Wild rice grains are dark brownish-black in color and look like short pine needles. They have a nice chewy texture. Wild rice is a rich source of fiber and niacin.

The grain works particularly well when added to rice dishes or in combination with other grains as a side dish. According to Moose Lake Wild Rice, wild rice grain takes longer to cook than other grains do. It cooks in approximately 35 to 50 minutes at a ratio of 1 part wild rice grain to 3 parts fluid.

Wild rice grain and flour may be available in natural foods stores or mail-ordered from Lundberg Family Farms. Try the recipes for savory Wild Rice Pilaf (page 150) or Wild Rice Spring Rolls (page 139). For more gluten-free recipes using wild rice, see the Web sites of Gibb's Wild Rice (www.gibbswildrice.com) and Moose Lake Wild Rice (www.mooselakewildrice.com).

Nutritional information

Amount: ¼ cup (40 grams) raw wild rice
Calories: 143
Fat: 0.4 grams
Carbohydrates: 30.0 grams
Protein: 5.9 grams
Dietary fiber: 2.5 grams
Thiamine: 0.05 milligrams
Riboflavin: 0.11 milligrams
Niacin: 2.7 milligrams
Folate: 38 dietary folate equivalents
Calcium: 8 milligrams
Iron: 0.78 milligrams

Here are some supersimple ways to incorporate millet, teff, sorghum, and wild rice into your meals:

1. The next time you make a rice dish, substitute ¼ cup of whatever rice you normally use for wild rice. You will have to increase the amount of liquid because wild rice requires more water to cook. This may take a bit of experimenting, but it is better to use too much, rather than too little, liquid. You can always drain the extra liquid when the rice is cooked, and return the pot to the heat to remove the excess water (just as you do with pasta).

2. The next time you make soup, throw in a handful of wild rice. It will add a nice chewy texture.

3. When you feel like eating popcorn, pop sorghum grain instead of corn—really! Sorghum pops best when it's done in a skillet—add a small amount of vegetable oil, cover the bottom of the pan with a single layer of sorghum, cover it, and pop. When sorghum is popped, it looks like "baby" popcorn. Your children will love how cute it looks. Because sorghum does not pop to the volume of corn, when using popped sorghum as a snack, it's best to mix it with dried fruit, such as raisins, or even some chopped dark chocolate.

4. When you make quick bread or muffins that usually include nuts, fold a tablespoon or two of teff grain into the mixture instead (or, alternatively, include both the nuts and the teff!).

5. If you like hot cereal, instead of your usual variety, cook teff or sorghum grain instead. Just follow the directions for cooking on the package. Keep in mind that when you cook sorghum, you will decrease the cooking time substantially if you first soak it overnight.

6. The next time you make chili, add a handful of millet grits to the pot. If you are making cornbread to go along with your chili, substitute millet flour for some of the cornmeal in your recipe.

Buckwheat, Amaranth, and Quinoa: The Psuedocereals

You may also be unfamiliar with buckwheat, amaranth, and quinoa, although they are being used more frequently in both gluten-free and mainstream foods and recipes. As stated at the beginning of this chapter, these "pseudocereals" are not really grains. Nonetheless, they are often called grains because their seeds are used in baking and cooking in a manner similar to grains. Like all of the gluten-free grains, they are healthy, easy to use, and delicious.

As was recommended with millet, sorghum, teff, and wild rice, cook up a small batch each of buckwheat, amaranth, and quinoa. Think about the dishes you already make that would benefit from their added flavor and texture. Like the grains, each of these pseudocereals can be used in any dish that typically calls for rice, such as rice medleys, salads, stuffed vegetables (peppers, eggplant, and tomatoes), soups, chili, and hot breakfast cereals.

Beguiling Buckwheat

Buckwheat was domesticated in Asia thousands of years ago. Buckwheat has been grown in the United States for hundreds of years and is currently grown primarily as a food crop. It is available in the United States as buckwheat groats, kasha (roasted buckwheat groats), and buckwheat flour. Buckwheat groats are light brown in color with a triangular shape. The flour is fine and powdery. This pseudocereal is a rich source of fiber and niacin.

Kasha works well in salads, chili, pilaf, and other side dishes. According to the Whole Grains Council, it cooks at a ratio of 1 part kasha to 2 parts liquid in approximately 20 minutes. Buckwheat flour works well in a variety of recipes, such as pancakes.

Buckwheat groats, kasha, and flour may be available in natural foods stores and can be mail-ordered from the Birkett Mills, Arrowhead Mills, and Bob's Red Mill. Try the tasty recipes for Buckwheat Banana Pancakes (page 68), Lentil and Kasha Salad (page 103), and Chocolate Buckwheat Crepes with Raspberry Ricotta Filling (page 200). For additional gluten-free recipes using kasha and buckwheat flour, see the Web sites of the Birkett Mills and Bob's Red Mill.

Nutritional information

Amount: ¼ cup (41 grams) buckwheat groats, roasted, dry (kasha)
Calories: 142
Fat: 1.1 grams
Carbohydrates: 30.7 grams

Protein: 4.8 grams
Dietary fiber: 4.2 grams
Thiamine: 0.09 milligrams
Riboflavin: 0.11 milligrams
Niacin: 2.11 milligrams
Folate: 17 dietary folate equivalents
Calcium: 7 milligrams
Iron: 1.01 milligrams

Amazing Amaranth

Amaranth is native to South America, Central America, and Mexico, where large amounts were grown by the Aztec people. Amaranth is grown in the United States, primarily in Illinois, and is available as a seed, as flour, and as puffed amaranth. Amaranth seeds are small, round, and cream-colored. The flour is fine and powdery. This pseudocereal is a rich source of fiber and iron.

Amaranth seeds may be used in a variety of recipes, including soups and chili. According to the Whole Grains Council, amaranth cooks at a ratio of 1 part amaranth to 2 parts water in about 20 minutes. Amaranth flour works well in many recipes, such as quick breads.

Amaranth seeds, puffed amaranth, and amaranth flour may be available in health food stores or can be mail-ordered from Nu-World Amaranth, Arrowhead Mills, and Bob's Red Mill. Use amaranth to make delicious Toasted Amaranth–Crusted Chicken Salad (page 99) and Amaranth-Stuffed Peppers (page 145). For additional gluten-free recipes using amaranth seeds and flour, see the Web sites of Nu-World Amaranth and Bob's Red Mill.

Nutritional information
Amount: ¼ cup (48 grams) uncooked amaranth seed
Calories: 179
Fat: 3.4 grams
Carbohydrates: 31.5 grams
Protein: 6.5 grams

Dietary fiber: 3.2 grams
Thiamine: 0.06 milligrams
Riboflavin: 0.10 milligrams
Niacin: 0.45 milligrams
Folate: 40 dietary folate equivalents
Calcium: 77 milligrams
Iron: 3.67 milligrams

Quirky Quinoa

This pseudocereal is native to Bolivia, Chile, and Peru, where it has been eaten for thousands of years. Quinoa (*keen*-wah) is currently not grown in the United States. Most of the quinoa available in the United States is grown in South America; some of it comes from Canada. Quinoa is available as a seed, a flour, and flakes. Depending on the variety, quinoa seed may be cream-colored or red. It is a disk-shaped seed with a mild flavor. This pseudocereal is a rich source of fiber, iron, thiamine, and folate.

Quinoa seeds are easy to prepare. It is important to buy prewashed quinoa, however, or you'll have to wash it yourself. Quinoa seeds contain a bitter substance called saponin in their outer coating. This outer coating must be removed before you eat the quinoa. If you are using unwashed quinoa, put it in a fine mesh sieve and rinse it thoroughly for several minutes under running water.

In any recipe where you would normally use rice or another grain, you can substitute quinoa seeds. According to the Quinoa Corporation, quinoa seeds cook at a ratio of 1 part quinoa to 2 parts liquid in about 15 minutes. Quinoa flour and quinoa flakes work well in baked goods such as breads, muffins, and bars.

Quinoa seeds, flakes, and flour may be available in natural food stores and also can be mail-ordered from the Quinoa Corporation, the Northern Quinoa Corporation, Arrowhead Mills, and Bob's Red Mill. Try the recipes for Spiced Quinoa Cereal (page 62), Quinoa with Sautéed Onions and Lima Beans (page 131), and Quinoa and Cheddar–Stuffed Eggplant (page 176). For more gluten-free recipes using quinoa seeds, flour, and flakes, see the Web sites of the

Quinoa Corporation, the Northern Quinoa Corporation, and Bob's Red Mill.

Nutritional information
Amount: ¼ cup (42.5 grams) uncooked quinoa seed
Calories: 156
Fat: 2.6 grams
Carbohydrates: 27.3 grams
Protein: 6.0 grams
Dietary fiber: 3.0 grams
Thiamine: 0.15 grams
Riboflavin: 0.14 grams
Niacin: 0.65 grams
Folate: 78 dietary folate equivalents
Calcium: 20 milligrams
Iron: 1.94 milligrams

Here are some supersimple ways to incorporate these pseudocereals into your meals:

1. The next time you make a dried bean salad (with kidney beans or black beans, for example), cook up some kasha (roasted buckwheat groats) to mix into the salad. The kasha will add a nice nutty flavor to your dish.
2. When you make a rice medley, substitute a little uncooked kasha for some of the uncooked rice. A medley of brown rice, wild rice, and kasha is a delicious combination.
3. If you are a fan of stuffed bell peppers, stuffed tomatoes, and so on, substitute cooked amaranth for some or all of the grain you normally use. Cook the amaranth according to the package directions.
4. Whenever you make soups or chili, throw in a handful of amaranth seeds.
5. If you plan to serve a rice pilaf, make a quinoa pilaf instead—simply substitute the quinoa for the rice.
6. If you miss tabbouleh, which is typically made with bulgur wheat, make it by substituting cooked quinoa for the bulgur.

Commingling of Grains

Contamination of gluten-free foods with gluten-containing ones is always a concern, even at the basic level of grains and flour. Naturally gluten-free grains may be processed in a variety of facilities: some of these handle only gluten-free grains and others produce both gluten-free and gluten-containing grains. Companies that process both types may have a separate room, area, or production line for gluten-free grains. Alternatively, naturally gluten-free grains may be processed in the same area and on the same lines as gluten-containing grains. If this is the case, the company may have extensive safeguards in place, such as the cleaning of shared equipment and timed product turnovers. Regardless of the type of facility, all manufacturers should follow current good manufacturing practices to decrease the likelihood of contaminating one food with the ingredients of another.

Unfortunately, naturally gluten-free grains may come into the processing plant already contaminated with wheat, barley, or rye. Whether the commingling of grains takes place depends on several factors, such as what crop was grown in the field prior to the gluten-free grain or which crops were growing adjacent to it. If these crops were wheat, barley, or rye, it is likely that some gluten-containing grain will be growing alongside the gluten-free crop. This foreign grain will be harvested along with the gluten-free grain. Contamination may also occur during harvesting or transporting if equipment is shared to handle both gluten-containing and gluten-free grains.

A load of grain that arrives at a processing plant is not processed as is. Several safeguards are in place to make sure the grain is as pure as possible. These measures may include extensive cleaning to remove foreign grain. Grain may also be passed through sizing equipment to separate foreign grain (which presumably is a different size and shape from the main grain) from the grain being processed.

Issues with contamination do not mean you should avoid naturally gluten-free grains, but it does mean you should carefully choose the brands you buy. Many producers of naturally gluten-free grains and flours specifically market to the gluten-free community. These manufacturers are well aware of your needs. Many of these companies take several steps to limit contamination, such as growing the grain themselves, contracting with specific growers, and routinely testing products for gluten. Often, the company's Web site will include information about its contamination safeguards. If you have any questions or concerns, contact the company to ask what precautions are taken to limit contamination.

Remember that under the FDA's proposed rule for labeling of food as gluten-free, a naturally gluten-free grain or flour that bears a gluten-free label must contain less than 20 parts per million of gluten, and this includes gluten from cross-contamination. The proposed rule will also require companies that market naturally gluten-free foods, such as rice, corn, and millet, to declare on their labels that all foods of that type are gluten-free (for example, "Corn, a gluten-free food"). It is hoped that this facet of the rule will change in the final version. Regardless, it is best to choose naturally gluten-free grains and flours that carry a gluten-free claim over those that don't, whenever possible. Products labeled gluten-free are more likely to have been tested for gluten contamination.

What to Keep in Your Pantry

An increasing number of grocery stores are stocking gluten-free grains and flours. Most natural food stores also carry these products, but they still may not be readily available in your area. All of them can be mail-ordered. Depending on your specific situation, you may want to keep the following ingredients (gluten-free versions, of course) on hand to help simplify your gluten-free cooking.

Grains
Amaranth seed
Brown rice
Buckwheat groats
Hulled millet
Instant brown rice
Instant polenta
Kasha (buckwheat groats)
Millet grits

Polenta
Puffed amaranth
Quinoa
Rolled oats (labeled gluten-free only)
Sorghum
Teff
Wild rice

Flour
Amaranth flour
Brown rice flour
Buckwheat flour
Millet flour
Oat flour (labeled gluten-free only)
Quinoa flakes
Sorghum flour
Teff flour (both white and brown)
White rice flour
Whole-grain cornmeal

Starches
Corn starch
Potato starch
Tapioca starch/flour

Note: Tapioca starch and tapioca flour are the same, but potato starch is not the same as potato flour.

Pasta
Brown rice pasta
Quinoa pasta
Soba (100% buckwheat noodles)

Other cooking and baking ingredients
Almond flour/meal
Almond paste

Bean flour
Brown rice crackers
Corn tortillas
Gluten-free cornflakes
Gluten-free granola
Ground flaxseeds/flax meal
Rice Chex
Rice wrappers
Xanthan gum

Note: Almond flour and almond meal are the same, as are ground flaxseed and flax meal.

Condiments

Gluten-free chicken/beef/vegetable stock
Gluten-free curry paste
Gluten-free soy/tamari sauce
Gluten-free Worcestershire sauce

Part Two

Recipes and
Meal Plans

As we mentioned in the preface, the recipes in this book are organized along traditional lines: breakfast, breads, soups and salads, starters, sides, main courses, and "sweet somethings." We've included serving suggestions for many of the recipes, which appear at the end of the recipe and are not part of the ingredients list. These suggestions are meant to introduce you to the wide variety of eating options available to you, but note that they are not included in the nutritional information at the end of the recipe. If the ingredient is not in the ingredients list, its nutritional values must be considered separately.

Within each section, recipes are separated into two main types—quick and easy gluten-free and creative gluten-free. Sometimes you may have only 30 minutes to throw together a meal, and you want a recipe you can make without a lot of fuss. Other times, you might like to spend more time creating a special dish for your family and friends. Either way, in the pages that follow you will find recipes to suit all of your needs.

When you purchase foods to make these recipes, it's important to read the labels and make sure all of the items you use are free of gluten-containing ingredients. Most of the required ingredients for these recipes are usually gluten-free, but always check the labels to be sure. For foods that often contain gluten, such as soy sauce, gluten-free varieties are listed in the Resources section.

Many recipes in this book call for gluten-free grains and flours, such as amaranth, buckwheat, quinoa, millet, teff, sorghum, and wild rice. These grains and flours generally can be bought in natural foods stores and increasingly are available in grocery stores. All of them can be mail-ordered. Please see the Resources section for sources.

In chapter 11, we've included four weeks of meal plans with many recipes from this book, to help you put together daily menus. Enjoy!

4

Breakfast

You've heard it before, but it really is true: breakfast is the most important meal of the day. Although some of these recipes are meant to be cooked when you have plenty of time, many others, such as Spiced Quinoa Cereal (page 62) and Hot Mixed-Grain Cereal with Berries (page 62), are quick enough to fit into any morning routine. A few, such as the Peanut Butter Oatmeal Granola Bars (page 70), can be made ahead of time and eaten on the run.

Quick and Easy Gluten-Free

Egg and Cheese Tostadas
Cheddar and Bacon Drop Biscuits
Spiced Quinoa Cereal
Hot Mixed-Grain Cereal with Berries
Blueberry Yogurt Belgian Waffles
French Toast
Eggs on Toast
Yogurt Breakfast Shake

Creative Gluten-Free

Polenta with Cinnamon Sugar
Buckwheat Banana Pancakes

Chicken Sausage Scramble
Peanut Butter Oatmeal Granola Bars
Homemade Granola
Parfaits with Homemade Granola

QUICK AND EASY GLUTEN-FREE

Egg and Cheese Tostadas
Serves 4

*Eggs on toast, the deluxe version! To cut down on fat
and cholesterol, use gluten-free egg substitute and
reduced-fat cream cheese and sour cream.*

4 corn tostadas

¼ cup whipped cream cheese

¼ teaspoon cumin

⅛ teaspoon chili powder

4 eggs

1 teaspoon dried cilantro

Vegetable oil or gluten-free
  cooking spray

¼ cup shredded Colby and
  Monterey Jack cheese blend

¼ cup gluten-free salsa

4 teaspoons sour cream

1. Preheat the oven to 350 degrees. Warm the tostadas for about
   5 minutes.
2. Meanwhile, mix the cream cheese with the cumin and the chili
   powder.
3. Beat the eggs with the cilantro. Coat a nonstick skillet with
   cooking spray or a small amount of vegetable oil. Scramble the
   eggs. Remove from heat.
4. Spread 1 tablespoon of the cream cheese mixture on each tostada.
   Top it with ¼ egg mixture, 1 tablespoon cheese, 1 tablespoon
   salsa, and 1 teaspoon sour cream.
5. Serve immediately.

Tip: If you're using soft corn tortillas, toast them in a skillet first.

Nutritional information per serving: 212 calories, 9.7 g protein, 10.7 g carbohydrate,
14.6 g fat, 229 mg cholesterol, 264 mg sodium, less than 1 g fiber, 95.8 mg calcium,
1.2 mg iron

Cheddar and Bacon Drop Biscuits

Makes 18 biscuits

The bacon and cheese add a delicious flavor to these savory biscuits. Enjoy them warm from the oven. These biscuits make a nice addition to any brunch.

Gluten-free cooking spray or vegetable oil

2 ounces Canadian bacon

1 cup brown rice flour

¼ cup sorghum flour

½ cup tapioca flour

¼ teaspoon salt

½ teaspoon baking soda

3 tablespoons unsalted butter

⅓ cup shredded sharp cheddar cheese

½ cup buttermilk (or combine ½ cup milk minus ½ tablespoon with ½ tablespoon vinegar)

¼ cup plain seltzer

1. Preheat the oven to 400 degrees. Coat a baking sheet with gluten-free cooking spray or vegetable oil.
2. Dice the Canadian bacon into small pieces. Place bacon in a small skillet over medium heat and cook until lightly browned. Remove from heat and set aside.
3. In a large bowl, mix the various flours, salt, and baking soda. Cut in the butter with a pastry blender or 2 knives until the mixture is crumbly.
4. Stir in the cheese and bacon. Add the buttermilk and seltzer and stir just until the dough is moist.
5. Drop the dough by 2 level tablespoons, 1 inch apart, onto the prepared baking sheets.
6. Bake for 10 to 12 minutes or until biscuits are golden brown.

Tip: For a tasty variation, use turkey bacon and Swiss cheese instead of Canadian bacon and cheddar.

Nutritional information per biscuit: 79 calories, 2 g protein, 10.7 g carbohydrate, 3 g fat, 9 mg cholesterol, 120 mg sodium, less than 1 g fiber, 25 mg calcium, less than 1 mg iron

Spiced Quinoa Cereal

Serves 4 (Serving size: ½ cup dry cereal or ¾ cup cooked cereal)

Make a large batch of this cereal so that you can have it anytime. The recipe calls for quinoa flakes, which are especially suited to hot cereal.

2 cups quinoa flakes

½ cup dried fruit (mix and match as desired or use a single variety)

2 tablespoons sugar (optional)

2 tablespoons brown sugar

½ teaspoon cinnamon

¼ teaspoon salt

⅛ teaspoon nutmeg

⅛ teaspoon allspice

1. Mix all ingredients together and store the cereal in an airtight container.
2. When you're ready to eat the cereal for breakfast, mix ½ cup of the dry mix with 1 cup water (or milk, if desired) in a deep dish.
3. Microwave for 2 to 3 minutes.

Tip: You may also add nuts for a crunchy texture.

Nutritional information per serving: 194 calories, 4.6 g protein, 39 g carbohydrates, 2 g fat, 0 mg cholesterol, 111 mg sodium, 3.5 g fiber, 11.7 mg calcium, 1.7 mg iron

Hot Mixed-Grain Cereal with Berries

Serves 8 (Serving size: ½ cup)

An easy-to-prepare, fiber-packed, stick-to-your ribs breakfast!

½ cup uncooked hulled millet

½ cup uncooked teff grain

½ teaspoon salt

3 cups 1% milk

1 cup blueberries

2 teaspoons cinnamon

¼ teaspoon nutmeg

4 tablespoons brown sugar

4 tablespoons hulled sunflower seeds

1. In a large saucepan, mix together the millet, teff, salt, and milk. Bring to a boil over medium heat. Reduce heat and simmer until the mixture is creamy and the milk is absorbed.

2. Stir in the blueberries, cinnamon, and nutmeg.
3. Pour the cereal into individual serving bowls and sprinkle it with brown sugar and sunflower seeds. Serve immediately.

Tip: Use frozen berries or dried fruit in place of the fresh berries.

Nutritional information per serving: 185 calories, 7 g protein, 31 g carbohydrates, 4.1 g fat, 4.5 mg cholesterol, 189.5 mg sodium, 3.2 g fiber, 146 mg calcium, 1.7 mg iron

---

Blueberry Yogurt Belgian Waffles

Serves 6 (Serving size: 2 4 × 4-inch waffles)

Why eat frozen waffles when you can so easily make your own? Every waffle maker is different, so be sure to follow the cooking instructions that came from the manufacturer.

3 eggs
1½ cups fat-free vanilla yogurt
1 teaspoon vanilla extract
1 cup brown rice flour
½ cup tapioca flour
½ teaspoon xanthan gum

1 teaspoon baking soda
2 teaspoons baking powder
¼ teaspoon salt
¼ teaspoon nutmeg
2 tablespoons butter, melted
¾ cup fresh or frozen blueberries

1. In a large bowl, beat together the eggs, yogurt, and vanilla. Add the dry ingredients, flour through nutmeg; then add the butter and mix everything well.
2. Stir in the blueberries until just combined.
3. Heat a waffle iron.
4. Pour enough batter for one waffle onto the waffle iron, and cook until golden on both sides.
5. Serve immediately. These waffles are delicious plain or served with apple butter or warm maple syrup.

Tip: Waffles also make nice "bread" for Eggs on Toast (page 65).

Nutritional information per serving: 227.5 calories, 6.8 g protein, 33.7 g carbohydrates, 7.1 g fat, 116.7 mg cholesterol, 457 mg sodium, 1.9 g fiber, 103.7 mg calcium, 1 mg iron

French Toast

Serves 4 (Serving size: 4 triangles)

Although you may think of French toast as a weekend breakfast, it really is fast and simple to make—perfect for on-the-go mornings.

3 eggs

½ cup skim milk

1½ teaspoons cinnamon

1 teaspoon vanilla extract

2 tablespoons brown sugar

8 slices of your favorite gluten-free whole-grain or gluten-free enriched bread

Gluten-free cooking spray (or 1 teaspoon vegetable oil)

2 teaspoons butter

1. Beat the eggs, milk, cinnamon, vanilla, and brown sugar together by hand until creamy.
2. Soak the bread in the egg mixture until well saturated.
3. Spray a large skillet with cooking spray (or coat with vegetable oil) and heat over medium heat until hot. Lower the flame, add the butter, and melt it.
4. Add the bread to the hot skillet and cook until golden brown on each side.
5. Set aside each piece of toast, keeping it covered, until all of the bread is toasted.
6. Slice each piece in half on an angle (into a triangle shape). Serve with warm maple syrup or apple butter and a sprinkle of cinnamon sugar.

Tip: French toast can be made ahead of time and frozen on a cookie sheet. Store it in zipper-lock freezer bags. Whenever you want quick and easy French toast, just place pieces on a cookie sheet and place them in a 350-degree oven until heated through.

Nutritional information per serving: 308 calories, 7.8 g protein, 42 g carbohydrate, 13.8 g fat, 164 mg cholesterol, 240 mg sodium, 4 g fiber, 103 mg calcium, 3.6 mg iron

Eggs on Toast

Makes 4 servings

*This breakfast is simple to prepare and
is a classic favorite.*

4 slices gluten-free whole-grain or
   gluten-free enriched bread

Gluten-free cooking spray (or
   1 teaspoon vegetable oil)

1½ tablespoons butter, softened

4 eggs

4 2 × 2-inch slices roasted red
   peppers (from a jar is fine)

¼ teaspoon salt

Dash of pepper

1. Tear out a 1½-inch-diameter hole from the center of each piece of bread (reserve the bread circles for another use).
2. Coat a large skillet with cooking spray or vegetable oil and heat over medium heat until the pan is hot, then reduce heat to low.
3. Meanwhile, lightly butter both sides of each piece of bread and place bread in the pan, making sure not to overcrowd.
4. Crack each egg, being careful not to break the yolk, and drop it into the center of each piece of bread.
5. Mix the salt and pepper.
6. When the white starts to cook through, top each egg with a piece of roasted pepper and sprinkle it with ¼ of the salt and pepper mixture.
7. When the white is almost completely cooked, carefully turn each piece of egg on toast over, cook until brown on the other side, and serve.

Tip: Save the mini circles of bread in the freezer to use for gluten-free croutons or breadcrumbs.

Nutritional information per serving: 210 calories, 7.4 g protein, 19 g carbohydrate, 12.5 g fat, 219 mg cholesterol, 311 mg sodium, 2.2 g fiber, 48 mg calcium, 2.4 mg iron

Yogurt Breakfast Shake

Makes 4 9-ounce shakes

*This yogurt shake is easy to prepare, and
you can drink it on the run!*

1 8-ounce plain nonfat yogurt	1 large banana, cut into 2-inch pieces
1 6-ounce low-fat vanilla yogurt	2 tablespoons ground flaxseed
1½ cups 1% milk	2 tablespoons brown sugar
1 cup strawberries	4 ice cubes

1. In a blender, process all ingredients together, except the ice cubes, until smooth.
2. Add the ice cubes and blend until the shake is frothy.
3. Add additional sweetener, if desired.

Tip: Other types of fruit and flavors of yogurt can be used to create your yogurt shake—you can even add nut butter! Make it your masterpiece, based on the ingredients you have available at home.

Nutritional information per shake: 181 calories, 9.6 g protein, 30.5 g carbohydrate, 3 g fat, 7 mg cholesterol, 115 mg sodium, 2.9 g fiber, 326 mg calcium, less than 1 mg iron

---

CREATIVE GLUTEN-FREE

Polenta with Cinnamon Sugar

Serves 4 (Serving size: 3 to 4 pieces, depending on the size of the cookie cutter that you use)

Polenta is made from coarse-grain cornmeal and is a popular dish in Italy. In general, polenta should be free of gluten-containing ingredients, but check the label just in case.

2½ cups water

¾ cup instant gluten-free polenta (see the box below for help with regular polenta)

2 tablespoons real maple syrup

½ cup whole milk

Gluten-free cooking spray or 1 teaspoon vegetable oil (some cooking sprays contain flour, so read labels carefully)

2 tablespoons butter, melted

2 tablespoons sugar

1 teaspoon cinnamon

1. Bring water to a boil in a medium saucepan. Add the polenta and cook for 3 to 4 minutes, stirring frequently.
2. Add the maple syrup and milk. Continue to cook for 1 minute longer.
3. Spray a 9 × 13-inch dish with cooking spray, or coat with vegetable oil. Pour the mixture into the dish and refrigerate for about 30 minutes, or until the polenta is cool and hard.
4. Preheat the oven to 350 degrees. Line a baking sheet with parchment paper.
5. Using a cookie cutter, cut the polenta into your desired shapes and transfer each piece to a baking sheet. Brush with melted butter and bake in the preheated oven for 10 minutes. Remove the polenta from the oven.
6. Turn on the broiler. Combine the sugar and cinnamon in a small bowl, and sprinkle the mixture over the polenta. Broil for 1 to 2 minutes, just until the sugar starts to melt. Remove from oven and serve polenta with blueberries, raspberries, or blackberries.

Tip: You can make your own cooking spray by purchasing a spray pump bottle at a kitchen supply store and adding your favorite oil.

Nutritional information per serving: 214 calories, 2.5 g protein, 36 g carbohydrate, 7 g fat, 18 mg cholesterol, 54 mg sodium, 1 g fiber, 50 mg calcium, 1.3 mg iron

Using Regular Polenta Instead of Instant

If you don't have instant polenta, follow the directions on the package of regular polenta for 4 servings, using ½ cup less water than recommended.

Buckwheat Banana Pancakes

Serves 4 (Serving size: 2 pancakes)

*Although this delectable recipe has a lot of ingredients,
it is well worth the effort.*

½ cup buckwheat flour

¼ cup brown rice flour

¼ cup finely ground almond flour
or meal (see box below)

2 tablespoons cornstarch

1 tablespoon finely ground
flaxseed

2 teaspoons baking powder

½ teaspoon baking soda

1 teaspoon cinnamon

¼ teaspoon allspice

¼ teaspoon salt

1 egg

½ cup plain nonfat yogurt

½ cup skim milk

2 tablespoons honey

2 tablespoons vegetable oil

1 ripe banana, mashed

Gluten-free cooking spray or
2 teaspoons vegetable oil (some
cooking sprays contain flour,
so check labels carefully)

1. In a large bowl, combine the dry ingredients, from the buckwheat flour through the salt. In a medium bowl, mix the egg, yogurt, milk, honey, oil, and banana; add them to the dry ingredients and stir the batter until just moistened.
2. Coat a hot griddle with cooking spray or vegetable oil. Pour the batter by ¼ cupfuls onto the griddle. When bubbles form on top of each pancake and it is browned on the bottom, flip it over. Cook until the other side is also brown. Serve with warm maple syrup, fruit butter, or fruit topping.

Tip: To save time, premix the dry ingredients, and store them in an airtight container in the refrigerator. This way, you will

Grinding Your Own Almond Flour or Flaxseed

Almond flour or meal is simply ground almonds. You can buy almond flour or make your own by finely grinding almonds in a food processor. You can do the same thing with whole flax in a coffee grinder.

have the mix available for whenever you want quick, delicious, whole-grain pancakes. This recipe takes 1¼ cups of premixed dry ingredients.

Nutritional information per serving: 320 calories, 8 g protein, 51 g carbohydrate, 10 g fat, 54 mg cholesterol, 560 mg sodium, 4 g fiber, 165 mg calcium, 2 mg iron

Chicken Sausage Scramble

Serves 6 (Serving size: ½ cup scramble and
¼ cup tomato mixture)

*Why buy processed chicken sausage when you can
so easily make your own?*

1 tablespoon dehydrated minced onion

½ teaspoon dried sage

½ teaspoon fennel seed

¼ teaspoon black pepper

¼ teaspoon salt

2 tablespoons vegetable oil, divided

½ pound ground chicken

2 tomatoes, chopped

2 green onions, sliced

1 tablespoon balsamic vinegar

4 eggs

2 tablespoons whipped cream cheese

1. In a spice mill or a coffee grinder, blend all of the spices, from the onion through the salt.
2. Heat 1 tablespoon of the oil in a large skillet over medium heat. Add the chicken and the spice blend, and cook until the chicken is cooked through. Use a large spoon to break up the chicken and blend in the spices as the chicken browns.
3. In a small saucepan, cook the tomatoes, onions, and vinegar, in the remaining tablespoon of oil until the vegetables are heated through and the onions and tomatoes are slightly softened, about 5 minutes.
4. Meanwhile, in a small bowl, beat the eggs with the cream cheese. Add them to the skillet with the chicken and scramble them together until the eggs are cooked through.
5. Serve the chicken sausage scramble with the tomato mixture.

Tip: The chicken scramble can be served with warmed corn tortillas or Teff Flatbread (see recipe on page 74).

Nutritional information per serving: 171 calories, 11.6 g protein, 4.3 g carbohydrates, 12 g fat, 176.8 mg cholesterol, 185.5 mg sodium, less than 1 g fiber, 31.7 mg calcium, 1.2 mg iron

Peanut Butter Oatmeal Granola Bars

Serves 12 (Serving size: 1 2 × 3-inch piece)

When made ahead of time, these bars are great for a grab-and-go breakfast or a snack. Any crunchy nut butter may be used in place of the peanut butter.

Gluten-free cooking spray or 2 teaspoons vegetable oil

½ cup brown sugar

¼ cup crunchy peanut butter

2 tablespoons vegetable oil

1 egg

1 teaspoon vanilla extract

1 cup gluten-free oats

¼ cup sorghum flour

¼ cup tapioca flour

½ teaspoon baking soda

¼ teaspoon cinnamon

¼ cup chopped dates

¼ cup chopped dried plums

1. Preheat the oven to 350 degrees. Spray a 9 × 9-inch pan with cooking spray (or coat it with vegetable oil).
2. In a large bowl, beat together the brown sugar, peanut butter, oil, egg, and vanilla extract until well combined.
3. Stir in all of the remaining ingredients.
4. Spread the mixture evenly on the bottom of the pan with a spatula.
5. Bake for 20 to 25 minutes until cooked through and browned.
6. Let bars cool in the pan. Cut into squares to serve. Store the unused bars in an airtight container.

Nutritional information per serving: 174 calories, 4.6 g protein, 25.8 g carbohydrate, 6.4 g fat, 17.6 mg cholesterol, 128.4 mg sodium, 3.8 g fiber, 20.5 mg calcium, 1 mg iron

Homemade Granola

Serves 12 (Serving size: about ⅓ cup)

Enjoy this crunchy granola on its own, in a breakfast parfait (page 72) or sprinkled on ice cream. If you make it ahead of time, it's an easy, quick breakfast.

¼ cup uncooked millet grits

3 tablespoons unsalted butter

3 tablespoons agave nectar (see box on page 72)

1 teaspoon vanilla extract

¼ teaspoon ground nutmeg

½ teaspoon cinnamon

3 cups gluten-free cornflakes

⅓ cup sunflower kernels

¼ cup chopped walnuts

½ cup slivered almonds

½ cup shredded coconut

¼ cup raisins

¼ cup dried cranberries

1. In a small skillet, toast the millet over medium heat until fragrant (about 5 minutes). Remove from heat and set aside.
2. In a small saucepan, melt the butter with the agave nectar, vanilla, nutmeg, and cinnamon.
3. Preheat the oven to 350 degrees. Line a large baking sheet with parchment paper.
4. In a large bowl, mix the cornflakes, millet, sunflower kernels, nuts, coconut, raisins, and dried fruit. Pour the butter mixture over the cereal and stir gently to combine.
5. Spread the mixture out on the baking sheet. Bake for 20 minutes until browned and crispy.
6. Let granola cool on the baking pan. When it's cool enough to handle, break it apart and store it in an airtight container.

Tip: This granola is very versatile—you can use honey or maple syrup instead of agave nectar, substitute any gluten-free whole-grain cereal for the cornflakes, or use any fruit and nut combination you like.

Nutritional information per serving: 160.5 calories, 2.9 g protein, 20 g carbohydrate, 8.4 g fat, 7.6 mg cholesterol, 66.4 mg sodium, 1.9 g fiber, 13.7 mg calcium, 2.6 mg iron

---

What Is Agave Nectar?

Agave nectar comes from the agave plant, which is widely grown in Mexico. You can usually find it in natural foods stores. If it is not available in your area, you can substitute honey.

Parfaits with Homemade Granola

Serves 4 (Serving size: 1 parfait glass)

This parfait makes a light, delicious breakfast. Put it in a coffee cup with a cover so you can enjoy it on mornings when you need to eat on the run.

2 cups low-fat vanilla yogurt
2 cups sliced strawberries
1⅓ cups gluten-free granola (see the recipe on page 71 or use store-bought gluten-free granola)
4 mint sprigs

1. In a parfait glass, layer ¼ cup vanilla yogurt, ¼ cup strawberries, and ¼ cup granola.
2. Top with ¼ cup strawberries, ¼ cup yogurt, and the remaining granola (about 1 heaping tablespoon for each parfait), and garnish each parfait with a mint sprig.

Tip: You may substitute any flavor of gluten-free yogurt or another type of berry or fruit, if desired.

Nutritional information per serving: 287.7 calories, 9.4 g protein, 42 g carbohydrate, 10 g fat, 13.7 mg cholesterol, 148 mg sodium, 3.4 g fiber, 234 mg calcium, 3 mg iron

5

Breads

Bread! Everyone on a gluten-free diet wants good-tasting breads. The bread recipes in this section include sweet and savory quick breads, flatbreads, sandwich bread, pizza crust, and crackers.

Many of the recipes in this section call for xanthan gum, which is frequently used in gluten-free baked goods to increase volume and improve texture. It is sometimes available in health food stores and can be mail-ordered. For sources of xanthan gum, please see the Resources section.

Quick and Easy Gluten-Free

Teff Flatbread
Citrus Millet Muffins
Cheese and Herb Bread
Apple Honey Walnut Flat Bread
Brown Rice and Flaxseed Pizza Crust
Cheese Crisp Crackers
Lemon Poppy Seed Mini Muffins
Savory Teff Pie Crust

Creative Gluten-Free

Carrot Raisin Pineapple Muffins
Mexican Cornbread

Sweet Potato Rolls
Sorghum with Garlic and Flax Bread
Multigrain Bread
Oatmeal Pear Spice Muffins
Chocolate Chip Banana Bread

QUICK AND EASY GLUTEN-FREE

Teff Flatbread
Serves 8 (Serving size: 1 piece)

*This bread is lighter than traditional Ethiopian
injera bread and quick to make. Serve it with
soup or stew to really soak up the broth.*

1 cup teff flour

¼ cup brown rice flour

¼ cup tapioca starch (flour)

¾ teaspoon baking soda

¼ teaspoon salt

¼ cup buttermilk (or combine ¼
cup milk minus ¼ tablespoon
with ¼ tablespoon of vinegar)

1¼ cups plain seltzer water

Gluten-free cooking spray or
about 2 teaspoons vegetable oil

1. Mix the dry ingredients together in a large bowl.
2. Mix the buttermilk and seltzer, then add them to the dry
   ingredients. Blend with a wire whisk until well combined.
3. Heat a large nonstick skillet over medium heat. Coat it with
   cooking spray (or vegetable oil).
4. Pour about ⅓ cup of the batter into the skillet in a spiral, starting
   in the center. The batter will not cover the entire surface. Cook
   the flatbread for 20 seconds.
5. Flip the flatbread over, using a spatula, and cook for an additional
   20 seconds or until just set. Remove to a platter and cover.
6. Repeat with the remaining batter.

Nutritional information per serving: 88 calories, 2.6 g protein, 17.8 g carbohydrate, less
than 1 g fat, less than 1 mg cholesterol, 201 mg sodium, 2.2 g fiber, 34.4 mg calcium,
1.3 mg iron

Citrus Millet Muffins

Makes 12 muffins

These easy-to-prepare muffins are light and delicately sweet with the flavor of citrus—a real treat.

Gluten-free cooking spray or paper muffin liners
1 cup millet flour
½ cup sorghum flour
½ cup almond flour or meal (see box on page 68)
2 teaspoons baking powder
½ teaspoon baking soda
¼ teaspoon salt

1 teaspoon grated lemon zest
1 egg
⅓ cup honey
½ cup plain yogurt
¾ cup orange juice, divided
¼ cup vegetable oil
½ teaspoon lemon extract
2 tablespoons sugar

1. Preheat the oven to 400 degrees. Spray a muffin tin with cooking spray or line with paper muffin liners.
2. In a large bowl, combine the flours, almond flour, baking powder, baking soda, salt, and lemon zest.
3. In a separate bowl, combine the egg, honey, yogurt, ½ cup of the orange juice, oil, and lemon extract.
4. Stir the wet ingredients into the flour mixture until just combined. Pour the batter, evenly dividing it among the individual muffin tin cups.
5. Bake the muffins for 15 to 20 minutes, until browned and a toothpick inserted in the center of a muffin comes out clean.
6. In a small saucepan, combine 2 tablespoons sugar and the remaining ¼ cup orange juice. Bring to a boil, stirring until the sugar dissolves.
7. Pour the syrup over the warm muffins while they are still in the muffin tin.
8. Let the muffins sit in the pan for 5 minutes, then remove them to a serving platter. Serve warm with orange marmalade.

Nutritional information per muffin: 167 calories, 4.7 g protein, 23.7 g carbohydrate, 6.8 g fat, 18.9 mg cholesterol, 152.6 mg sodium, less than 1 g fiber, 54 mg calcium, 1.5 mg iron

Cheese and Herb Bread

Serves 10 (Serving size: 1 wedge, approximately 1-inch)

You can make this bread very quickly. It is so full of flavor, there is no need to add butter. The recipe calls for Greek yogurt, which has a creamier consistency than regular yogurt. It is generally available in supermarkets.

Gluten-free cooking spray or 1 teaspoon vegetable oil
¾ cup sorghum flour
½ cup brown rice flour
¼ cup nonfat dry milk
½ cup potato starch
2 tablespoons ground flaxseed
1 tablespoon sugar
½ teaspoon baking soda
2 teaspoons baking powder
½ teaspoon salt
1 cup shredded sharp cheddar cheese
½ teaspoon dried thyme leaves
¼ teaspoon ground sage
½ teaspoon dill weed
¼ teaspoon dried chives
3 tablespoons cold unsalted butter
1 egg
½ cup plain Greek yogurt (or nonfat plain yogurt)
½ cup skim milk
¼ teaspoon poppy seeds
¼ teaspoon sesame seeds
½ teaspoon onion powder
½ teaspoon garlic powder

1. Preheat the oven to 400 degrees. Spray a 9-inch round cake pan with cooking spray or coat it with vegetable oil.
2. In a large bowl, combine the next 14 ingredients, from the sorghum flour to the chives; mix well.
3. Using a pastry blender or two knives, cut in the butter until the mixture resembles fine crumbs.
4. In a separate bowl, beat the egg, yogurt, and milk. Stir the wet ingredients into the dry ingredients until just moistened.
5. Spoon the dough into the prepared pan. Sprinkle with the poppy seeds, sesame seeds, and onion and garlic powders.
6. Bake for 20 minutes or until golden brown and a toothpick inserted in the center comes out clean. Cool the bread in the pan.
7. Cut into wedges to serve.

Nutritional information per serving: 175 calories, 6.8 g protein, 25 g carbohydrate, 5.7 g fat, 35 mg cholesterol, 325.8 mg sodium, less than 1 g fiber, 157 mg calcium, less than 1 mg iron

Apple Honey Walnut
Flatbread

Serves 6 (Serving size: 1 piece, approximately 2½ × 1½-inch)

*This dense flatbread is full of fiber and has a delicious
sweet flavor! It's a great bread to have for breakfast
or an afternoon snack with a cup of tea.*

Gluten-free cooking spray or 2
  teaspoons vegetable oil

1 cup ground flaxseed

½ cup sorghum flour

½ cup almond flour or meal (see
  box on page 68)

2 teaspoons baking powder

½ teaspoon baking soda

½ teaspoon salt

1 teaspoon cinnamon

½ cup chopped walnuts

2 tablespoons honey

3 eggs

½ cup unsweetened applesauce

¼ cup vegetable oil

1 teaspoon vanilla extract

½ cup sparkling apple cider or
  plain seltzer

1 green apple, peeled and finely
  chopped

1. Preheat the oven to 350 degrees. Line a 15 × 10-inch pan with
   parchment paper, and lightly spray with cooking spray (or lightly
   coat with vegetable oil).
2. Mix the dry ingredients, from the flaxseed to the walnuts.
3. In a separate bowl, beat together the honey, eggs, applesauce, oil,
   vanilla, and cider.
4. Make a well in the center of the dry ingredients. Pour in the wet
   ingredients and stir until just combined.
5. Stir in the chopped apple. Pour the batter into the prepared pan,
   spreading it out to the edges as evenly as possible.
6. Bake for 15 to 20 minutes, until the bread is puffed up in the
   middle and springs back when pressed.

Tip: For variety, try pears and almonds instead of the apples and
walnuts.

Nutritional information per serving: 368.4 calories, 14.2 g protein, 28.7 g carbohydrate,
23.8 g fat, 105.7 mg cholesterol, 416 mg sodium, 6.8 g fiber, 99.8 mg calcium, 2.2 mg iron

Brown Rice and Flaxseed Pizza Crust

Makes 1 crust (about 6 servings)

This is a hearty crust that can hold a multitude of toppings.

Gluten-free cooking spray or 2 teaspoons vegetable oil
½ cup brown rice flour
½ cup ground flaxseed
1 teaspoon baking powder
½ teaspoon salt
1 teaspoon garlic powder

1 teaspoon onion powder
¼ cup water
3 eggs
3 tablespoons olive oil
½ cup cooked long grain brown rice

1. Preheat the oven to 425 degrees. Line a 15 × 10-inch pan with parchment paper and spray with cooking spray (or lightly coat with vegetable oil).
2. Mix the dry ingredients, from the flour to the onion powder, together in a large mixing bowl.
3. Mix the wet ingredients, from the water to the olive oil, in a separate bowl.
4. Add the wet ingredients to the dry ingredients and stir until well combined. Let sit for 2 to 3 minutes.
5. Stir in the brown rice.
6. Spread the batter on the prepared pan and bake for 15 minutes. Add whatever pizza toppings you'd like and cook until crisp (about another 10 minutes).

Tip: Add herbs with the dry ingredients to flavor the crust, based on the type of pizza you are making: for Italian, add basil and oregano; for Mexican, add cilantro; for BBQ chicken, add chili powder.

Nutritional information per serving: 204 calories, 6.6 g protein, 17.2 g carbohydrate, 12.7 g fat, 105.7 mg cholesterol, 271 mg sodium, 3.6 g fiber, 31.5 mg calcium, less than 1 mg iron

Cheese Crisp Crackers

Makes 18 crackers (Serving size: 3 crackers)

Serve these tasty crackers with any soup or stew.
Asiago cheese is generally available in large
supermarkets or specialty cheese shops.

1 cup arepa flour (see box below)

2 tablespoons potato starch

¼ teaspoon salt

½ teaspoon baking powder

½ teaspoon garlic powder

½ teaspoon dried basil

½ cup part-skim ricotta cheese

1¼ cups plain seltzer

Gluten-free cooking spray or 2 teaspoons vegetable oil

2 tablespoons grated asiago cheese (or grated Parmesan or Romano)

1. Preheat the oven to 400 degrees.
2. Sift together the arepa flour, potato starch, salt, baking powder, and garlic powder. Blend in the basil and ricotta cheese until well combined.
3. Warm the seltzer in the microwave for about 1 minute; you want the water warm, not hot or boiling.
4. Add the seltzer to the dry mixture. Stir to combine and form a soft dough.
5. Spray a griddle with cooking spray or lightly coat with vegetable oil. Take 1 rounded tablespoon of dough and flatten it into a round shape, about 2 inches across. Repeat with the remaining dough.

Where Can I Find Arepa Flour?

Arepa flour is precooked corn flour. It is sold in Latin American markets under the names masarepa, harina precocida, or masa al intante. If you cannot find arepa flour, masa harina may be substituted. Masa harina is usually found in the grocery store or can be mail-ordered from Bob's Red Mill.

6. Place the flattened dough circles on the lightly oiled griddle and brown them on both sides, about 2 to 3 minutes. Transfer them to an ungreased baking sheet. Sprinkle with grated cheese and bake for 15 to 20 minutes, until the crackers are crisp.

Nutritional information per serving: 125 calories, 5 g protein, 20.6 g carbohydrates, 3.2 g fat, 8.4 mg cholesterol, 171 mg sodium, 2 g fiber, 110 mg calcium, less than 1 mg iron

---

Lemon Poppy Seed Mini Muffins

Makes 12 mini muffins.

This recipe is easy is to make, and the muffins are light, with a lemony flavor and aroma.

Gluten-free cooking spray or paper muffin liners
½ cup sorghum flour
¼ cup whole-grain cornmeal
¼ cup tapioca starch
⅓ cup sugar
1 teaspoon baking powder
½ teaspoon baking soda
¼ teaspoon salt
2 teaspoons grated lemon zest
2 tablespoons poppy seeds
1 egg
1 6-ounce container lemon yogurt
2 tablespoons melted butter
3 tablespoons lemon juice

1. Preheat the oven to 400 degrees. Spray a mini muffin pan with cooking spray or line it with paper liners.
2. In a large bowl, combine the dry ingredients, from the flour to the poppy seeds.
3. In a separate bowl, blend the egg, yogurt, butter, and lemon juice. Add to the flour mixture and stir until just combined. Do not overmix.
4. Pour the batter into the prepared muffin tin. Fill each muffin cup to the top. Place the muffin tin in the preheated oven. Bake for 15 to 20 minutes or until a toothpick inserted in the center of a muffin comes out clean.

Tip: For a nice variation, substitute orange yogurt, orange zest, and orange juice for lemon yogurt, lemon zest, and lemon juice.

Nutritional information per muffin: 101 calories, 2 g protein, 16 g carbohydrate, 3.3 g fat, 23 mg cholesterol, 149 mg sodium, less than 1 g fiber, 53 mg calcium, less than 1 mg iron

Savory Teff Pie Crust

Serves 8 (Serving size: ⅛ pie crust).

Use this pie crust as an alternate to any plain pie crust when you make quiche or another savory pie.

1 cup teff flour
¼ cup sorghum flour
¼ teaspoon salt
¼ teaspoon black pepper
½ teaspoon dried basil

2 tablespoons grated Parmesan cheese
3 tablespoons vegetable oil
⅓ cup cold water

1. Preheat the oven to 375 degrees.
2. In a large bowl, combine the flours, salt, pepper, basil, and Parmesan cheese.
3. Mix the vegetable oil and water into the dry ingredients; the dough will be dry and crumbly.
4. Press the dough into a 9-inch pie plate. It will stick together when you are pushing and shaping it into the pie pan. If the dough is too dry to press into the pan, wet your hands.
5. Bake for 10 minutes.

Tip: See page 194 for a teff pie crust recipe that you can use with sweet pies.

Nutritional information per serving: 126.4 calories, 3.2 g protein, 15.5 g carbohydrate, 6.1 g fat, 1.1 mg cholesterol, 94.6 mg sodium, 2.4 g fiber, 41 mg calcium, 1.5 mg iron

CREATIVE GLUTEN-FREE

Carrot Raisin Pineapple Muffins
Makes 12 muffins

These muffins are a clever way to get your children to eat fruits and vegetables! The muffins are chock full of carrots, raisins, and pineapple. You can also add nuts if you like.

Paper muffin cups
1 cup brown rice flour
½ cup finely ground almond flour or meal (see box on page 68)
1 teaspoon xanthan gum
2 teaspoons baking powder
¼ teaspoon salt
½ cup sugar
2 eggs
¼ cup orange juice
¼ cup vegetable oil
1 cup finely grated carrots
½ cup golden raisins
1 8-ounce can crushed pineapple

1. Preheat the oven to 400 degrees. Line a muffin pan with paper cups.
2. In a large mixing bowl, blend the dry ingredients, from the brown rice flour to the sugar.
3. In a separate bowl, mix the eggs, orange juice, and oil until well blended.
4. Add the egg mixture to the flour mixture. Stir until just moistened.
5. Stir in the carrots, raisins, and pineapple.
6. Divide the batter evenly among the muffin cups.
7. Bake the muffins for 20 minutes or until a toothpick inserted in the center of a muffin comes out clean.
8. Cool the muffins in the pan before serving.

Tip: You can also try this recipe with grated zucchini—just add about 2 tablespoons less liquid to the mix.

Nutritional information per muffin: 193 calories, 2.85 g protein, 33 g carbohydrate, 6 g fat, 35 mg cholesterol, 112 mg sodium, 1.75 g fiber, 6.5 mg calcium, 0.75 mg iron

Mexican Cornbread

Makes 16 2 × 2-inch squares

*One great thing about this recipe is the texture—
the diced red pepper and whole kernels of corn
make it truly unique. You can use another type
of pepper for more variety.*

1 tablespoon butter
¾ cup whole-grain cornmeal
1 cup brown rice flour
½ teaspoon xanthan gum
3 tablespoons sugar
2 teaspoons baking powder
¼ teaspoon salt

1 egg
½ cup skim milk
½ cup low-fat sour cream
¼ cup vegetable oil
1 cup frozen corn kernels,
   thawed
½ cup diced red bell pepper

1. Preheat the oven to 400 degrees.
2. Place the butter in an 8-inch square baking pan and put it in the oven to melt. Remove the pan from the oven and set aside.
3. In a large bowl, mix all of the dry ingredients, from the cornmeal to the salt.
4. In a separate bowl, mix the wet ingredients, from the egg to the oil.
5. Add the wet ingredients to the dry, and stir until just blended. Add the corn and red pepper, and stir until combined.
6. Pour the batter into the prepared pan and bake for 25 to 30 minutes.
7. Cool the cornbread in the pan on a cooling rack before cutting it.

Tip: If you want a more basic cornbread, prepare the recipe without the pepper.

Nutritional information per square: 133 calories, 2.5 g protein, 20 g carbohydrate, 5.5 g fat, 18 mg cholesterol, 84 mg sodium, 1 g fiber, 31 mg calcium, 0.5 mg iron

Sweet Potato Rolls

Makes 12 rolls

These rolls have a subtle sweet potato flavor without being too sweet. They are delicious hot from the oven.

4 tablespoons toasted pumpkin seeds

Gluten-free cooking spray or 2 teaspoons vegetable oil

2 cups brown rice flour

⅔ cup potato starch

⅓ cup tapioca starch

1 teaspoon xanthan gum

½ teaspoon baking soda

½ teaspoon cream of tartar

½ teaspoon cinnamon

¼ teaspoon allspice

1 package (¼ ounce) rapid-acting dry yeast

½ cup 1% milk

½ cup water

1 tablespoon butter

1 tablespoon honey

½ teaspoon salt

1 medium sweet potato, peeled, cooked, and mashed (about ¾ cup; or substitute baby food sweet potatoes)

1 teaspoon apple cider vinegar

1. Toast the pumpkin seeds in a hot skillet coated with cooking spray or a small amount of vegetable oil until they start to brown. Be careful not to burn them.
2. Sift together the dry ingredients, from the flour to the yeast.
3. In a medium saucepan, heat the milk, water, butter, honey, salt, and sweet potato until very warm (120 degrees).
4. Put 2 cups of the flour mixture into a large mixing bowl. Add the sweet potato mixture and vinegar all at once and beat at medium speed for 2 minutes, until smooth.
5. Stir in the remaining flour mixture to make a stiff dough.
6. Shape the dough into 12 equal-size balls, and press some pumpkin seeds on top of each roll.
7. Place the rolls on a baking sheet that has been coated with gluten-free cooking spray or vegetable oil.
8. Cover them and let them rise for 1 hour.
9. Preheat the oven to 400 degrees. Bake the rolls for 25 to 30 minutes until lightly browned and cooked through. Serve with apple butter. To keep unused rolls fresh, freeze until ready to use.

Tip: If you prefer browner rolls, brush them with egg yolks before baking.

Nutritional information per roll: 184 calories, 3.3 g protein, 36.5 g carbohydrate, 3.1 g fat, 1.9 g fiber, 3 mg cholesterol, 172 mg sodium, 26 mg calcium, 1.6 mg iron

---

Sorghum with Garlic and Flax Bread

Serves 8 (Serving size: 1 thick 1-inch slice
or 2 thin ½-inch slices)

If you like garlic, you will love this bread!

1 cup lukewarm water

1 packet (¼ ounce) dry yeast

1 teaspoon sugar

1 tablespoon olive oil

3 cloves garlic, minced

1 cup sorghum flour

⅔ cup tapioca starch

⅔ cup corn starch

⅓ cup nonfat dry milk powder

1 teaspoon xanthan gum

1 teaspoon baking powder

½ teaspoon baking soda

½ teaspoon salt

1 teaspoon unflavored gelatin

2 tablespoons ground flaxseeds

2 eggs

1 teaspoon apple cider vinegar

Gluten-free cooking spray or
  vegetable oil

1. In a large bowl, mix the water, yeast, and sugar. Let stand for about 10 minutes.
2. Meanwhile, heat the olive oil in a small skillet over medium heat. Add the garlic and sauté until softened. Be careful not to burn the garlic. Remove from heat.
3. Sift together the dry ingredients, from the flour to the flaxseed.
4. Add the eggs, vinegar, and garlic with olive oil to the yeast. Beat the batter on medium speed for 1 to 2 minutes.
5. Turn the mixer to a low speed and add the combined dry ingredients, ¼ cup at a time. The mixture will be thick. When all of the dry ingredients have been added, turn the mixer to medium and beat for 2 to 3 minutes.

6. Spray an 8½ × 4½-inch loaf pan with gluten-free cooking spray or lightly coat with vegetable oil. Spoon the batter into the pan and cover with a dish towel. Let the dough rise in a warm place for 1 to 1½ hours.
7. Preheat the oven to 400 degrees. Bake the bread for 50 minutes. Cover the pan with foil about halfway through.
8. Remove the bread from the pan and cool it on a wire rack. Serve warm with herb butter or herb cream cheese.

Nutritional information per serving: 213 calories, 6.5 g protein, 39 g carbohydrate, 4.8 g fat, 1.4 g fiber, 53 mg cholesterol, 296 mg sodium, 69 mg calcium, 1.7 mg iron

Multigrain Bread
Makes 18 ½-inch slices

This bread is hearty and flavorful and will really liven up your sandwich. As an added bonus, your house will smell great, too! Please make sure oat flour is labeled gluten free.

½ cup sorghum flour

¾ cup brown rice flour

⅓ cup gluten-free oat flour (see the box on page 87)

¾ cup millet flour (see the box on page 87)

½ cup tapioca starch (flour)

⅓ cup potato starch

½ cup almond meal or flour

⅛ cup white teff flour

⅛ cup flax meal

2 teaspoons salt

3 tablespoons brown sugar

2 teaspoons xanthan gum

3 eggs

2 teaspoons apple cider vinegar

2 tablespoons molasses

3 tablespoons butter, melted

½ cup applesauce or prune puree

1 packet (¼ ounce) dry yeast

2 teaspoons sugar

⅓ cup warm water

Gluten-free cooking spray or about 2 teaspoons vegetable oil

2 tablespoons olive oil

1. Mix together the first 12 dry ingredients in a medium bowl, from the sorghum flour to the xanthan gum.
2. Whisk together the eggs, vinegar, molasses, butter, and applesauce or prune puree in a large bowl.

3. In a small cup, mix the yeast, sugar, and warm water until foamy, about 3 minutes.
4. Spray a 9 × 5-inch loaf pan with cooking spray or lightly coat with vegetable oil and set aside.
5. Fold the yeast mixture into the egg mixture.
6. Slowly add the dry mixture into the wet mixture until thoroughly combined.
7. Mix the dough using the paddle attachment on a stand mixer for 6 to 8 minutes. The dough will have a thick, grainy consistency and should be moist but not too wet or sticky. Add additional brown rice flour if the dough is too wet. If it's too dry, add a few tablespoons of warm water.
8. Mold the dough into the loaf pan and flatten it with a wet spatula. Cover with a towel and keep in a warm place for about 1½ hours until the dough has doubled in size.
9. Preheat the oven to 350 degrees.
10. Drizzle the olive oil over the bread right before putting it into the oven.
11. Bake for about 40 minutes.

Tips:

1. If you cannot have nuts, omit the almond meal and substitute an equal amount of bean flour or tapioca starch.

2. If you're not using all of the bread right away, slice and freeze individual slices. Leftover bread also makes great gluten-free breadcrumbs.

Nutritional information per slice: 120 calories, 2.4 g protein, 17.9 g carbohydrate, 4.8 g fat, 40 mg cholesterol, 289 mg sodium, 1.3 g fiber, 22 mg calcium, 1.2 mg iron

---

Making Your Own Gluten-Free Oat Flour

Put gluten-free oats in a coffee grinder and process them for a few seconds. The same technique can be used to make millet flour as well.

Oatmeal Pear Spice
Muffins

Makes 12 muffins

*These muffins are a delicious way to get your oatmeal fix.
Just make sure your oats are labeled gluten-free.*

Paper muffin cups or gluten-free cooking spray

1 cup uncooked gluten-free rolled oats

¼ cup butter

½ cup pure maple syrup

1 cup buttermilk (or combine 1 cup of milk, minus 1 tablespoon, with 1 tablespoon of vinegar)

1 teaspoon vanilla

½ cup gluten-free liquid egg substitute or 4 large egg whites

⅔ cup brown rice flour

⅓ cup sorghum flour

½ teaspoon baking soda

1 teaspoon baking powder

¼ teaspoon salt

½ teaspoon ground ginger

¼ teaspoon nutmeg

½ teaspoon allspice

1 teaspoon cinnamon

2 pears, peeled, cored, and chopped

1 tablespoon sugar

½ teaspoon cinnamon

1. Preheat the oven to 375 degrees. Line a muffin tin with paper liners or coat with cooking spray.
2. In a food processor, process the oats until finely ground. Put them in a large bowl.
3. Heat the butter and syrup over low heat until the butter is melted. Pour it over the oats. Add the buttermilk, vanilla, and egg substitute or egg whites. Beat with a hand mixer until well combined.
4. Mix the next 9 dry ingredients, from the flour to the cinnamon, in a separate medium bowl. Stir into the oatmeal mixture until just combined.
5. Stir in the chopped pears.
6. Pour the batter into the prepared muffin cups, filling each cup to the top.
7. Mix the sugar and cinnamon together. Sprinkle them on top of each muffin.
8. Bake for 15 to 20 minutes or until a toothpick inserted in the center of a muffin comes out clean.

Tip: You may add raisins, dried cranberries, or nuts if you like. Apples or peaches also work nicely in this recipe (in place of the pears).

Nutritional information per muffin: 182.6 calories, 4 g protein, 30.8 g carbohydrate, 5.4 g fat, 11 mg cholesterol, 191 mg sodium, 2.4 g fiber, 54.5 mg calcium, 1.2 mg iron

Chocolate Chip Banana Bread

Makes 10 slices (¾-inch thick)

This dark-colored, rich, and flavorful banana bread works well as a dessert or a breakfast bread. If well covered, this bread will stay fresh for several days.

⅓ cup butter

¾ cup dark brown sugar

¼ cup granulated sugar

¼ cup sour cream

½ cup applesauce

1 egg

1 teaspoon vanilla extract

3 soft bananas, pureed

½ cup buckwheat flour

¼ cup sorghum flour

¼ cup teff flour (light or dark)

⅓ cup tapioca flour

½ teaspoon baking soda

½ teaspoon baking powder

½ teaspoon salt

½ teaspoon cinnamon

¼ cup finely chopped dark chocolate

¼ cup chopped walnuts (optional)

Gluten-free cooking spray or 2 teaspoons vegetable oil

2 tablespoons powdered sugar (for garnish)

1. Preheat the oven to 350 degrees.
2. In a large bowl, cream the butter, then mix in the brown and the granulated sugars until well combined.
3. To the butter mixture, add the sour cream, applesauce, egg, vanilla extract, and pureed bananas, and mix until creamy.
4. Combine the dry ingredients, from the buckwheat flour to the cinnamon, and slowly add them into the wet ingredients until the batter is creamy.
5. Fold in the chocolate and walnuts, if using.

6. Spray a 9 × 5-inch loaf pan or a 9-inch round cake pan with cooking spray or coat with vegetable oil. Pour the batter into the pan and bake for about 40 to 50 minutes or until a knife inserted in the center comes out clean.
7. Cool the banana bread, remove from the pan, sprinkle with powdered sugar, and serve.

Tip: Use low-fat sour cream and fewer nuts to reduce the amount of fat in this recipe.

Nutritional information per slice: 240 calories, 3 g protein, 40.4 g carbohydrate, 8.5 g fat, 39.4 mg cholesterol, 249 mg sodium, 2.5 g fiber, 35.5 mg calcium, 1 mg iron

---

6

Soups and Salads

Mmm-mmm, good! Some of these soups and salads are hearty enough to be served on their own as a meal.

Quick and Easy Gluten-Free

Black Bean Soup with Yogurt Garnish
Chopped Salad
Gazpacho with White Beans
Grilled Romaine Salad
Scallop and Arugula Salad
Chili Lime Shrimp Salad Bowls
Blue Cheese Turkey Salad with Sliced Apples
Toasted Amaranth–Crusted Chicken Salad

Creative Gluten-Free

Hearty Three-Bean Soup
Lentil and Millet Soup
Lentil and Kasha Salad
Caribbean Stew
Pumpkin and Millet Soup with Toasted Coconut
Tomato Vegetable Soup with Quinoa
Waldorf Quinoa Salad

QUICK AND EASY GLUTEN-FREE

Black Bean Soup with Yogurt Garnish

Serves 6 (Serving size: about 1 cup)

This bean soup may be served year-round—the yogurt and cucumber garnish gives it a nice summer touch. If you like your black bean soup spicy, add ½ teaspoon cumin and a few dashes of cayenne pepper.

2 tablespoons olive oil
2 tablespoons minced garlic
1 cup finely chopped carrots
2 large onions, chopped
½ teaspoon salt
½ teaspoon black pepper

2 15-ounce cans black beans, drained and rinsed
24 ounces gluten-free chicken stock
6 tablespoons nonfat plain yogurt
¼ cup chopped seedless cucumber

1. Heat the oil in a large soup pot over medium heat. Add the garlic and sauté for 2 to 3 minutes.
2. Add the carrots and onions to the pot and cook for about 5 minutes, until the onions are soft and translucent.
3. Add the salt, black pepper, beans, and chicken stock.
4. Cover and cook for about 20 minutes.
5. Puree the soup in a blender (see tip).
6. Mix the yogurt with the cucumber, and top each serving of soup with 1 tablespoon of the yogurt mixture.

Tip: When pureeing hot soup, take care that you don't overfill the blender, and make sure that the lid is tightly closed. If the lid is not secure, you could burn yourself. Try a practice run with cold water first to be safe.

Nutritional information per serving: 200 calories, 10.8 g protein, 29 g carbohydrate, 5.3 g fat, less than 1 mg cholesterol, 621 mg sodium, 7.1 g fiber, 102 mg calcium, 2.1 mg iron

Chopped Salad

Serves 4 (Serving size: approximately 2 to 3 cups)

We don't know what it is about chopping ingredients that makes these salads so delicious, but it does! For a zesty balsamic dressing to serve with this salad, see the recipe for Blue Cheese Turkey Salad on pages 98–99.

6 cups chopped romaine

2 cucumbers, peeled and chopped

2 tomatoes, chopped

2 carrots, chopped

1 small red onion, chopped

1 small jar chopped beets (drained, approximately 1 cup)

2 stalks celery, chopped

1 cup canned or cooked dried chickpeas (cooled)

4 ounces cheddar cheese, cut into ½-inch chunks

4 ounces cooked turkey breast or ham, chopped into ½-inch-thick squares

Combine the ingredients and serve the salad with your favorite dressing. For best taste, toss with dressing immediately before serving.

Tip: You may substitute different meats, vegetables, and cheeses in this recipe as desired.

Nutritional information per serving (does not include dressing): 289 calories, 18 g protein, 29 g carbohydrate, 11.7 g fat, 41.8 mg cholesterol, 592 mg sodium, 9 g fiber, 308.6 mg calcium, 4 mg iron

Gazpacho with White Beans

Serves 4 (Serving size: about 1 cup)

This is gazpacho with a twist—white beans! If you're looking for ways to add more beans to your diet, this is an easy way to do it. This light, flavorful soup can easily be made ahead and stored in the refrigerator for three to four days.

1½ pounds (about 4 large) firm ripe tomatoes

1 large cucumber, peeled and chopped

1 stalk celery, coarsely chopped

2 green onions, chopped

1 green pepper, chopped

3 cloves garlic, peeled

1 tablespoon fresh chopped basil

2 tablespoons balsamic vinegar

2 teaspoons olive oil

1 teaspoon salt

¼ teaspoon pepper

2 cups canned or cooked dried white beans

1 small cucumber, peeled and chopped

1 green onion, chopped (include both the bulb and the greens)

Hot sauce (to taste)

1. Place the tomatoes in boiling water until the skins start to soften. Remove them from the water, peel off the skins, cut them in half, and remove the seeds.
2. In a food processor, chop the tomatoes.
3. Next, add the remaining ingredients, except the garnish and the beans, to the food processor and coarsely chop until soup is liquid and thick.
4. Fold in the beans and taste the soup to see whether the seasonings are correct; add more seasoning if desired. Chill the soup at least one hour before serving it; for the best flavor chill it overnight.
5. Serve the soup cold. Garnish with chopped cucumber, scallions, and hot sauce.

Tip: Fresh tomatoes make a zesty gazpacho. If you are lucky enough to have heirloom tomatoes, they are a special treat. For another variation, substitute cooked quinoa, millet, or brown rice for the beans.

Nutritional information per serving: 207 calories, 11.4 g protein, 36 g carbohydrate, 3.1 g fat, 0 mg cholesterol, 610 mg sodium, 9.3 g fiber, 133 mg calcium, 4.4 mg iron

Grilled Romaine Salad

Serves 4 (Serving size: ½ heart of romaine with topping)

*This creative salad may be quick to make,
but the presentation is impressive enough
to serve at a dinner party.*

3 tablespoons orange juice

2 tablespoons lemon juice

2 tablespoons olive oil

1 teaspoon gluten-free Dijon
mustard

¼ teaspoon salt

⅛ teaspoon black pepper

1 teaspoon grated lemon zest

1 cup canned small white beans,
drained and rinsed

2 romaine hearts, halved

2 tablespoons olive oil

¼ teaspoon black pepper

¼ teaspoon salt

1 cup ruby red grapefruit
sections (fresh or canned)

1. In a small bowl, whisk together the orange and lemon juices, olive oil, mustard, salt, and black pepper. Pour into a small saucepan. Add the lemon zest and beans and simmer for about 10 minutes, until heated through.
2. Heat a stove-top grill pan over medium heat. Brush the cut side of the romaine with the olive oil and sprinkle the salt and pepper on top. Place the cut side down on the grill pan, and cook the romaine for 3 to 4 minutes, until it is just starting to brown and wilt slightly.
3. Remove the romaine from the pan. Place the cut side up on a serving plate. Top with the white beans and dressing and the grapefruit sections.

Tip: Mandarin oranges make a nice substitute for the grapefruit.

Nutritional information per serving: 198.6 calories, 4.5 g protein, 18.5 g carbohydrate, 13.8 g fat, 0 mg cholesterol, 433 mg sodium, 4.4 g fiber, 62 mg calcium, 1.4 mg iron

Scallop and Arugula Salad

Serves 4 (Serving size: about 2 cups)

Serving seafood over a mixed green salad can work as a side salad or, served with a gluten-free grain like quinoa, can stand alone as a meal. You can add the grain to the salad along with the scallops or toss it with the arugula and basil dressing.

12 ounces sea scallops, fresh or thawed if frozen

3 tablespoons olive oil, divided

¾ teaspoon salt, divided

⅜ teaspoon black pepper, divided

½ teaspoon dried thyme leaves

4 tablespoons fresh lemon juice

¼ cup fresh basil leaves

6 cups arugula leaves

1. Preheat the broiler. Toss the scallops in 1 tablespoon of the olive oil, then sprinkle with ½ teaspoon of the salt, ¼ teaspoon of the pepper, and the thyme. Place them on a baking sheet and broil for 8 to 10 minutes, or just until they are opaque and firm and beginning to brown.

2. In a blender or a small food processor, combine the lemon juice, the remaining oil, the remaining salt (¼ teaspoon) and pepper (⅛ teaspoon), and the basil. Process the dressing until the ingredients are well combined.

3. Toss the arugula with the basil dressing. Top the salad with the scallops.

Tip: Arugula has a strong peppery flavor. You can substitute spinach or romaine if you'd like a lighter flavor.

Nutritional information per serving: 165.5 calories, 14 g protein, 2.6 g carbohydrate, 11 g fat, 30 mg cholesterol, 594.9 mg sodium, less than 1 g fiber, 120.2 mg calcium, 2.3 mg iron

---

Chili Lime Shrimp Bowls

Serves 4 (Serving size: 2 tortilla shells)

*These stuffed tortilla shells are crispy and delicious.
The next time you want to serve shrimp cocktails,
make these instead—they are sure to be a hit.*

Gluten-free cooking spray or
  1 teaspoon vegetable oil
8 corn tortillas, warmed
1 cup frozen corn
1 tablespoon vegetable oil
1 pound small uncooked shrimp,
  peeled and deveined

¼ teaspoon black pepper
2 teaspoons chili powder
1 teaspoon grated lime zest
1 cup shredded lettuce
1 avocado, chopped
2 tablespoons chopped fresh
  cilantro

1. Preheat the oven to 400 degrees. Spray 8 muffin cups with cooking spray or coat lightly with vegetable oil. Place and fold a tortilla into each muffin cup, pressing out the edges (see tip). Bake for about 10 minutes, or until crisp.
2. Cook the corn in the microwave for about 3 minutes, until heated through.
3. Heat 1 tablespoon vegetable oil in a large nonstick skillet. Add the shrimp and cook for 3 to 4 minutes, or until pink. Add the pepper, chili powder, and lime zest. Remove from heat.
4. Place 2 tortilla shells on each serving plate. Add the lettuce, and top it with the shrimp, corn, avocado, and cilantro.

Tip: If you warm the tortillas before pressing them into the muffin tins, they become more pliable and less likely to tear.

Nutritional information per serving: 359.7 calories, 28 g protein, 36.4 g carbohydrate, 12.5 g fat, 172.3 mg cholesterol, 208.7 mg sodium, 7.3 g fiber, 116 mg calcium, 4.1 mg iron

Blue Cheese Turkey Salad with Sliced Apples

Serves 4 (Serving size: 3½ cups)

This salad can stand alone as a great side or as lunch, with or without the quinoa. To make your own balsamic salad dressing, use the recipe that follows. If you don't have quinoa or want to try a variation, you can substitute brown rice, millet, wild rice, or cooked beans.

6 ounces cooked turkey breast, diced into ½-inch squares (purchase turkey breast unsliced)

1 cup cooked quinoa (see the box below)

2 apples, peeled and sliced

8 cups mixed greens

2 scallions, chopped

2 ounces crumbled blue cheese (see glossary)

2 tablespoons slivered almonds

1 cup cherry tomatoes

1 cucumber, peeled, sliced, and cut into half moons

½ cup gluten-free balsamic dressing

Combine the ingredients and serve.

Tip: For quick and easy salads, keep the chopped ingredients in your refrigerator in plastic containers or zipper-lock bags and toss them together for fabulous fresh salad blends.

Nutritional information per serving: 320 calories, 15.5 g protein, 34.5 g carbohydrate, 14.7 g fat, 28 mg cholesterol, 642 mg sodium, 7 g fiber, 160 mg calcium, 3 mg iron

Rinsing Quinoa

It's helpful to buy prerinsed quinoa for convenience. If you don't, you must rinse the quinoa several times before using it. Quinoa contains an outer coating of saponin that is very bitter. Use a fine colander, and rinse the quinoa under cold water.

Balsamic Salad Dressing

Makes 1 cup or 16 1-tablespoon servings

½ cup balsamic vinegar

1 tablespoon gluten-free soy or tamari sauce

2 tablespoons honey or sugar

1 teaspoon garlic powder

½ teaspoon onion powder

½ teaspoon dried Italian seasoning herbs

¼ cup olive oil

Whisk all ingredients together and refrigerate until ready to use.

Nutritional information per serving: 38 calories, less than 1 g protein, 5 g carbohydrate, 6.4 g fat, 0 mg cholesterol, 1 mg sodium, less than 1 g fiber, 0.85 mg calcium, less than 1 mg iron

Toasted Amaranth–Crusted Chicken Salad

Serves 4 (Serving size: approximately 2 cups salad and 3 ounces chicken)

Amaranth seeds are a clever and healthy way to add some crunch to your chicken. This recipe also calls for gorgonzola cheese, which is an Italian blue cheese (see glossary).

12 ounces skinless, boneless chicken breasts

½ cup uncooked amaranth seed

2 tablespoons grated Parmesan cheese

1 teaspoon garlic powder

1 teaspoon onion powder

½ teaspoon salt

Gluten-free cooking spray or 2 teaspoons vegetable oil

1 egg, beaten

6 cups chopped mixed lettuce

4 ounces gorgonzola cheese

½ cup dried cranberries or raisins

1 cup chopped tomato

1 cup chopped cucumber

1 cup chopped red pepper

1 cup chopped carrots

1. Clean the chicken breasts and pound to 1 inch thickness (or purchase thin chicken cutlets).
2. In a skillet, toast the amaranth seeds for about 3 to 4 minutes until they start to brown; take care not to burn them. The seeds will make a popping noise while they're toasting.
3. Preheat the broiler.
4. In a medium bowl, mix together the Parmesan cheese, garlic powder, onion powder, salt, and toasted amaranth seeds.
5. Spray a baking sheet with cooking spray or lightly coat with vegetable oil.
6. Pour the beaten egg into a soup bowl; dip the chicken into the egg and then into the amaranth mixture, pressing the amaranth seeds into the chicken.
7. Place the chicken on a baking sheet and spray the top of the chicken with gluten-free cooking spray (or drizzle it with vegetable oil).
8. Broil the chicken until it starts to brown on one side, turn it over, and spray the second side with gluten-free cooking spray or drizzle it with vegetable oil and bake until that side is brown as well.
9. Slice the chicken into 2-inch strips.
10. In a large bowl, mix the chopped lettuce and vegetables and the dried fruit, and serve with balsamic vinegar or your favorite gluten-free salad dressing. Place the chicken strips over the entire salad, or serve the salad on four individual plates, with the chicken strips evenly divided among them.

Tip: Amaranth makes a great crunchy topping for any baked or broiled item.

Nutritional information per serving: 418 calories, 34 g protein, 45 g carbohydrate, 12.3 g fat, 131 mg cholesterol, 790 mg sodium, 7.5 g fiber, 238 mg calcium, 3 mg iron

CREATIVE GLUTEN-FREE

Hearty Three-Bean Soup

Serves 6 (Serving size: 1 cup)

This soup is a tasty way to eat your fiber. It is chock full of vegetables and legumes. Although this recipe calls for white beans and kidney beans, feel free to experiment with other types, such as black beans and pinto beans.

1 teaspoon olive oil

2 carrots, peeled and chopped

2 stalks celery, chopped

½ large onion, chopped

2 cloves garlic, minced

1 15-ounce can white beans, drained and rinsed

1 15-ounce can red kidney beans, drained and rinsed

1 8-ounce can tomato sauce

2 cups gluten-free vegetable or chicken broth

2 cups water

2 cups frozen green beans

¼ teaspoon black pepper (or to taste)

1. In a large stockpot, heat the oil over medium heat.
2. Add the carrots, celery, onion, and garlic and cook for 10 minutes or until tender.
3. Add the beans, tomato sauce, broth, and water. Heat to a boil. Reduce the heat to simmer and cook for 30 minutes.
4. Remove 1 cup of the soup, and puree in a food processor or a blender. Return soup to pot.
5. Add the green beans and simmer for 5 to 10 minutes longer. Season with pepper to taste and garnish with lemon, vinegar, or hot sauce for a little extra burst of flavor.

Tip: To reduce the sodium content, use tomato sauce with no added salt and/or reduced-sodium broth.

Nutritional information per serving: 201 calories, 10.7 g protein, 38 g carbohydrate, 1.6 g fat, 0 mg cholesterol, 605 mg sodium, 10.7 g fiber, 119 mg calcium, 4 mg iron

Lentil and Millet Soup

Serves 8 (about 1¼ cups per serving).

This soup calls for millet, but if you don't have it on hand, you can substitute amaranth, quinoa, or brown rice.

2 teaspoons vegetable oil or gluten-free cooking spray

1 cup chopped onions

½ cup chopped celery

2 carrots, chopped

2 tablespoons minced garlic

½ teaspoon ground cumin

1 teaspoon salt

½ teaspoon black pepper

2 tablespoons brown sugar

¼ cup tomato paste

2 bay leaves

4 cups (32 ounces) low-sodium, gluten-free beef broth

3 cups water

½ cup uncooked hulled millet

1 pound dried lentils, picked through to remove any damaged lentils

1. Spray a medium saucepan with gluten-free cooking spray or add the vegetable oil. Sauté the onions, celery, carrots, and garlic until the onions are translucent (if the pan begins to dry out, add water, 2 tablespoons at a time).
2. Add the cumin, salt, pepper, brown sugar, and tomato paste and heat for 2 to 3 minutes.
3. Add the remaining ingredients and cook for 40 minutes to 1 hour or until the lentils are soft.
4. Add additional water, if needed, to give the soup the desired thickness.
5. Remove the bay leaves before serving.

Tip: If you'd like a creamier soup, use a stick blender to puree the soup.

Nutritional information per serving: 298 calories, 19 g protein, 52 g carbohydrate, 1.9 g fat, 0 mg cholesterol, 411 mg sodium, 19.6 g fiber, 58 mg calcium, 5.3 mg iron

---

Lentil and Kasha Salad

Serves 4 (Serving size: about 1 cup)

*Kasha, or roasted buckwheat groats, is a common staple
in many Eastern European countries.*

1 teaspoon grated lemon zest
2 tablespoons fresh lemon juice
½ teaspoon red pepper flakes
  (or to taste)
¼ teaspoon black pepper
½ teaspoon salt
1 7-ounce jar roasted red bell
  peppers in olive oil, drained,
  reserving the oil

1 cup cooked kasha (cooked
  according to package
  instructions)
2 cups cooked lentils (see tip)
1 10-ounce package frozen
  chopped broccoli
⅓ cup shredded Parmesan
  cheese

1. In a large bowl, mix the lemon zest, lemon juice, red pepper
   flakes, black pepper, salt, and 2 tablespoons of olive oil from the
   roasted red peppers.
2. Microwave the broccoli for about 3 to 4 minutes until
   defrosted.
3. Add the red bell peppers, kasha, lentils, and broccoli to the lemon
   and oil dressing in the bowl. Stir gently to combine.
4. Stir in the cheese and serve warm or cold.

Tip: If you have uncooked lentils, put approximately ⅔ cup dried
lentils in a medium pot of water and boil until the lentils are
cooked through; drain the lentils and proceed with the recipe.

Nutritional information per serving: 269 calories, 15 g protein, 34 g carbohydrate,
9.4 g fat, 12 g fiber, 4.7 mg cholesterol, 415 mg sodium, 131 mg calcium, 4.3 mg iron

Caribbean Stew

Serves 4 (Serving size: about 1½ cups)

In this recipe, the flavorful butternut squash blends well with the coconut and spices to make a rich and satisfying stew.

2 tablespoons olive oil

½ cup chopped onion

2 cloves garlic, minced

2 medium tomatoes, chopped

1 small butternut squash (about 1½ pounds), peeled, seeded, and cut into 1-inch pieces

3 cups gluten-free, low-sodium vegetable broth

¼ teaspoon cinnamon

½ teaspoon coriander

½ teaspoon cumin

¼ teaspoon paprika

½ teaspoon salt

½ teaspoon black pepper

4 cups fresh baby spinach

½ cup coconut milk (or plain yogurt)

1. Heat the oil in a large saucepan over medium heat. Add the onion and garlic, and cook until softened, about 5 minutes.
2. Add the tomatoes and squash. Cook for another 3 minutes.
3. Add the broth, cinnamon, coriander, cumin, paprika, salt, and pepper.
4. Reduce heat to a low simmer. Cook for 45 minutes to 1 hour or until the squash is fork tender.
5. Add the spinach and coconut milk. Cook until the spinach is wilted, about 3 minutes.
6. Serve the stew over cooked quinoa or with a side of Teff Flatbread (see page 74).

Nutritional information per serving: 316 calories, 11.7 g protein, 39.6 g carbohydrate, 16 g fat, 0 mg cholesterol, 432 mg sodium, 13 g fiber, 411 mg calcium, 6 mg iron

Pumpkin and Millet Soup with Toasted Coconut

Serves 6 (Serving size: 1 cup soup and
1 teaspoon toasted coconut)

*This hearty, delicious soup can be served as either a side
dish or a meal. It is so satisfying on a cool fall day!*

2 tablespoons olive oil

1 tablespoon minced garlic

1 large onion, chopped

1 teaspoon salt

½ teaspoon cinnamon

¼ teaspoon cumin

¼ teaspoon black pepper

Dash ground nutmeg

¼ teaspoon dried thyme leaves

2 cups canned or cooked fresh pumpkin (see tip)

3 tablespoons brown sugar

4 cups gluten-free chicken stock

1 cup water

¼ cup uncooked hulled millet

2 tablespoons sweetened grated coconut (for garnish)

1. In a large pot, heat the oil over medium heat and sauté the garlic for 2 to 3 minutes.
2. Add the onion to the pot, and sauté until the onions are translucent.
3. Add the salt, cinnamon, cumin, pepper, nutmeg, thyme, pumpkin, and brown sugar. Heat for about 5 minutes.
4. Add the chicken stock and cook for about 15 minutes.
5. Meanwhile, boil the water in a small pot, add the millet, cover it, and simmer until the liquid is absorbed.
6. Add the cooked millet to the soup, put the soup into the blender, and blend until creamy.
7. Put the soup back into the pot and continue cooking for about 5 minutes more.
8. In a small nonstick skillet, toast the coconut over a low heat for about 5 minutes.
9. Serve the soup topped with coconut.

Tip: To prepare fresh pumpkin, cut a medium pumpkin in half, scoop out the seeds, and slice the pumpkin into wedges. Cover a cookie sheet with aluminum foil. Place the pumpkin slices cut side down on the cookie sheet, and bake in a 350-degree oven for about 30 minutes, until the pumpkin pierces easily with a fork. Scoop the pumpkin pulp out of the pumpkin skin and mash it.

Nutritional information per serving: 161.7 calories, 5.5 g protein, 21.4 g carbohydrate, 6.5 g fat, 0 mg cholesterol, 916 mg sodium, 3.8 g fiber, 42.7 mg calcium, 1.9 mg iron

Tomato Vegetable Soup with Quinoa

Serves 8 (Serving size: 1 cup)

This soup brings back that warm, cozy feeling of eating vegetable soup as a child.

Gluten-free cooking spray or 1 teaspoon vegetable oil

2 tablespoons butter or nonhydrogenated margarine

I large onion, finely chopped

1 tablespoon minced garlic

2 tablespoons brown rice flour

1 28-ounce can whole peeled tomatoes

3 cups gluten-free, low-sodium chicken broth

2 teaspoons sugar

1 teaspoon salt

½ teaspoon black pepper

1 teaspoon dried thyme

1 10-ounce package frozen mixed vegetables (or 2 cups chopped fresh vegetables of your choice)

1 cup cooked quinoa (see box on page 166)

½ cup sour cream

1. Spray the inside of a large soup pot with cooking spray or lightly coat with vegetable oil, add the butter, and heat on a low heat until the butter melts.
2. Add the onion and garlic, and cook until the onion is soft and translucent.
3. Add the flour, and mix together well.
4. In a blender, process the canned tomatoes, juice and all.

5. To the onion mixture, add the broth, tomatoes, sugar, salt, pepper, thyme, and frozen vegetables, stirring frequently.
6. Bring the soup to a simmer, and cook for about 30 to 40 minutes; mix in the cooked quinoa and cook the soup for 10 minutes more.
7. Top soup with a dollop of sour cream and serve.

Nutritional information per serving: 159 calories, 5.5 g protein, 21 g carbohydrate, 6.5 g fat, 12.9 mg cholesterol, 266 mg sodium, 4.3 g fiber, 54 mg calcium, 1.2 mg iron

Waldorf Quinoa Salad

Serves 4 (Serving size: about ¾ cup)

The quinoa in this recipe puts a distinctive twist on the classic favorite.

½ cup uncooked quinoa (see box on page 166)

¼ cup mayonnaise

¼ cup plain Greek-style yogurt (or nonfat plain yogurt)

1 teaspoon grated lemon zest

¼ teaspoon salt

1 tablespoon minced dried onion flakes

1 green apple (any type, or pear), cored and chopped

1 cup chopped fennel

¼ cup golden raisins

1. Cook the quinoa according to the package directions. Let cool.
2. In a small bowl, mix the mayonnaise, yogurt, lemon zest, salt, and onion flakes.
3. Put the chopped apple, chopped fennel, quinoa, and raisins in a large serving bowl.
4. Mix in the dressing and serve.

Nutritional information per serving: 240.3 calories, 4.4 g protein, 30.5 g carbohydrate, 11.9 g fat, 6.9 mg cholesterol, 260.5 mg sodium, 3.7 g fiber, 53.9 mg calcium, 1.4 mg iron

7

Starters

If you're having a party—big or small—you won't have to rack your brain anymore trying to figure out good-tasting gluten-free appetizers. Trust us; no one will miss the gluten!

Quick and Easy Gluten-Free

Garlic and Herb–Stuffed Cucumber Rounds
Layered Eggplant and Goat Cheese Tower
Bruschetta with Corn Tortilla Triangles
Dates Stuffed with Brie and Almonds
Navy Bean Peach Salsa
Marinated Antipasto Kabobs
Endive Stuffed with Garlic Edamame Spread
Orange and Yellow Potato Dippers
Hot Spinach and Millet Dip
Goat Cheese and Currants on Brown Rice Crackers

Creative Gluten-Free

Homemade Hummus with Spicy Salsa
Asian Chicken Lettuce Wraps
Plantain Chips

Crabmeat Cocktail with Papaya Salsa
Crab Cakes with Herbed Mayonnaise
Amaranth and Rice Cracker–Stuffed Mushrooms
Mini Frittatas
Crispy Fish Sticks with Cocktail Sauce
Honey BBQ Chicken Nuggets
Arepas with White Bean Pimento Spread

QUICK AND EASY GLUTEN-FREE

Garlic and Herb–Stuffed Cucumber Rounds

Serves 8 (Serving size: about 3 pieces)

Seedless cucumbers are also known as English cucumbers.
They generally come wrapped in plastic. We like them
because they are not coated in wax.

2 seedless cucumbers
4 ounces low-fat cream cheese
1 teaspoon garlic powder
1 tablespoon butter
½ teaspoon salt

1 green onion, chopped (bulb and greens)
½ red pepper, chopped
4 ounces goat cheese
Parsley sprigs (optional)

1. Use a vegetable peeler to cut lengthwise stripes into the cucumbers. If you run a vegetable peeler down the sides of the cucumber, leaving some green in between each peeled area, it creates a nice design.
2. Cut off the ends of the cucumbers and slice in half lengthwise. Completely scoop out the middle. A melon baller does the trick nicely.
3. Mix together the cream cheese, garlic powder, butter, salt, green onion, red pepper, and goat cheese until creamy.
4. Stuff the filling into the cucumbers, making sure to fill the entire length, and chill them for 15 minutes or more.
5. Cut the cucumbers into 1½-inch-long pieces, garnish with parsley sprigs, and serve.

Tip: If there is extra filling left over, try the following: Cut small rounds out of gluten-free bread with a biscuit cutter and toast them in the oven. Top the rounds with cheese filling, put them under the broiler, and heat until bubbling. Garnish with parsley and serve.

Nutritional information per serving: 112 calories, 5 g protein, 5 g carbohydrate, 8.2 g fat, 23 mg cholesterol, 273 mg sodium, less than 1 g fiber, 73 mg calcium, less than 1 mg iron

---

Layered Eggplant and Goat Cheese Tower

Serves 6

This recipe calls for roasted red peppers. You can find them in a grocery store or you can roast your own.

1 large eggplant, peeled and sliced into ½-inch rounds

2 tablespoons minced garlic

1 teaspoon salt

½ teaspoon black pepper

2 tablespoons olive oil

1 cup gluten-free marinara or tomato sauce, heated

12 slices roasted red pepper (approximately 3 inches long, 1½ inches wide; see box on page 112)

3 beefsteak tomatoes, thinly sliced

6 ounces goat cheese (or any kind of soft cheese)

4 tablespoons minced fresh basil

1. Mix the eggplant slices with the garlic, salt, pepper, and olive oil, and marinate them in a zipper-lock bag for about 10 minutes.
2. Cook the eggplant slices on a countertop or stovetop grill until just cooked through. The eggplant will pierce easily with a fork; be careful not to burn it.
3. Spoon 2 to 3 tablespoons of tomato sauce on each of 6 small plates.
4. On each plate, place an eggplant slice on top of the sauce, then add alternating layers of the roasted peppers, tomatoes, and goat cheese.
5. Garnish each dish with minced basil and serve.

Roasting Your Own Peppers

Preheat the oven to 450 degrees. Cover a baking sheet with aluminum foil, and place the red peppers on the sheet. Bake for about 35 to 45 minutes until the peppers are blackened on the outside, with some areas still red. Remove them from the oven and cool them, covered tightly. Peel off the outside skin and pop out the seeds. The roasted peppers are ready to use. If there are any leftover peppers, they can be stored in the refrigerator in a jar for up to 5 days.

Tip: Use extra sauce if you like. Pesto sauce works nicely in this recipe as well.

Nutritional information per serving: 220 calories, 8.6 g protein, 15.7 g carbohydrate, 14.4 g fat, 23 mg cholesterol, 710 mg sodium, 5.4 g fiber, 113 mg calcium, 1.3 mg iron

Bruschetta with Corn Tortilla Triangles

Serves 6 (Serving size: about 2/3 cup)

Everyone loves bruschetta. It's quick and easy to make and can be prepared one to two days ahead. Best made with vine-ripened tomatoes, bruschetta is typically served with crusty bread, but tortilla triangles work just as well.

3 cups chopped plum tomatoes

¼ cup chopped pitted black olives (such as Kalamata olives)

1 small red onion or 2 shallots, finely chopped

2 tablespoons chopped basil

3 tablespoons olive oil

3 garlic cloves, chopped (use more if you like garlic)

1 tablespoon balsamic vinegar

2 roasted red bell peppers, chopped (see box above)

1 teaspoon kosher salt

½ teaspoon black pepper

1 tablespoon capers (optional)

1. Combine the ingredients and refrigerate at least 15 minutes.
2. To make corn tortilla triangles, preheat oven to 350 degrees. Cut each corn tortilla into 8 triangles, slicing as you would a pizza. Place triangles on a cookie sheet, spray with cooking oil or toss with a small amount of vegetable oil, and bake for about 10 minutes or until crisp.
3. Serve the triangles topped with bruschetta.

Tip: This bruschetta is also a great topping for grilled fish or chicken.

Nutritional information per serving (bruschetta): 86 calories, less than 1 g protein, 4.5 g carbohydrate, 7.5 g fat, 0 mg cholesterol, 417 mg sodium, less than 1 g fiber, 17.4 mg calcium, less than 1 mg iron

Nutritional information (bruschetta with 8 corn triangles): 153 calories, 2.3 g protein, 16.1 g carbohydrate, 7.8 g fat, 0 mg cholesterol, 429 mg sodium, less than 1 g fiber, 38.4 mg calcium, less than 1 mg iron

Dates Stuffed with Brie and Almonds
Serves 6 (Serving size: 2 dates)

These stuffed dates are easy to make and oh, so delicious!
You may substitute other nuts for the almonds
or leave out the nuts entirely.

12 dates, pitted
12 roasted almonds

3 tablespoons low-fat cream cheese
3 tablespoons Brie cheese

1. Roast raw almonds in a dry skillet for about 3 to 5 minutes until golden brown and fragrant, taking care not to burn them. Remove from heat and let cool.
2. Remove the pits from 12 dates.
3. Stuff an almond into each date.
4. Cream together the cream cheese and Brie.
5. Fill each date with about ½ tablespoon of the cheese mixture.

Nutritional information per serving: 128 calories, 4.7 g protein, 13 g carbohydrate, 6.6 g fat, 18.4 mg cholesterol, 111 mg sodium, 1.5 g fiber, 49 mg calcium, less than 1 mg iron

Navy Bean Peach Salsa

Serves 6 (Serving size: about ⅔ cup)

This recipe is an appetizing way to add more beans to your diet and is a nice combination of sweet and savory flavors. Mangoes, papaya, pears, and apples also work well in this recipe.

2 10¾-ounce cans navy (or black) beans, drained and rinsed

1 small red onion, chopped

1 green pepper, chopped

1 small jalapeño pepper, chopped (optional)

½ cup cilantro, chopped

1 cup peaches or nectarines, peeled and chopped (or other fruits, as desired)

¼ cup lime juice

1 tablespoon olive oil

½ teaspoon salt

1. Combine the ingredients.
2. Chill the salsa overnight and serve it with Plantain Chips (page 121).

Nutritional information per serving: 164 calories, 8 g protein, 28 g carbohydrate, 2.3 g fat, 0 mg cholesterol, 439 mg sodium, 6.4 g fiber, 56 mg calcium, 2 mg iron

Marinated Antipasto Kabobs

Serves 4 (Serving size: 2 kabobs)

These kabobs are delicious, quick, and festive. If you have more time and would like to make your own marinated mushrooms, a recipe is provided in the tip on the next page.

1 cup marinated button mushrooms (most are gluten-free, but be sure to check the labels)

½ pound small mozzarella balls (cut larger pieces in half)

1 cup cherry tomatoes

1 12-ounce jar marinated artichoke hearts (if artichoke hearts are very large, cut them in half)

16 large green pitted olives

8 6-inch wooden kabob skewers

Alternate all of the ingredients on skewers and serve.

Tip: To make your own marinated mushrooms, take about 1½ cups of small button mushrooms and dip them in boiling water for about 15 seconds. Remove them from the boiling water and mix them in a small bowl with about ¼ cup gluten-free Italian salad dressing. Refrigerate until ready to use. To make your own Italian dressing, use the recipe below.

Nutritional information per serving: 259 calories, 13.7 g protein, 11 g carbohydrate, 21 g fat, 30 mg cholesterol, 754 mg sodium, 4.4 g fiber, 13.7 mg calcium, less than 1 mg iron

ITALIAN SALAD DRESSING
Makes 1 cup dressing or 16 1-tablespoon servings

⅔ cup olive oil

¼ cup vinegar (such as red wine vinegar)

2 tablespoons grated Parmesan cheese

2 teaspoons sugar

1 teaspoon salt

1 teaspoon onion powder

1 teaspoon garlic powder

¼ teaspoon black pepper

¼ teaspoon paprika

1 teaspoon gluten-free Italian seasoning

½ teaspoon gluten-free dry mustard

Whisk the ingredients together and reserve the dressing until ready to use.

Nutritional information per serving: 86 calories, less than 1 g protein, 0.85 g carbohydrate, 9 g fat, less than 1 mg cholesterol, 155 mg sodium, less than 1 g fiber, 8.5 mg calcium, less than 1 mg iron

Endive Stuffed with Garlic Edamame Spread
Serves 8 (Serving size: 2 stuffed endive leaves)

Endive makes a lovely appetizer and is a perfect way to serve the garlicky edamame beans. Edamame beans are simply green soybeans that are harvested before they have ripened.

2 cups frozen shelled edamame beans (available in most supermarkets)

½ cup fresh parsley

1 tablespoon fresh lemon juice

1 tablespoon olive oil

2 teaspoons minced roasted garlic (available in jars in the produce section of the supermarket)

½ teaspoon salt

¼ teaspoon black pepper

¼ cup water

16 fresh endive leaves

1. Place the edamame in a medium saucepan. Cover with water and bring to a boil. Cook for 4 to 5 minutes. Drain and rinse the beans with cold water.
2. Place the cooked edamame, parsley, lemon juice, olive oil, garlic, salt, and pepper in a food processor. Pulse several times to blend.
3. With the food processor on, pour in ¼ cup water. Continue to blend until a paste is formed.
4. Put 1½ tablespoons of the mixture in each endive leaf, and place two leaves on each individual plate to serve.

Tip: If you like spicy food, garnish this dish with hot sauce or dried red pepper flakes.

Nutritional information per serving: 81 calories, 5.6 g protein, 6.4 g carbohydrate, 4.3 g fat, 0 mg cholesterol, 150 mg sodium, 7.4 g fiber, 47 mg calcium, 1.2 mg iron

Orange and Yellow Potato Dippers

Serves 4 (Serving size: about 6 potato slices with 2½ tablespoons dip)

Everyone starts a party with chips and dips, and this creative combo is sure to delight your guests. This recipe can be doubled or tripled to serve a crowd. Add purple or white potatoes for a more colorful presentation.

1 medium sweet potato

1 medium Yukon gold potato

1 tablespoon vegetable oil

¼ teaspoon salt

¼ teaspoon black pepper

3 tablespoons whipped cream cheese

3 tablespoons sour cream

¼ cup plain Greek yogurt

1 tablespoon grated Parmesan cheese

¼ teaspoon garlic powder

1 green onion, thinly sliced

½ cup chopped roasted red peppers

1. Preheat the oven to 400 degrees.
2. Slice the potatoes into ⅛-inch slices. Place them in a large gallon-size zipper-lock bag. Add the oil, salt, and pepper. Close the bag and gently shake until all the potatoes are coated.
3. Place the potatoes in a single layer on a large cookie sheet. Cook for 20 to 25 minutes, turning once, until just tender.
4. While the potatoes are cooking, prepare the dip.
5. In a small bowl, combine the cream cheese, sour cream, yogurt, Parmesan cheese, and garlic powder. Beat with a whisk until well combined. Stir in the green onion and red peppers. Serve the dip with the potatoes.

Tip: If you want to reduce the fat in this recipe, substitute low-fat cream cheese for the whipped cream cheese, low-fat sour cream for the regular sour cream, and low-fat Greek yogurt for the regular Greek yogurt.

Nutritional information per serving: 144 calories, 3 g protein, 14.5 g carbohydrate, 8.5 g fat, 14.5 mg cholesterol, 231 mg sodium, 1.9 g fiber, 60.7 mg calcium, less than 1 mg iron

---

Hot Spinach and Millet Dip
Serves 24 (Serving size: 2 tablespoons)

Toasted millet adds a tasty, crunchy texture to this dip.
Serve the dip hot or cold on homemade Cheese
Crisp Crackers (page 79).

½ cup hulled millet
10-ounce package frozen chopped spinach, thawed
1 cup mayonnaise
1 cup plain nonfat yogurt

½ cup shredded Monterey Jack cheese
1 teaspoon onion powder
1 teaspoon garlic powder

1. Preheat the oven to 350 degrees.
2. Toast the millet in a small skillet over medium heat until fragrant, about 5 minutes.
3. Drain the spinach and squeeze dry.

4. Mix all ingredients in a large bowl. Pour into a 2-quart casserole dish.
5. Bake for 15 to 20 minutes, until hot and bubbly.
6. Serve with raw vegetables or gluten-free crackers.

Nutritional information per serving: 94 calories, 2 g protein, 4.5 g carbohydrate, 7.6 g fat, 5.6 mg cholesterol, 89.5 mg sodium, less than 1 g fiber, 54 mg calcium, less than 1 mg iron

Goat Cheese and Currants on Brown Rice Crackers

Serves 6 (Serving size: 4 crackers)

This topping is sweet and creamy, with a hint of savory, and will undoubtedly become a party favorite. You can reduce the fat in this recipe by substituting light cream cheese.

2 ounces goat cheese
4 ounces cream cheese
½ teaspoon garlic powder
1 tablespoon balsamic vinegar

1 teaspoon sugar
2 tablespoons currants or chopped dried cranberries
24 gluten-free brown rice crackers

1. Cream together the goat cheese, cream cheese, garlic powder, balsamic vinegar, and sugar.
2. Fold the currants into the cheese mixture.
3. Spread ½ tablespoon of the cheese mixture on each cracker and serve immediately.

Tip: This recipe also works well stuffed in grapes or on apple wedges (leave out the currants, when spreading it on fruit). If you're stuffing grapes, cut a thin slice off each grape lengthwise with a sharp knife so that the grape will lie flat, then make a slit lengthwise on the other side, halfway open, and spread the filling in the opening (yum).

Nutritional information per serving: 158.2 calories, 4.7 g protein, 13.2 g carbohydrate, 9.5 g fat, 25 mg cholesterol, 206.4 mg sodium, 1.1 g fiber, 40.4 mg calcium, less than 1 mg iron

CREATIVE GLUTEN-FREE

Homemade Hummus
with Spicy Salsa

Serves 6 (Serving size: approximately ½ cup)

Hummus is a Middle Eastern specialty made with garbanzo beans (also called chickpeas) and tahini (a paste made from ground sesame seeds). You can find tahini in your supermarket. Hummus makes a great dip or sandwich spread.

Spicy Salsa:

4 plum tomatoes, cut into quarters

½ red onion, cut into quarters

1 jalapeño pepper, seeded

1 tablespoon red wine vinegar

1 tablespoon fresh cilantro, chopped

1 clove garlic, peeled

1 teaspoon ground cumin

¼ teaspoon salt

Hummus:

16-ounce can garbanzo beans, drained, reserving ¼ cup liquid

1½ tablespoons tahini

2 cloves garlic, peeled and crushed

Juice of 1 lemon

½ teaspoon salt

1 tablespoon olive oil

½ teaspoon ground cumin

2 tablespoons fresh cilantro, chopped (for garnish)

1. Put the salsa ingredients in a food processor, cover, and process until chunky. Set aside.
2. Put the hummus ingredients (except the reserved bean liquid and the cilantro) into the food processor. Cover and blend until smooth and thoroughly mixed.
3. Add the reserved liquid, 1 tablespoon at a time, and process until creamy.
4. Fold in the salsa ingredients and sprinkle the hummus with the cilantro.
5. Serve hummus on sliced cucumbers, baby carrots, gluten-free rice crackers, or corn chips.

Nutritional information per serving: 134 calories, 4 g protein, 17.3 g carbohydrate, 6 g fat, 0 mg cholesterol, 461 mg sodium, 4.4 g fiber, 48 mg calcium, 1 mg iron

Asian Chicken Lettuce Wraps

Serves 8 (Serving size: 1 lettuce wrap)

*Lettuce leaves are a great way to whip up a quick meal.
You can also stuff them with your favorite cold cuts,
hummus, or leftover chili. Use your imagination!*

12 ounces thinly cut, boneless, skinless chicken breasts (or regular chicken breasts pounded to ¼-inch thickness with a rolling pin)

1 teaspoon olive oil

1 teaspoon gluten-free grill seasoning blend (or a blend of black pepper, salt, and Italian herbs)

½ cup apricot preserves

1 teaspoon sesame oil

2 teaspoons garlic powder

½ teaspoon rice wine vinegar

2 tablespoons gluten-free chicken broth or water

3 green onions, chopped

½ cup slivered almonds

8 whole iceberg lettuce leaves

2 cups coleslaw blend (or 2 cups shredded cabbage)

1. Heat a grill pan over medium-high heat. Brush the chicken with the olive oil and sprinkle it with the grill seasoning.
2. Cook the chicken 3 to 4 minutes on each side until cooked through. Cover and set aside.
3. In a small saucepan, blend the apricot preserves, sesame oil, garlic powder, vinegar, and broth. Bring to a boil over medium heat. Remove from heat and stir in the green onions.
4. Toast the almonds in a small skillet over medium heat, stirring frequently until browned and fragrant.
5. Slice the chicken into thin strips. Place the chicken strips in the lettuce leaves with the coleslaw mix and almonds. Top each stuffed leaf with the sauce and serve.

Nutritional information per serving: 297 calories, 25 g protein, 23 g carbohydrate, 12 g fat, 49 mg cholesterol, 295 mg sodium, 3.2 g fiber, 82 mg calcium, 2.3 mg iron

Plantain Chips

Serves 6 (Serving size: ½ plantain with 2 tablespoons salsa)

Plantain chips are fabulous—they taste both sweet and savory at the same time. When choosing a plantain for this recipe, find one that has turned mostly yellow, with a few spots of black on it, for the sweetest taste.

3 tablespoons corn oil

3 plantains, ripe and yellow

1 tablespoon granulated sugar

½ teaspoon salt

¾ cup gluten-free tomato salsa

1. Heat the corn oil.
2. Peel and slice the plantains into ¼-inch rounds.
3. Fry the plantains on one side, flatten them with a fork, turn them over, and brown them on the other side.
4. When the plantains are cooked through, crispy, and golden, remove them from the heat.
5. Sprinkle the plantains with the sugar and salt, and serve with your favorite gluten-free tomato salsa.

Nutritional information per serving: 183 calories, 1.4 g protein, 31.8 g carbohydrate, 7.1 g fat, 0 mg cholesterol, 332 mg sodium, 5.9 mg calcium, 0.6 mg iron

Crabmeat Cocktail with Papaya Salsa

Serves 4

This recipe is a nice alternative to shrimp cocktail and is a festive dish to serve during the holidays or at dinner parties. Salsa can be made the day before you plan to use it.

1 cup loose lettuce leaves

1 cup diced fresh papaya (pineapple, mango, or peaches also work well)

⅓ cup roasted red bell peppers, drained and diced

½ jalapeño pepper, seeded and minced (less, if you don't like it too hot)

1 small cucumber, peeled and diced

2 tablespoons fresh cilantro, chopped

1 small red onion, chopped

½ teaspoon salt

½ teaspoon black pepper

2 tablespoons fresh lime juice

1 pound fresh cooked crabmeat (do not use imitation crabmeat—it is not gluten-free)

4 lime slices (optional garnish)

1. Arrange the lettuce leaves in 4 small bowls.
2. Combine the remaining ingredients, except the crabmeat and the lime slices, and toss them together.
3. Place ¼ of the papaya salsa in the middle of each bowl.
4. Arrange the crabmeat over the salsa and serve with a lime slice, if desired.

Tip: Leftover chicken cut into 1 × ½-inch pieces can be substituted for the crab in this recipe as a money-saving alternative.

Nutritional information per serving: 155 calories, 24 g protein, 9.4 g carbohydrate, 2.2 g fat, 113 mg cholesterol, 612 mg sodium, 2 g fiber, 143 mg calcium, 1.4 mg iron

Crab Cakes with Herbed Mayonnaise

Serves 4 (Serving size: 1 crab cake with 1 tablespoon mayonnaise)

These succulent panfried crab cakes will make you feel as if you're in the Caribbean! Chilling the crab cakes before you fry them helps hold them together.

2 6-ounce cans lump crabmeat, drained

¼ cup crushed plain potato chips (gluten-free rice crackers or corn chips also work well)

2 green onions, chopped

2 tablespoons mayonnaise

1 teaspoon gluten-free dry mustard

¼ teaspoon salt

¼ teaspoon lemon juice

1 egg

¼ cup millet flour

1 teaspoon paprika

2 tablespoons vegetable oil

1. Mix the crabmeat with the potato chips and onions.
2. In a small bowl, combine the mayonnaise, mustard, salt, lemon juice, and egg. Whisk until smooth.
3. Carefully stir the mayonnaise mixture into the crabmeat until just combined.
4. Combine the millet flour with the paprika on a paper plate.
5. Form the crabmeat into four patties. Dip each patty in the millet flour and place it on a cookie sheet. Refrigerate the patties for 1 hour before cooking them.
6. Heat the oil in a large skillet over medium heat. Carefully place the crab cakes in the skillet. Cook them for about 5 minutes on each side until golden brown.
7. Serve the crab cakes with Herbed Mayonnaise.

HERBED MAYONNAISE

Use any fresh herb or combination of herbs that you have on hand for this delicious mayonnaise.

¼ cup mayonnaise

1 teaspoon minced dried onion

1 teaspoon capers

¼ teaspoon lemon juice

1 tablespoon chopped fresh flat-leaf parsley

Process the ingredients in a food processor. Serve the mayonnaise with the warm crab cakes.

Tip: To decrease the fat content of this recipe, serve the crab cakes with a spicy salsa instead of the Herbed Mayonnaise. The Papaya Salsa from the Crabmeat Cocktail recipe (page 121) would work nicely, as would the Navy Bean Peach Salsa (page 114).

Nutritional information per serving: 367.3 calories, 20.6 g protein, 11.3 g carbohydrate, 26.2 g fat, 136 mg cholesterol, 632 mg sodium, 2.1 g fiber, 102 mg calcium, 1.5 mg iron

Amaranth and Rice Cracker–Stuffed Mushrooms

Serves 6 (Serving size: 4 to 5 mushrooms, depending on the size of the mushrooms)

Amaranth seeds and brown rice crackers make a great stuffing for mushrooms. Brown rice crackers are available in grocery stores and natural food stores.

2 8-ounce packages baby portobello mushrooms (or substitute your favorite type of mushroom)

⅓ cup uncooked amaranth seeds

1½ cups gluten-free chicken broth

1 teaspoon onion powder

1 teaspoon garlic powder

¾ teaspoon dried thyme leaves

⅓ cup finely ground gluten-free brown rice crackers (any flavor)

1½ tablespoons unsalted butter

1 tablespoon grated Parmesan cheese

1. Wipe the mushrooms clean with a damp paper towel. Carefully separate the stems from the caps, keeping the caps intact.
2. Finely chop the stems and set aside ½ cup.
3. In a small saucepan, combine the amaranth, 1 cup of the broth, onion powder, garlic powder, thyme, and the reserved mushroom stems. Bring to a boil. Reduce the heat, cover, and simmer until the liquid is absorbed and the amaranth is tender, about 20 minutes.
4. Remove from heat and stir in the cracker crumbs.
5. Preheat the oven to 375 degrees.
6. Stuff ½ to 1 tablespoon of mixture into each mushroom cap. Place the mushrooms in a shallow baking dish in a single layer. Dot with butter and sprinkle with Parmesan cheese.
7. Pour the remaining ½ cup broth into the bottom of the baking dish. Cover the dish tightly with aluminum foil and bake in preheated oven for 30 minutes.
8. Let stand for 10 minutes before serving.

Nutritional information per serving: 140 calories, 6 g protein, 19 g carbohydrate, 5 g fat, 8.4 mg cholesterol, 290 mg sodium, 2.8 g fiber, 42 mg calcium, 1.6 mg iron

Mini Frittatas

Serves 5 (Serving size: 6 frittatas)

These frittatas are great when you're cooking breakfast for a crowd. They also make a tasty appetizer or a nice addition to a brunch buffet.

Gluten-free cooking spray or vegetable oil

2 tablespoons chopped sun-dried tomatoes (not oil packed)

1½ cups skim milk

¼ cup white rice flour

½ tablespoon garlic powder

½ tablespoon onion powder

1 teaspoon gluten-free Italian seasoning (or any combination of dried basil, oregano, thyme, and parsley)

¼ teaspoon black pepper

3 eggs

3 egg whites

½ cup shredded Parmesan, asiago, and Romano cheese blend

½ cup water-packed, canned artichoke hearts, drained and chopped

1. Preheat the oven to 350 degrees. Coat 30 mini muffin cups with gluten-free cooking spray or vegetable oil.
2. Put the sun-dried tomatoes in a small bowl. Pour ½ cup boiling water over the tomatoes and let sit for 5 minutes. Drain and set aside.
3. Combine the milk, rice flour, garlic powder, onion powder, Italian seasoning, and black pepper in a large mixing bowl.
4. Beat in the eggs and egg whites with a wire whisk until well blended.
5. Stir in the sun-dried tomatoes, cheese, and artichokes.
6. Fill the muffin cups with the egg and vegetable mixture (about 2 tablespoons each).
7. Bake for 20 minutes, or until frittatas are browned around the edges and firm in the middle.
8. Serve immediately.

Tip: You can find sun-dried tomatoes in the produce section—they will be in a plastic package, not in a jar. You may be able to find some that are soft and recipe-ready. If you use these, you can skip the second step.

Nutritional information per serving: 147 calories, 11.7 g protein, 13.5 g carbohydrate, 5 g fat, 115 mg cholesterol, 283.5 mg sodium, 1 g fiber, 179 mg calcium, less than 1 mg iron

Crispy Fish Sticks with Cocktail Sauce

Serves 4 (Serving size: 4 to 5 fish sticks with 2 tablespoons sauce)

These fish sticks are a real treat and, oh, so easy to prepare.

Gluten-free cooking spray or about 2 teaspoons vegetable oil

1 pound fish fillets, such as tilapia, cod, or sole

1 cup gluten-free cornflakes, processed into crumbs (see tip)

1 tablespoon dried parsley

1 teaspoon onion powder

¼ teaspoon salt

¼ teaspoon black pepper

1 egg

2 egg whites

½ cup brown rice flour

½ cup gluten-free chili sauce

1 tablespoon horseradish (or more to taste)

1 tablespoon lemon juice

1. Preheat the oven to 425 degrees. Coat a large baking pan with the cooking spray or vegetable oil.
2. Cut the fish into strips, about 2 inches long by ½-inch wide.
3. Mix the cornflakes with the parsley, onion powder, salt, and pepper.
4. In a separate dish, beat together the egg and egg whites.
5. Place the brown rice flour in a gallon-size zipper-lock bag. Add the fish, a few pieces at a time; coat each piece with flour, then dip it in the egg, then into the cornflake mixture, making sure to coat the fish stick completely. Place the fish on the prepared tray.
6. Bake for 12 to 15 minutes, or until fish is cooked through.
7. To make cocktail sauce, mix the chili sauce, horseradish, and lemon juice in a small bowl. Serve with the fish. If you prefer tartar sauce with your fish, simply mix ½ cup mayonnaise with 1 tablespoon pickle relish and 1 tablespoon lemon juice.

Tip: To crush cornflakes, put them in a gallon-size zipper-lock bag, close the top, and pound them gently with a mallet or a rolling pin until they're crushed to coarse crumbs.

Nutritional information per serving: 323 calories, 30.4 g protein, 40.6 g carbohydrate, 3.8 g fat, 109.5 mg cholesterol, 825 mg sodium, 2.9 g fiber, 35.5 mg calcium, 5.4 mg iron

Honey BBQ Chicken Nuggets

Serves 4 (Serving size: about 6 to 8 pieces)

*Your kids (and the adults in your household)
will love these chicken nuggets! The recipe
can be doubled to serve a crowd.*

1 tablespoon vegetable oil

1 tablespoon butter

¼ cup brown rice flour

½ teaspoon salt

¼ teaspoon black pepper

1 pound chicken tenders, cut into 1-inch pieces

1 8-ounce can low-sodium tomato sauce

1 tablespoon white distilled vinegar

1 tablespoon dark brown sugar

1 tablespoon gluten-free Dijon mustard

2 tablespoons honey

1. Heat the oil and butter in a large skillet over medium-high heat.
2. Mix the flour with the salt and pepper in a shallow dish.
3. Dredge the chicken in the flour, shaking off the excess, and place each piece in the skillet.
4. Cook the nuggets for 4 to 5 minutes, until the chicken is cooked through and browned.
5. Mix the tomato sauce, vinegar, sugar, mustard, and honey in a small saucepan with a wire whisk until well combined. Heat over low heat until the sauce just reaches a simmer.
6. When the chicken is done, dip each piece into the sauce to coat it and place the nuggets on a serving plate.

Nutritional information per serving: 287 calories, 27.7 g protein, 23.8 g carbohydrate, 8 g fat, 73.3 mg cholesterol, 483.5 mg sodium, 1.4 g fiber, 26.4 mg calcium, 1.6 mg iron

Arepas with White Bean Pimento Spread

Serves 6 (Serving size: 4 arepas)

Arepas, a flatbread made with corn flour, are a staple in South American diets. They make a tasty, sturdy base for any number of toppings.

½ cup arepa flour (see box on page 79)

¼ teaspoon salt

¾ cup warm water

2 tablespoons vegetable oil

15-ounce can white beans, rinsed and drained

2 cloves garlic

4 green onions (scallions)

3 tablespoons diced pimento

1. Blend the arepa flour with the salt. Stir in the water until well mixed. Let the dough sit for about 10 minutes.
2. Take 1 tablespoon of the dough and make a ball in your hands. Flatten it to a round patty about 2 inches wide and ¼-inch thick. Place the patty on waxed paper and repeat with the remaining dough.
3. Heat a griddle to medium heat. Brush with oil. Place the arepas on the griddle and cook for 5 to 6 minutes on each side until browned.
4. In a food processor, blend the beans, garlic, three of the green onions (the bulbs and the greens) and 2 tablespoons of the pimento until well blended and smooth.
5. Top each arepa with about 1 tablespoon of the spread. Slice the remaining green onion (green only) into thin slices. Sprinkle the arepas with the sliced green onion and 1 tablespoon diced pimento.

Tip: If you do not have either arepa flour or masa harina on hand you can substitute corn tortillas for the arepas. Bake 12 tortillas in the oven at 400 degrees for about 10 minutes until they start to crisp. Spread each with about 2 tablespoons of the bean spread and cut them into quarters to serve

Nutritional information per serving: 127 calories, 5.2 g protein, 20 g carbohydrate, 5.3 g fat, 0 mg cholesterol, 262 mg sodium, 4.7 g fiber, 56.2 mg calcium, 1.3 mg iron

8

Sides

The next time you go to a potluck or a family gathering, take along any of these side dishes. They are sure to please!

Quick and Easy Gluten-Free

Black Beans and Rice in a Tomato Green Chili Sauce
Quinoa with Sautéed Onions and Lima Beans
Asparagus Parmesan
Zucchini Noodles
Smashed Cauliflower with Parmesan Amaranth
Brown Rice with Dried Fruit and Hazelnuts
Spicy Peanut Noodles
Baked Onion Rings
Roasted Parsnips
Sesame Tofu Stir-Fry
Wild Rice Spring Rolls
Green Beans in Black Bean Sauce
Sweet Potato Pancakes

Creative Gluten-Free

Cheesy Rice and Beans Casserole

Corn Pudding
Roasted Mashed Sweet Potatoes and Red Beets
Apricot Noodle Kugel
Amaranth-Stuffed Peppers
Millet Pilaf with Pine Nuts
Savory Cornbread Stuffing
Macaroni and Cheese with Fire-Roasted Red Peppers
Mixed Grain and Vegetable Casserole
Wild Rice Pilaf
Fra Diavolo over Quinoa Pasta
Broccoli Pasta Bake

QUICK AND EASY GLUTEN-FREE

Black Beans and Rice in a Tomato Green Chili Sauce

Serves 4 (Serving size: about 1 cup)

Although you might be used to eating white rice with your meals, you will probably like brown rice just as well. It has a nuttier, more flavorful taste than white rice. This recipe calls for black beans, but you can substitute any kind of bean.

2 teaspoons vegetable oil
½ cup finely chopped onion
2 cloves garlic, minced
10-ounce can diced tomatoes with green chilies
15-ounce can black beans, drained

½ teaspoon dried oregano
1 cup instant brown rice
1 cup water
2 tablespoons chopped fresh cilantro

1. Heat the oil in a large saucepan over medium heat. Add the onion and garlic and cook until softened, about 5 minutes.

2. Add the remaining ingredients, except the cilantro, and bring to a boil. Reduce heat, cover and simmer for 10 minutes until the liquid is absorbed.
3. Remove from heat and let stand, covered, for 5 minutes.
4. Sprinkle the beans and rice with fresh cilantro and serve.

Tip: If you have leftover vegetables, you can chop them and add them at step one of this recipe.

Nutritional information per serving: 221 calories, 7 g protein, 42 g carbohydrate, 3 g fat, 0 mg cholesterol, 524 mg sodium, 6 g fiber, 67 mg calcium, 2.7 mg iron

Quinoa with Sautéed Onions and Lima Beans
Serves 4 (Serving size: about 1 cup)
This dish is a rich and satisfying side, but it can also stand alone as a meal.

2 teaspoons vegetable oil
½ cup diced onion
1 teaspoon turmeric
½ teaspoon ground coriander
¼ teaspoon ground cinnamon

¼ teaspoon allspice
1 cup quinoa (see box on page 98)
2 cups gluten-free vegetable or chicken broth
1 cup lima beans

1. Heat the oil in a large saucepan over medium-high heat. Add the onions and sauté for 3 to 4 minutes until softened.
2. Add the spices and quinoa and stir to coat.
3. Add the broth and bring to a boil. Reduce heat and simmer for 10 to 15 minutes.
4. Stir in the lima beans and continue to simmer for another 5 to 10 minutes until the quinoa is tender and the liquid is absorbed.

Nutritional information per serving: 259 calories, 9.4 g protein, 44.5 g carbohydrate, 5 g fat, 0 mg cholesterol, 261 mg sodium, 6 g fiber, 58 mg calcium, 5.3 mg iron

Asparagus Parmesan

Serves 4 (Serving size: 3–4 stalks)

*This delicious vegetable is the perfect side
for almost any meal.*

Gluten-free cooking spray or
  2 teaspoons vegetable oil
1 pound asparagus (about 1 bunch)
2 tablespoons olive oil
4 tablespoons grated Parmesan
  cheese

2 teaspoons garlic powder
1 teaspoon onion powder
1 teaspoon oregano
4 tablespoons toasted
  amaranth seeds (see box on
  page 133)

1. Preheat the broiler.
2. Spray a cookie sheet with cooking spray or coat lightly with vegetable oil.
3. Snap off the ends of the asparagus stems, and place the trimmed asparagus on a cookie sheet. Asparagus ends will snap off easily at the spot where the stem should be discarded. Brush the asparagus with olive oil.
4. Combine the Parmesan cheese with the garlic powder, onion powder, oregano, and toasted amaranth seeds. Sprinkle the amaranth blend over the asparagus.
5. Drizzle the asparagus with the remaining olive oil, and broil until the asparagus is cooked through, about 4 minutes (it will pierce easily with a fork when it's done). When broiling asparagus, do not set the pan too close to the broiler or the asparagus may burn before it's cooked through.

Nutritional information per serving: 161 calories, 6.4 g protein, 15 g carbohydrate, 9.4 g fat, 4.4 mg cholesterol, 79.5 mg sodium, 2.7 g fiber, 127 mg calcium, 2.9 mg iron

Toasting Amaranth Seeds

To toast amaranth seeds, put them in a hot skillet for 3 to 4 minutes until they start to brown, taking care not to burn them. Amaranth seeds will make a popping sound while they're toasting.

Zucchini Noodles

Serves 6 (Serving size: about 1 cup)

This rich and creamy dish is a great way to eat zucchini!

8 ounces 100% buckwheat soba noodles (if soba noodles are not available, try brown rice noodles)

3 medium zucchini, coarsely shredded

1 tablespoon olive oil

1 clove garlic, minced

¼ cup sour cream

¼ cup plain Greek yogurt (or gluten-free plain yogurt)

½ cup shredded mild cheddar cheese

½ teaspoon salt

¼ teaspoon black pepper

1. Cook the soba noodles according to the package directions.
2. Drain the zucchini in a colander, squeezing out as much liquid as possible.
3. Heat the oil in a large nonstick skillet over medium heat. Add the zucchini and sauté for 2 minutes. Add the garlic and sauté for 2 to 3 minutes longer or until the zucchini is tender.
4. Remove the zucchini from heat and transfer to a large bowl. Add the sour cream, yogurt, cheese, salt, and pepper.
5. Drain the soba noodles; add to the zucchini and toss to coat.

Tip: If you'd like to reduce the fat in this recipe, use low-fat sour cream instead of regular sour cream, 2% plain Greek yogurt instead of regular, and low-fat cheddar cheese instead of regular.

Nutritional information per serving: 230 calories, 8.1 g protein, 33 g carbohydrate, 8.1 g fat, 14.8 mg cholesterol, 279 mg sodium, 3.1 g fiber, 117.7 mg calcium, 1.1 mg iron

---

Smashed Cauliflower with Parmesan Amaranth

Serves 4 (Serving size: ½ cup)

*Using amaranth in this recipe adds a nice crunch
to the creamy cauliflower.*

1 teaspoon uncooked amaranth seeds

1 tablespoon grated Parmesan cheese

10-ounce package frozen cauliflower

2 tablespoons half-and-half

2 tablespoons 2% cottage cheese

1 tablespoon sour cream

¼ teaspoon salt

¼ teaspoon white pepper

4 tablespoons gluten-free chicken broth

1. Heat a small skillet over medium-high heat. Add the amaranth seeds. Cover and shake the skillet until the amaranth pops. Remove from heat and sprinkle with Parmesan cheese.
2. Microwave the cauliflower until tender. Drain the excess liquid and place the cauliflower in a food processor.
3. Add the half-and-half, cottage cheese, sour cream, salt, and pepper. Process until smooth, gradually adding the broth to reach the desired consistency.
4. Pour the cauliflower into a serving bowl. Sprinkle with the amaranth/cheese mixture.

Tip: Fresh cauliflower can be used instead of the frozen. Steam it on the stove or in the microwave until tender.

Nutritional information per serving: 51 calories, 3.5 g protein, 4.5 g carbohydrate, 2.4 g fat, 5.7 mg cholesterol, 257 mg sodium, 1.8 g fiber, 44 mg calcium, less than 1 mg iron

Brown Rice with Dried Fruit and Hazelnuts

Serves 6 (Serving size: about ½ cup)

This is a simple and sweet side dish. It's great with roast pork or chicken. Try different combinations of dried fruit and nuts—whatever you like.

1¾ cups water   10 dried apricots, chopped
¼ cup orange juice   5 dried plums, chopped
2 cups instant brown rice   2 tablespoons chopped hazelnuts

1. Bring the water and orange juice to a boil in a medium saucepan. Stir in the rice and dried fruit. Return to a boil.
2. Reduce heat, cover, and let simmer for 5 to 10 minutes, until the liquid is absorbed.
3. Stir in the nuts and serve.

Nutritional information per serving: 293 calories, 6 g protein, 60 g carbohydrate, 3 g fat, 0 mg cholesterol, 34 mg sodium, 4.3 g fiber, 13 mg calcium, 1.4 mg iron

Spicy Peanut Noodles

Serves 4 (Serving size: about 1 cup)

We love peanut noodles. Because this dish can be served cold, it is perfect for potluck dinners. Just make sure you serve yourself early, because it disappears fast!

8 ounces dry brown rice noodles   1 tablespoon honey
1 tablespoon sesame oil   3 green onions, chopped
½ cup smooth peanut butter   1 tablespoon garlic powder
1 tablespoon gluten-free soy   ½ teaspoon red pepper flakes
  sauce or tamari sauce   (or to taste)
1 tablespoon cider vinegar   ½ cup chopped peanuts

1. Cook the rice noodles in boiling water until tender. Drain, reserving ½ cup of the cooking liquid. Rinse the noodles and toss them with the sesame oil. Set aside.
2. In a blender, combine the peanut butter, soy sauce, vinegar, honey, 2 green onions, garlic powder, red pepper flakes, and ¼ cup of the reserved cooking liquid. Blend until smooth. Add a little additional cooking liquid to reach a nice, smooth, creamy consistency.
3. Stir the sauce into the noodles in a large bowl. Sprinkle with the remaining chopped onion and peanuts.

4. Serve warm or cold.

Nutritional information per serving: 427.5 calories, 10.5 g protein, 60.5 g carbohydrate, 16.6 g fat, 0 mg cholesterol, 507 mg sodium, 3.6 g fiber, 37 mg calcium, 1.3 mg iron

---

Baked Onion Rings

Makes 4 servings (Serving size: 5 to 6 rings)

*Mmm-mmm, good! You will love these
gluten-free onion rings!*

1 large Vidalia onion

Gluten-free cooking spray
  or 2 teaspoons olive oil

1 cup gluten-free brown rice
  cracker crumbs

½ teaspoon paprika

¼ teaspoon salt

¼ teaspoon black pepper

1 egg

1 egg white

1. Peel and cut the onion into ¼-inch slices and separate them into rings. Soak the rings in a large bowl of cold water for about 15 minutes.
2. Preheat the oven to 400 degrees. Spray a large baking sheet with cooking spray (or coat it with olive oil).
3. Mix the cracker crumbs, paprika, salt, and pepper in a shallow dish.
4. Beat the egg and egg white together in a separate dish.
5. Drain the onions and pat them dry with a paper towel. Dip the onion rings, a few at a time, into the egg, then into the crumbs. Place the onion rings on the prepared baking sheet.
6. Bake for 10 to 15 minutes, until crisp and brown.
7. Onion rings are delicious served with ketchup, or with a simple dipping sauce made from ½ cup mayonnaise, 2 tablespoons gluten-free chili sauce, and 1 tablespoon pickle relish.

Nutritional information per serving: 143 calories, 5.5 g protein, 23.8 g carbohydrate, 2.9 g fat, 52.8 mg cholesterol, 363 mg sodium, 2.4 g fiber, 40.5 mg calcium, 1.1 mg iron

Roasted Parsnips

Serves 4 (Serving size: ½ cup)

A parsnip is a delicately flavored root vegetable that looks like a pale carrot. If you have never tried parsnips, this recipe makes a great introduction.

1 pound parsnips (or ½ pound parsnips and ½ pound sweet potatoes), peeled and cut into ¼-inch rounds

½ teaspoon salt

¼ teaspoon black pepper

3 tablespoons olive oil

2 cloves garlic, sliced

1 teaspoon dried rosemary

¼ teaspoon grated lemon zest

1. Preheat the oven to 425 degrees.
2. Spread the parsnips on a large baking sheet and sprinkle with salt and pepper.
3. Heat the oil with the garlic and rosemary in a small saucepan over low heat for about 5 minutes to let the flavors infuse the oil.
4. Remove the garlic from the oil with a slotted spoon. Pour the oil with the rosemary over the parsnips. Stir to make sure that all of the parsnips are coated.
5. Roast in the oven for 15 to 20 minutes, stirring halfway through.
6. Remove from the oven and sprinkle the parsnips with lemon zest. Serve immediately.

Nutritional information per serving: 142.7 calories, less than 1 g protein, 12.7 g carbohydrate, 10.4 g fat, 0 mg cholesterol, 298 mg sodium, 3.4 g fiber, 31.4 mg calcium, less than 1 mg iron

Sesame Tofu Stir-Fry

Serves 6 (Serving size: 1 cup)

Coating the tofu with sesame seeds and brown rice flour adds extra flavor and texture to this stir-fry.

Gluten-free cooking spray or 4 teaspoons olive oil

1 14-ounce package extra-firm tofu

⅓ cup brown rice flour

2 tablespoons sesame seeds

2 teaspoons vegetable oil

1 teaspoon minced garlic

1 teaspoon minced ginger
½ cup chopped onion
2 cups mixed fresh vegetables
1 cup shredded cabbage
½ cup gluten-free vegetable broth

¼ cup gluten-free, low-sodium soy sauce
2 teaspoons sesame oil
1 teaspoon cornstarch

1. Preheat the broiler. Spray a baking sheet with cooking spray (or coat with 2 teaspoons olive oil). Drain the tofu and pat dry with paper towels. Slice into ¼-inch slices.
2. Mix the brown rice flour and sesame seeds in a shallow dish. Coat the tofu on each side with the brown rice mixture, pressing it into the tofu to coat it. Place the tofu on the prepared baking sheet.
3. Spray the top of the tofu with cooking spray (or brush it with 2 teaspoons olive oil) and broil for 2 to 3 minutes. Turn it over and spray it again with cooking spray. Broil for 2 to 3 minutes longer. Remove from the oven, cut it into ½-inch cubes, and set aside.
4. Heat a large skillet or wok over medium-high heat. Add the vegetable oil, garlic, ginger, and onion. Cook, stirring constantly, for 2 to 3 minutes. Add the mixed vegetables and continue to cook for 3 to 4 minutes, or until the vegetables begin to soften. Add the cabbage and tofu.
5. In a small bowl, whisk together the broth, soy sauce, sesame oil, and cornstarch. Pour over the vegetables and cook for an additional 2 to 3 minutes until the sauce is thickened and the vegetables are tender. Serve immediately.

Tip: Check the produce section in your supermarket for prepackaged stir-fry vegetable blends that will make this recipe very easy to prepare.

Nutritional information per serving: 155 calories, 8.5 g protein, 15.3 g carbohydrate, 7.7 g fat, 0 mg cholesterol, 467 mg sodium, 3.2 g fiber, 189.7 mg calcium, 2.2 mg iron

Wild Rice Spring Rolls
Makes 8

These spring rolls are a fun way to get your children to eat more vegetables. They are delicious on their own or served with Asian Dipping Sauce (page 140). This recipe can be doubled or tripled as needed. You can even cut each roll in half to serve them on an appetizer platter.

1 teaspoon vegetable oil

1 teaspoon minced garlic

1 teaspoon minced ginger

¼ cup chopped onion

¼ cup chopped green pepper

¼ cup frozen corn kernels, thawed

1 cup cooked wild rice

1 cup shredded cabbage

½ teaspoon salt

¼ teaspoon black pepper

8 100% rice paper spring roll wrappers or 8 iceberg lettuce leaves

1. Heat the oil in a large skillet over medium heat. Add the garlic, ginger, onion, and pepper. Sauté for 3 to 4 minutes.
2. Add the corn, rice, cabbage, salt, and pepper. Cook for 3 to 4 more minutes, or until heated through.
3. Cover a baking sheet with parchment paper.
4. Dip a rice paper wrapper, one at a time, in hot water for a couple of seconds to soften. Place 2 tablespoons of the vegetable mixture in the center of the wrapper, fold in the sides, and roll it up. Place the rolls on the baking sheet. Repeat with the remaining wrappers.
5. Place the rolls in the refrigerator to cool for about 10 to 15 minutes, or until ready to serve.

Tip: Iceberg lettuce leaves work well in place of the spring roll wrappers. Just separate the large leaves from the outside of the lettuce, and serve the lettuce leaves with the filling on the side. Each diner will then roll his or her own spring roll at the table.

Nutritional information per serving: 78.8 calories, 1.8 g protein, 16.6 g carbohydrate, less than 1 g fat, 0 mg cholesterol, 152 mg sodium, 1.5 g fiber, 10.6 mg calcium, less than 1 mg iron

Asian Dipping Sauce

Makes ½ cup (Serving size: 1 tablespoon)

This sauce goes great with any Asian recipe and also works well as a coating for chicken, fish, or pork. If you're using it as a coating, brush the sauce on during the last few minutes of cooking to prevent burning.

¼ cup apricot preserves

¼ cup peach preserves

1 tablespoon gluten-free soy sauce

½ teaspoon red pepper flakes (optional)

In a small food processor, blend all ingredients until well combined.

Nutritional information per serving: 45.4 calories, less than 1 g protein, 11.6 g carbohydrate, less than 1 g fat, 0 mg cholesterol, 130.8 mg sodium, less than 1 g fiber, 2.4 mg calcium, less than 1 mg iron

Green Beans in Black Bean Sauce

Serves 4 (Serving size: about ¾ cup)

This recipe is a fabulous way to eat green beans. If you prefer your sauce to have a little more texture, skip the blending step.

1 pound fresh whole green beans, ends removed

2 teaspoons vegetable oil

1 shallot, minced

1 teaspoon grated ginger

1 teaspoon minced garlic

1 cup canned black beans, rinsed and drained

2 teaspoons gluten-free red curry paste

¾ cup water

1 tablespoon gluten-free soy sauce

1 teaspoon sesame oil

1 teaspoon cornstarch

1. Microwave or steam the green beans for 3 to 4 minutes until crisp tender.
2. Heat the oil in a large skillet. Add the shallot, ginger, and garlic and sauté for 2 to 3 minutes.

3. Add the black beans and curry paste. Using the back of a spoon, mash the black beans into the shallot mixture.
4. In a small bowl, combine the water, soy sauce, sesame oil, and cornstarch. Pour over the black beans, and stir to combine. If the sauce is too thick, add more water.
5. Transfer the black bean mixture to a blender and blend until smooth.
6. Pour the sauce over the green beans to serve.

Nutritional information per serving: 123.6 calories, 4.8 g protein, 16.2 g carbohydrate, 3.7 g fat, less than 1 mg cholesterol, 355 mg sodium, 5.3 g fiber, 51.9 mg calcium, less than 1 mg iron

Sweet Potato Pancakes
Makes 6 pancakes

Serve these flavorful pancakes as a side dish with turkey or pork or as part of a brunch buffet. Heated whole-berry cranberry sauce is delicious served on top of the pancakes, especially when they accompany turkey.

¼ cup cornmeal

2 tablespoons sorghum flour

1 teaspoon baking powder

¼ teaspoon salt

¼ teaspoon baking soda

¼ teaspoon black pepper

¼ teaspoon nutmeg

½ cup mashed sweet potatoes

1 egg

¾ cup buttermilk

1 tablespoon agave nectar (or honey; see box on page 72)

Gluten-free cooking spray or 2 teaspoons olive oil

1. Sift the dry ingredients together, from the cornmeal to the nutmeg.
2. Mix the wet ingredients, from the potatoes to the nectar.
3. Add the wet ingredients to the dry ingredients and stir to combine.
4. Heat a griddle and coat it with cooking spray or olive oil.
5. Drop the batter by ¼ cupfuls onto the hot griddle. Cook each pancake for 2 to 3 minutes on each side until browned and cooked through.

6. Serve the pancakes with warm maple syrup or agave nectar, if these pancakes are part of a breakfast buffet, or with sour cream or applesauce if you're using them as a side dish with pork chops or turkey.

Nutritional information per serving: 80.8 calories, 3.1 g protein, 15.9 g carbohydrate, 1.3 g fat, less than 1 mg cholesterol, 240 mg sodium, less than 1 g fiber, 58.5 mg calcium, less than 1 mg iron

---

CREATIVE GLUTEN-FREE

Cheesy Rice and Beans Casserole

Serves 6 (Serving size: about 1 cup)

This is a true one-pot meal and a nice twist on rice and beans. Take the dish along to your next potluck for rave reviews.

1⅓ cups gluten-free vegetable or chicken broth

⅔ cup long-grain brown rice

2 green onions, chopped

½ cup grated carrots

1 cup low-fat plain yogurt

1 cup low-fat plain cottage cheese

1 15-ounce can small white beans, drained and rinsed

1 teaspoon dried parsley

1 cup (4 ounces) low-fat shredded cheddar cheese (or any type of low-fat cheese)

1. In a large saucepan, mix the broth, rice, onions, and carrots. Bring to a boil, reduce heat, and simmer for 40 to 45 minutes, until the liquid is absorbed and the rice is tender (if the rice is too hard, add additional liquid). Remove from heat.
2. Preheat the oven to 350 degrees.
3. Stir the yogurt, cottage cheese, beans, and parsley into the rice mixture until well combined.
4. Spread in a 1½-quart baking dish. Sprinkle with cheddar cheese and cover with aluminum foil.

5. Bake for 20 minutes. Remove the foil and bake for an additional 10 minutes until the cheese is melted and bubbly.

Tip: Other cooked chopped vegetables, such as broccoli, can be added to the dish when you're stirring in the cheese and beans.

Nutritional information per serving: 237 calories, 17.3 g protein, 33.3 g carbohydrate, 6 g fat, 18 mg cholesterol, 447 mg sodium, 5.1 g fiber, 406 mg calcium, 1.3 mg iron

Corn Pudding
Serves 4

*This recipe is definitely a step up from canned cream corn!
It is perfect served on a cool fall or winter evening. If corn is in
season, use fresh corn removed from the cob.*

Gluten-free cooking spray or about 2 teaspoons vegetable oil

1 tablespoon brown rice flour

½ cup gluten-free liquid egg substitute or 4 large egg whites

1 tablespoon sugar

½ teaspoon salt

¼ teaspoon white pepper

2 tablespoons butter, melted

1¾ cups frozen corn kernels, white or yellow

1. Preheat the oven to 375 degrees. Spray four 7-ounce individual ramekins with cooking spray (or coat them with vegetable oil).
2. Mix the flour, egg substitute, sugar, salt, pepper, and butter together until smooth.
3. Stir in the corn and divide the pudding evenly among the ramekins.
4. Place the ramekins in a deep pan, such as a 9 × 13-inch pan. Pour water into the pan until it's halfway up the sides of the ramekins.
5. Carefully place in the oven and cook for about 30 minutes or until set in the center.

Nutritional information per serving: 162 calories, 6.2 g protein, 20 g carbohydrate, 7 g fat, 15.5 mg cholesterol, 389 mg sodium, 1.8 g fiber, 22 mg calcium, 1 mg iron

Roasted Mashed Sweet Potatoes and Red Beets

Serves 8 (Serving size: approximately ½ cup)

*This dish is fabulous served with chicken
and steamed green vegetables.*

3 large sweet potatoes, cut into 2-inch pieces

3 fresh beets, peeled and cut into 2-inch pieces (or 1 cup canned beets)

1 peeled and cored apple cut into 2-inch pieces

1 cup gluten-free chicken stock

2 tablespoons butter or olive oil

1 tablespoon dark brown sugar

1 teaspoon onion powder

¼ teaspoon cinnamon

½ teaspoon dried thyme leaves

1 teaspoon salt

1. Preheat the oven to 400 degrees.
2. Place all ingredients in a medium casserole dish, and cover with aluminum foil.
3. Bake for about 1 hour until the vegetables are soft.
4. Process in a food processor until creamy.

Nutritional information per serving: 115 calories, 1.9 g protein, 20.4 g carbohydrate, 3.2 g fat, 7.6 mg cholesterol, 437 mg sodium, 3.3 g fiber, 19 mg calcium, less than 1 mg iron

Apricot Noodle Kugel

Serves 8 (Serving size: 2 × 3-inch piece)

*Kugel is a traditional Jewish side dish that's often served
on holidays and sold at Jewish delis. The sweet, creamy,
crunchy combination makes a delightful dish.
Any pasta shape will work in this recipe.*

Gluten-free cooking spray or about 2 teaspoons vegetable oil

8-ounce package uncooked quinoa pasta

2 cups low-fat (1%) small-curd cottage cheese

1 cup reduced-fat (2%) evaporated milk

½ cup sour cream

1½ teaspoons cinnamon
¼ teaspoon nutmeg
2 eggs
1 teaspoon vanilla extract

¾ cup sugar
12 canned apricot halves, drained
    and chopped. Reserve 2
    tablespoons of the juice.

1. Preheat the oven to 350 degrees. Spray a 9 × 13-inch dish with cooking spray (or coat it with vegetable oil).
2. Cook the pasta in boiling water until just tender. Do not overcook the pasta, or it will fall apart.
3. Mix the cottage cheese, evaporated milk, sour cream, 1 teaspoon of the cinnamon, nutmeg, eggs, vanilla, and sugar until well blended.
4. Add the noodles, apricots, and reserved apricot juice. Stir to mix.
5. Pour the noodles into the prepared dish. Sprinkle with the remaining ½ teaspoon cinnamon.
6. Bake the dish for about 1 hour, until the top is light brown and the kugel is firm.
7. Cut it into squares and serve hot or cold.

Nutritional information per serving: 316 calories, 11.8 g protein, 52 g carbohydrate, 5.3 g fat, 61.6 mg cholesterol, 266 mg sodium, 3.1 g fiber, 141.1 mg calcium, less than 1 mg iron

Amaranth-Stuffed Peppers

Serves 4 (Serving size: 1 pepper)

Stuffed peppers are a fun way to introduce yourself to gluten-free grains.

4 green bell peppers (or try red, orange, and yellow bell peppers for a colorful variety)
1 tablespoon vegetable oil
1 pound lean ground beef, such as sirloin (ground turkey or chicken will also work)
½ cup diced onion
½ cup diced carrot

1 14.5-ounce can tomatoes
1 tablespoon olive oil
2 teaspoons balsamic vinegar
1 teaspoon dried basil
2 cups puffed amaranth
1 teaspoon garlic powder
½ teaspoon black pepper

½ cup gluten-free, low-sodium
vegetable broth (or gluten-free
chicken broth)

2 slices thinly sliced provolone
cheese (or 3 tablespoons
slivered Parmesan, if desired)

1. Preheat the oven to 350 degrees.
2. Cut a slice from the top of each pepper, removing the stem and seeds.
3. Heat 1 tablespoon oil in a large skillet over medium-high heat.
4. Add the ground beef and cook, stirring occasionally, for 3 to 4 minutes.
5. Add the onion and carrots. Continue to cook until the meat is browned and the vegetables are softened.
6. Stir in the tomatoes, olive oil, balsamic vinegar, dried basil, amaranth, garlic powder, and pepper. Remove from heat.
7. Fill each pepper with ¼ of the meat mixture and stand them, top side up, in a medium casserole dish (that just fits the 4 peppers).
8. Pour the vegetable broth over the peppers and into the bottom of the dish. Cover with aluminum foil and bake for 55 minutes.
9. Remove the foil, and spoon the broth from the bottom of the dish over the peppers. Cut each slice of cheese into quarters and place 2 pieces on top of each pepper.
10. Bake peppers for an additional 10 minutes.
11. Remove the peppers from the oven and serve them immediately.

Nutritional information per serving: 369 calories, 31.5 g protein, 25 g carbohydrate, 16 g fat, 72 mg cholesterol, 656 mg sodium, 5 g fiber, 208.7 mg calcium, 4.4 mg iron

Millet Pilaf with Pine Nuts
Serves 6 (Serving size: ½ cup)

Believe it or not, you can make pilaf with just about any grain—not only rice. If you've never tried millet before, this is an easy and tasty way to do so. For added flavor, toast the pine nuts before adding them to the pilaf.

2 tablespoons butter
1 small onion, sliced thin
½ cup sliced carrots

1 cup hulled millet
2¼ cups low-sodium, gluten-free
chicken broth

½ teaspoon salt   Dash nutmeg
¼ teaspoon cumin   2 tablespoons pine nuts

1. Melt the butter in a small pot; add the onions, carrots, and millet and sauté for about 5 minutes.
2. Add the broth, salt, cumin, and nutmeg and cook for about 30 minutes or until the liquid is absorbed. If the millet is not soft enough, add a few tablespoons of water or broth and continue to cook until the millet becomes tender.
3. Sprinkle the pilaf with pine nuts and serve.

Nutritional information per serving: 203.6 calories, 6.1 g protein, 28 g carbohydrate, 7.8 g fat, 10 mg cholesterol, 257 mg sodium, 3.4 g fiber, 15 mg calcium, 1.4 mg iron

Savory Cornbread Stuffing

Serves 8 (Serving size: about ¾ cup)

This cornbread dressing can be served as a side dish or used as a stuffing for your next Thanksgiving dinner. The stuffing works even better with stale cornbread.

Gluten-free cooking spray or about 2 teaspoons vegetable oil
2 cups whole-grain cornmeal
1 tablespoon baking powder
1 teaspoon salt
½ teaspoon white pepper
1 tablespoon garlic powder
1 egg
1½ cups low-fat milk
¼ cup vegetable oil

2 tablespoons butter
1 cup diced onion
1 cup diced celery
1 tablespoon gluten-free poultry seasoning (or a mixture of dried thyme, sage, marjoram, rosemary, black pepper, and nutmeg)
2 cups gluten-free, low-sodium chicken stock

1. Preheat the oven to 400 degrees. Spray an 8-inch square baking pan with cooking spray (or coat it with vegetable oil).
2. Mix the dry ingredients, from the cornmeal to the garlic powder, together in a large bowl.
3. In a separate medium bowl, mix together the egg, milk, and vegetable oil.

4. Add the egg mixture to the dry ingredients. Stir to combine. Pour the cornbread batter into the prepared pan and bake for 25 to 30 minutes or until a toothpick inserted in the center comes out clean. Set aside until completely cool.
5. When you're ready to assemble the stuffing, preheat the oven to 350 degrees.
6. Melt the butter in a skillet over medium heat.
7. Add the onions and celery. Cook for 5 to 6 minutes until the vegetables have softened.
8. Break the cornbread into small pieces in a large bowl. Sprinkle with the poultry seasoning. Add the onions and celery.
9. Pour the broth over the bread, a little at a time. Stir carefully to combine. The mixture should be wet but not soggy.
10. Spray a 2-quart casserole dish with cooking spray or coat it with vegetable oil. Spoon the cornbread mixture into the dish. Cover with foil and bake for 30 minutes.

Tip: If your cornbread is fresh, just break it up and place it on a cookie sheet in a 350-degree oven for about 10 to 15 minutes.

Nutritional information per serving: 266 calories, 6.6 g protein, 33 g carbohydrate, 11.8 g fat, 36 mg cholesterol, 636 mg sodium, 2 g fiber, 108 mg calcium, 2 mg iron

Macaroni and Cheese with Fire-Roasted Tomatoes

Serves 8 (Serving size: about ½ cup)

This is a nice twist on a familiar dish. You can also use quinoa pasta shells or any small gluten-free pasta in this recipe.

Gluten-free cooking spray or
  1 teaspoon vegetable oil
1 8-ounce box uncooked
  spiral-shaped brown rice pasta
2 tablespoons unsalted butter
1 tablespoon brown rice flour
1 tablespoon cornstarch
1 cup skim milk

¾ cup gluten-free vegetable broth
¼ teaspoon white pepper
  (or black pepper)
⅛ teaspoon nutmeg
2 ounces provolone cheese,
  shredded
6 ounces reduced-fat cheddar
  cheese, shredded

1 14-ounce can fire-roasted tomatoes, drained (or 1 cup gluten-free salsa or 1 14-ounce can chopped tomatoes, or ½ cup fresh tomatoes, chopped)

1. Preheat the oven to 350 degrees.
2. Spray a 2-quart casserole dish with cooking spray or lightly coat it with vegetable oil.
3. Cook the pasta in boiling water until just tender. Do not overcook. Drain the pasta, rinse, and set aside.
4. In a medium saucepan, melt the butter over medium heat. Stir in the brown rice flour and cornstarch. Cook for 1 minute.
5. Using a wire whisk, add the milk and vegetable broth, whisking until smooth.
6. Bring to a boil over medium heat, stirring constantly, until thickened.
7. Remove from heat. Stir in the pepper, nutmeg, and cheese until melted.
8. Mix the pasta with the tomatoes and cheese sauce. Pour into the prepared casserole dish. Cover with foil and bake in preheated oven for 30 minutes until hot and bubbly.

Nutritional information per serving: 247 calories, 10.7 g protein, 30 g carbohydrate, 9.6 g fat, 28 mg cholesterol, 404 mg sodium, 1 g fiber, 403 mg calcium, 1.3 mg iron

---

Mixed Grain and Vegetable Casserole

Serves 10 (Serving size: ¾ cup)

This dish is very versatile. You can even make it ahead of time—just cover and refrigerate until you're ready to bake it. Use your favorite combination of vegetables, grains, beans, and cheese.

Gluten-free cooking spray or 1 teaspoon vegetable oil
10-ounce bag plain frozen mixed vegetables
1 cup chopped onion
½ cup buckwheat groats (kasha), uncooked and roasted
1 cup brown rice, uncooked

1 teaspoon salt

½ teaspoon black pepper

1 15-ounce can black beans, drained and rinsed

4 cups gluten-free, low-sodium vegetable broth

1 cup shredded Colby and Monterey Jack cheese combo

1. Preheat the oven to 350 degrees. Spray a 2-quart casserole with cooking spray or lightly coat it with vegetable oil.
2. In a small saucepan heat buckwheat groats over medium heat for about 5 minutes, turning a bit until they are slightly roasted and fragrant. Cool.
3. In a large bowl, combine the vegetables, onion, groats, brown rice, salt, and pepper.
4. Stir in the beans and broth. Pour into the prepared casserole dish.
5. Cover and bake for about 1 hour, until the grains are tender and the liquid is absorbed.
6. Remove the cover, and sprinkle the casserole with cheese. Bake for 5 minutes longer or until the cheese is melted.

Nutritional information per serving: 206 calories, 9.4 g protein, 32 g carbohydrate, 4.6 g fat, 12 mg cholesterol, 427 mg sodium, 4.7 g fiber, 110 mg calcium, 1.3 mg iron

Wild Rice Pilaf

Serves 10 (Serving size: ½ cup)

Using wild rice in this pilaf gives it a nice chewy texture and a nutty taste. You can also try adding wild rice to your salads and soups.

1 cup wild rice

1 pound asparagus, cut into ¼-inch pieces

2 tablespoons olive oil

1 clove garlic, minced

½ cup chopped onion

½ cup chopped green pepper

1 cup chopped mushrooms

2 tomatoes, chopped

⅔ cup gluten-free Italian dressing

¼ cup sunflower seed kernels

1. Cook the rice according to the package directions.
2. Microwave the asparagus for 3 minutes, until just tender.

3. Heat the oil in a large skillet over medium heat. Add the garlic, onion, and pepper, and sauté for 3 to 4 minutes until softened.
4. Add the mushrooms and cook for 1 to 2 minutes longer. Add the asparagus, tomatoes, rice, and dressing. Cook for 3 to 4 minutes until heated through.
5. Sprinkle with sunflower seeds and serve immediately, or let cool and serve cold.

Tip: Wild rice takes a long time to cook. You may find it convenient to cook up a larger amount than you need and store in the refrigerator for 2 to 3 days.

Nutritional information per serving: 168 calories, 4.8 g protein, 18.5 g carbohydrate, 9.5 g fat, 0 mg cholesterol, 261.4 mg sodium, 2.9 g fiber, 24 mg calcium, 1.7 mg iron

Fra Diavolo over Quinoa Pasta

Serves 8 (¾ cup per serving)

Fra Diavolo is a tomato sauce with a spicy kick.
This version is nice and creamy.

1 tablespoon olive oil
1 cup chopped onion
2 cloves garlic, minced
½ carrot, finely grated
1 teaspoon dried oregano
¼ teaspoon salt
¼ teaspoon black pepper
¼ to ½ teaspoon red pepper flakes (depending on how spicy you like it)
2 tablespoons tomato paste

1 28-ounce can fire-roasted crushed tomatoes (if fire-roasted are unavailable, use regular crushed tomatoes)
⅓ cup half-and-half
1 8-ounce box quinoa spaghetti (brown rice spaghetti or 100% buckwheat noodles may be substituted)
1 tablespoon chopped flat-leaf parsley

1. Heat the oil in a large pot over medium heat. Add the onion, garlic, and carrot, and sauté for about 5 minutes until softened.
2. Add the oregano, salt, pepper, red pepper, and tomato paste. Continue to stir and cook for about 2 minutes longer. Add the crushed tomatoes, and simmer the sauce for about 30 minutes.

3. Cook the pasta in boiling water until tender. Drain and rinse.

4. Blend the sauce with an immersion blender until smooth. If you do not have an immersion blender, use a regular blender and blend the sauce in small batches until smooth.

5. Stir the half-and-half into the sauce. Add the pasta and stir to combine the sauce and pasta. Sprinkle the dish with chopped parsley and serve.

Nutritional information per serving: 179.4 calories, 4.5 g protein, 34.6 g carbohydrate, 3.7 g fat, 3.6 mg cholesterol, 248.6 mg sodium, 4.8 g fiber, 58 mg calcium, 1.6 mg iron

Broccoli Pasta Bake
Serves 8 (Serving size: about ½ cup)

Gluten-free comfort food! This recipe is very versatile, so feel free to substitute your favorite nuts and cheese for delicious results. It is also hearty enough to be served as a main course.

8 ounces uncooked brown rice penne

1 10-ounce package frozen chopped broccoli

½ cup chopped red onion

Gluten-free cooking spray or 2 teaspoons vegetable oil

1 7-ounce jar roasted red bell peppers, chopped

½ cup part-skim ricotta cheese

2 eggs

¼ cup skim milk

¼ teaspoon black pepper

½ teaspoon paprika

½ teaspoon gluten-free dry mustard

½ teaspoon salt

½ cup shredded Monterey Jack cheese

2 tablespoons popped amaranth

2 tablespoons finely chopped hazelnuts

1. Add the pasta to a large pot of boiling water. Cook for 5 minutes.

2. Meanwhile, sauté the onions in a small skillet until tender but not quite fully cooked, about 4 minutes. Add broccoli and continue to cook until broccoli can be pierced with a fork.

3. Preheat the oven to 350 degrees. Spray a 2-quart casserole dish with cooking spray (or coat with the vegetable oil).

4. Put the pasta, broccoli, and onions in a large bowl. Stir in the red peppers and ricotta cheese.
5. In a separate bowl, beat the eggs, milk, pepper, paprika, mustard, and salt. Pour over the pasta and mix well.
6. Put the pasta into the prepared casserole dish. Top with the cheese.
7. Mix the amaranth and hazelnuts together. Sprinkle on top of the cheese. Place the casserole in the oven and bake for 30 minutes.

Nutritional information per serving: 205.6 calories, 8.9 g protein, 28.5 g carbohydrate, 6.3 g fat, 64 mg cholesterol, 240.2 mg sodium, 1.8 g fiber, 137.2 mg calcium, 1.9 mg iron

9

Main Courses

All of these meals are good enough to be served to guests. Your family will love them, too!

Quick and Easy Gluten-Free

Baked Salmon with Mustard Sauce
Falafel with Tahini Sauce
Homemade Veggie Burgers
Chicken with Chickpeas
Flank Steak with Homemade Teriyaki Sauce
Pork Kebabs over Apple Millet
Sweet Potato Quesadillas
Taco Pizza
Grilled Chicken Cordon Bleu
Chicken, Leeks, and Olives over Sun-Dried Tomato Quinoa
Tilapia with Artichokes and Tomatoes
Turkey Cutlets Marsala
Walnut-Crusted Orange Roughy with Fresh Herb Pesto
Chicken Fajitas with Black Beans
Potato-Crusted Grouper with Tarragon

Creative Gluten-Free

Crustless Quiche Lorraine

Baked Polenta with Tomato Sauce and Goat Cheese

Quinoa with Roasted Garlic and Shrimp

Turkey Chili with Cocoa

Quinoa and Cheddar–Stuffed Eggplant

Baked Quinoa Ratatouille

Amaranth-Crusted Chicken

Broccoli and Cheese and Rice Pie

Shrimp Scampi over Kasha and Onions

Sesame and Millet–Crusted Tuna and Pineapple Kabobs

Mediterranean Chicken with Sorghum, Feta, and Tomato Served
over Millet

Slow-Cooker Sloppy Joes

Sage Butter Sautéed Chicken Breasts and Pancetta over Millet

Turkey Meatloaf

Potato Lasagna

QUICK AND EASY
GLUTEN-FREE

Baked Salmon with
Mustard Sauce

Serves 4 (Serving size: ¼ salmon with ¼ cup sauce)

*Salmon is a great source of omega-3 fatty acids, which
are so beneficial for your health. To help decrease your
risk of coronary artery disease, you should consider
eating fatty fish, such as salmon, twice a week.*

1 pound salmon fillet (checked
for bones)

¼ cup white wine

1 teaspoon garlic powder

1 teaspoon onion powder

2 tablespoons whole amaranth
seeds, toasted (see the box on
page 133)

Mustard Sauce:

1 cup nonfat plain yogurt

3 tablespoons gluten-free grainy mustard (use 2 tablespoons if you don't want as much mustard flavor)

2 teaspoons sugar

2 teaspoons gluten-free Worcestershire sauce

2 tablespoons fresh chopped dill (optional)

1. Preheat the oven to 350 degrees.
2. On a cookie sheet, place the salmon skin side down.
3. Run your hand across the top of the salmon fillet, and pull out any bones that you find.
4. Sprinkle the salmon with the garlic powder, onion powder, and toasted amaranth. (If toasted amaranth is not available, you can use toasted gluten-free breadcrumbs.)
5. Mix together the sauce ingredients and pour over the salmon.
6. Bake for about 20 minutes until the salmon is cooked through and light pink in color.

Tip: To make gluten-free breadcrumbs, toast 1 to 2 slices of whole-grain gluten-free bread and put them through a food processor.

Nutritional information per serving: 303 calories, 27 g protein, 12.6 g carbohydrate, 12.8 g fat, 68 mg cholesterol, 329 mg sodium, less than 1 g fiber, 149 mg calcium, 1.2 mg iron

Falafel with Tahini Sauce

Serves 4 (Serving size: 3 falafel and 1 tablespoon tahini sauce)

Traditional falafel is fried, but this falafel is broiled, which substantially cuts down on the fat. This inexpensive and easy-to-prepare dish makes a hearty meal.

1 16-ounce can chickpeas, drained and rinsed

1 yellow onion, chopped

2 garlic cloves, chopped

2 tablespoons cornstarch

1 teaspoon coriander

1 teaspoon cumin

½ teaspoon salt

½ teaspoon black pepper

1 teaspoon grated lemon peel

3 tablespoons chopped fresh parsley

1. Process all of the ingredients in a food processor until the mixture forms a thick paste.
2. Line a cookie sheet with parchment paper. Preheat the broiler.

3. Form the chickpea mixture into small balls, about the size of a golf ball.
4. Place the balls on the cookie sheet, flattening them slightly.
5. Broil the falafel for 2 to 3 minutes. Turn the balls over and broil them for 1 to 2 minutes more or until just browned. Leave the oven door cracked open so that the falafel does not burn.
6. Serve with tahini sauce.

TAHINI SAUCE

Tahini sauce can be made ahead of time and stored in the refrigerator for about a week.

¼ cup tahini	1 teaspoon grated lemon peel
2 garlic cloves, minced	2 tablespoons fresh lemon juice
¼ teaspoon kosher salt	2 tablespoons hot water
1 tablespoon olive oil	1 teaspoon chopped fresh parsley

1. Combine the tahini, garlic, and salt in a food processor or a blender. Pulse until smooth.
2. Add the oil, lemon peel, and lemon juice. Continue to blend until smooth. Add the hot water, a little at a time, until the desired consistency is reached.
3. Stir in the parsley.
4. Store the tahini sauce refrigerated in an airtight container until ready to serve.

Nutritional information per serving: 317 calories, 13.1 g protein, 44 g carbohydrate, 11 g fat, 0 mg cholesterol, 430 mg sodium, 10 g fiber, 104 mg calcium, 4.4 mg iron

Homemade Veggie Burgers
Serves 4

Why eat processed veggie burgers when you can so easily make your own? These burgers are chock full of vegetables.

½ cup cooked long-grain brown rice (not instant)	1 cup grated zucchini
	1 cup grated carrot

½ cup chopped mushrooms

1 green onion, chopped

½ red bell pepper, chopped

1 egg

½ tablespoon molasses

2 tablespoons whole-grain cornmeal

¼ teaspoon salt

¼ teaspoon black pepper

Gluten-free cooking spray or 2 teaspoons vegetable oil

1 avocado, sliced

1 tablespoon fresh lime juice

1. Mix the burger ingredients, from the rice to the black pepper, in a medium bowl. Stir gently to combine.
2. Form the mixture into 4 patties.
3. Place the burgers on a hot griddle sprayed with cooking spray or lightly coated in vegetable oil.
4. Cook the burgers for 2 to 3 minutes on each side until golden brown.
5. Top with sliced avocado and lime juice. Other topping options include cheese, roasted peppers, sliced tomatoes, grilled onions, and grilled veggies. Serve with barbeque sauce, tomato sauce, ketchup, or mustard, as desired.

Tip: Although the burgers hold together better when they're cooked in a skillet, they can be baked on a cookie sheet coated with vegetable oil in a 350-degree oven. Take care when you turn the burgers over not to break them apart.

Nutritional information per serving: 165 calories, 4.6 g protein, 21 g carbohydrate, 8 g fat, 53 mg cholesterol, 193 mg sodium, 5 g fiber, 38.5 mg calcium, 1.2 mg iron

Chicken with Chickpeas
Serves 4 (Serving size: about 1 cup)

The turmeric in this recipe gives this dish a rich golden color and an exotic flavor. For a nice color contrast to the yellow, add spinach or peas when you add the chickpeas.

2 tablespoons vegetable oil

1 cup chopped onion

1 clove garlic, minced

1 teaspoon turmeric

½ teaspoon dried thyme

¼ teaspoon black pepper

1 pound boneless, skinless chicken breasts, cut into ½-inch pieces

1 15-ounce can chickpeas, drained and rinsed

2 teaspoons lemon juice

2 teaspoons honey

1 14-ounce can diced tomatoes

1. Heat the oil in a large skillet over medium heat. Add the onions and garlic and cook until tender, about 5 minutes.
2. Stir in the turmeric, thyme, and black pepper. Mix well.
3. Add the chicken. Cook for 5 to 10 minutes, stirring occasionally, until the chicken is cooked through.
4. Add the chickpeas, lemon juice, honey, and tomatoes. Cook for 10 more minutes or until heated through. Serve over brown rice or quinoa or with Teff Flatbread (page 74) to soak up the juices.

Nutritional information per serving: 324 calories, 31 g protein, 26.7 g carbohydrate, 9.5 g fat, 65.7 mg cholesterol, 313 mg sodium, 5 g fiber, 91 mg calcium, 3.7 mg iron

Flank Steak with Homemade Teriyaki Sauce

Serves 4 (Serving size: 4 to 5 slices)

This recipe calls for flank steak—a long, thin cut of beef that cooks quickly and is very versatile.

¼ cup gluten-free, low-sodium soy or tamari sauce

2 tablespoons brown sugar

¼ teaspoon ginger

¼ teaspoon onion powder

¼ teaspoon garlic powder

1 teaspoon cornstarch

2 tablespoons water

1 pound flank steak

¼ teaspoon salt

¼ teaspoon black pepper

1. Heat the soy sauce, brown sugar, ginger, onion powder, and garlic powder in a small saucepan over medium heat. Bring to a boil.

2. Reduce the heat. Mix the cornstarch and water together in a small dish. Whisk into the soy sauce and continue to simmer until thickened. If the mixture becomes too thick, add more water. Remove from heat.

3. Preheat the broiler. Season the steak with salt and pepper. Place it under the broiler and cook for 3 minutes on each side. Brush both sides with the teriyaki sauce and cook the steak for an additional 1 to 2 minutes or until the desired degree of doneness is reached. Keep a close eye on the steak after brushing on the sauce so that it does not burn.

4. Slice thinly, on a diagonal, across the grain, before serving. Serve with roasted potatoes and steamed broccoli.

Tip: Leftover flank steak makes a great main dish salad. Toss your favorite greens with gluten-free salad dressing and top them with tomatoes, sliced flank steak, and blue cheese crumbles. (See glossary for more information about blue cheese.)

Nutritional information per serving: 217 calories, 26 g protein, 6.8 g carbohydrate, 8.9 g fat, 53 mg cholesterol, 819 mg sodium, less than 1 g fiber, 14.5 mg calcium, 2.5 mg iron

---

Pork Kebabs over Apple Millet

Serves 4 (Serving size: 1 kebab with about ½ cup millet mixture)

This recipe is a unique version of the pork-chops-and-applesauce meals many of us ate as kids!

½ cup apple jelly
1 tablespoon minced ginger
1 tablespoon garlic powder
4 wooden skewers
1 pound pork tenderloin, cut into 1-inch cubes
½ teaspoon salt
½ teaspoon black pepper, divided
2 tablespoons butter

¼ cup finely chopped onion
1 medium apple, finely chopped
2 cups cooked hulled millet (cooked according to package directions)
¼ teaspoon allspice
2 tablespoons sour cream

1. In a small saucepan, melt the apple jelly over low heat. Stir in the ginger and garlic powder. Remove from heat and set aside.
2. Soak 4 wooden skewers in water for 5 minutes. Preheat the grill pan over medium-high heat.
3. Put the pork on the skewers. Sprinkle with salt and ¼ teaspoon pepper.
4. Spray a grill pan with gluten-free cooking spray or lightly coat it with vegetable oil. Place the pork in the grill pan and cook for 8 to 10 minutes, turning frequently, until the pork is almost cooked.
5. Brush on the apple jelly marinade and continue to grill, basting all of the sides with the marinade, until the pork is cooked through. Do not add the marinade until the pork is nearly cooked because the sugar in the apple jelly will burn. Remove from heat, and cover to keep warm.
6. Melt the butter in a large skillet. Add the onions and apples, and cook for about 5 minutes or until tender.
7. Stir in the millet, allspice, and the remaining ¼ teaspoon pepper. Continue to cook, stirring frequently, for 3 to 4 minutes or until heated through.
8. Remove the millet from the heat and stir in the sour cream.
9. Serve the millet with the pork.

Nutritional information per serving: 461 calories, 29 g protein, 64 g carbohydrate, 10.7 g fat, 91.6 mg cholesterol, 399 mg sodium, 2.9 g fiber, 26.3 mg calcium, 2 mg iron

Sweet Potato Quesadillas

Serves 8 (Serving size: 1 quesadilla)

These quesadillas are a tasty and nutritious twist on the traditional, and they make great leftovers—simply spray a small skillet with cooking spray or lightly coat with vegetable oil and heat them over medium heat until warm.

Gluten-free cooking spray (or 2 teaspoons vegetable oil)

1 cup cooked and mashed sweet potatoes or yams

2 teaspoons chili powder

1 teaspoon ground cumin

1 tablespoon canned green chilies

2 tablespoons sour cream

½ teaspoon salt

¼ teaspoon black pepper

1 cup gluten-free vegetarian refried beans

½ cup shredded Mexican cheese blend (a blend of Monterey Jack, cheddar, asadero, and quesadilla cheeses. If you

cannot find the blend, simply substitute Monterey Jack and cheddar or any combination of your favorite cheeses.)

16 corn tortillas

1. Preheat the oven to 350 degrees. Spray 2 large baking sheets with cooking spray or coat them with vegetable oil.
2. Mix the sweet potatoes with the chili powder, cumin, green chilies, sour cream, salt, and black pepper.
3. Use 8 tortillas as the bottom layers of the 8 quesadillas. Spread each one with 2 tablespoons of the refried beans, and top with 2 tablespoons of the sweet potato mixture and 1 tablespoon of the shredded cheese. Put another tortilla over the top layer of each one, and place them on the prepared baking sheets.
4. Bake for 15 minutes. Serve immediately with salsa and sour cream.

Nutritional information per serving: 189 calories, 6 g protein, 32.6 g carbohydrate, 5 g fat, 7.5 mg cholesterol, 371 mg sodium, 4.8 g fiber, 115.3 mg calcium, 1.4 mg iron

Taco Pizza

Serves 6 (Serving size: ⅙ of the pie)

Kids will love this pizza! It combines two of their favorite foods—pizza and tacos.

1 tablespoon canola oil

½ pound ground turkey breast

½ cup chopped onion

1 teaspoon chili powder

1 teaspoon cumin

1 cup red kidney beans

2 tablespoons tomato paste

½ cup gluten-free salsa

½ cup shredded Mexican blend cheese (a blend of Monterey

Jack, cheddar, asadero, and quesadilla cheeses. If you cannot find the blend, simply substitute Monterey Jack and cheddar, or any combination of your favorite cheeses.)

1 Pizza Crust (see page 78)

2 cups shredded lettuce

1 tomato, chopped

1 tablespoon chopped fresh cilantro

1. Heat the oil in a large skillet over medium heat. Add the meat, breaking it up and stirring until browned. Add the onion, chili powder, and cumin. Continue to cook the meat for 5 minutes longer.
2. Add the kidney beans and tomato paste. Continue to cook the meat, breaking up large pieces with a spatula. Remove from heat.
3. Follow the directions for baking the Pizza Crust in a 425-degree oven (see page 178), but before it's done, remove it partially cooked from the oven. Spread the salsa on top. Add the meat and bean mixture and then sprinkle it with cheese.
4. Return to oven and cook for about 10 minutes or until the cheese is melted and bubbly.
5. Top with lettuce, tomato, and cilantro, and serve immediately.

Tip: To reduce the fat in this recipe, use gluten-free cooking spray in place of the vegetable oil and substitute reduced-fat gluten-free cheese for regular cheese.

Nutritional information per serving: 360.4 calories, 20.7 g protein, 29.3 g carbohydrate, 18.7 g fat, 132.4 mg cholesterol, 594 mg sodium, 7.5 g fiber, 129 mg calcium, 2.2 mg iron

---

Grilled Chicken Cordon Bleu

Serves 4

Grilling the chicken instead of breading it is a great way to cut down on the fat in this French classic. You can substitute turkey cutlets for the chicken, if desired.

2 tablespoons balsamic vinegar
¼ cup olive oil
⅛ teaspoon salt
⅛ teaspoon black pepper
¼ teaspoon garlic powder
¼ teaspoon dried basil
4 4-ounce boneless, skinless chicken cutlets

2 ounces Swiss cheese
2 ounces ham
¼ cup popped amaranth seeds (about 2 tablespoons unpopped seeds)
1 tablespoon chopped fresh parsley
1 tablespoon melted butter

1. In a blender or a small food processor, combine the vinegar, oil, salt, pepper, garlic powder, and basil. Blend until well mixed.
2. Put the chicken into a gallon-size plastic bag. Pour the marinade over the chicken, and let stand for 5 minutes.
3. Preheat the broiler.
4. Heat an ovenproof grill pan on the stove over medium-high heat. Add the chicken cutlets and grill for 3 to 4 minutes on each side until cooked through.
5. Lay ½ ounce cheese and ½ ounce ham on each piece of chicken.
6. Mix the amaranth, parsley, and butter. Sprinkle on top of the chicken.
7. Transfer the grill pan to the broiler. Broil the chicken for 2 to 3 minutes, or until the cheese is melted and the topping is browned.

Nutritional information per serving: 294 calories, 3.3 g protein, 3.6 g carbohydrate, 15.4 g fat, 92.8 mg cholesterol, 371 mg sodium, less than 1 g fiber, 133 mg calcium, 1.3 mg iron

Chicken, Leeks, and Olives over Sun-Dried Tomato Quinoa

Serves 4 (Serving size: ½ cup quinoa with about ½ cup chicken and leek mixture)

Gluten-free comfort food! This hearty chicken dish is sure to bring raves.

1 3-ounce package sun-dried tomatoes (not packed in oil)

¼ cup olive oil

2 tablespoons tomato paste

1 tablespoon brown sugar

1 clove garlic

1 teaspoon dried oregano

⅓ to ½ cup warm water

2 cups hot, cooked quinoa (see the box on page 166)

1 tablespoon olive oil

1 tablespoon unsalted butter

¼ cup brown rice flour

¼ teaspoon salt

⅛ teaspoon black pepper

1 pound skinless, boneless chicken breasts, cut into 1-inch pieces

1 leek, cleaned and thinly sliced

½ cup sliced black olives

¼ cup gluten-free, low-sodium chicken broth

1. In a blender or a food processor, combine the tomatoes, olive oil, tomato paste, brown sugar, garlic, and oregano. Blend, gradually adding the water until a thick paste is formed. Stir into the quinoa, cover to keep warm, and set aside.
2. Heat the oil and butter in a large nonstick skillet over medium-high heat. Mix the salt and pepper with the brown rice flour. Toss the chicken in the seasoned flour and place it in the skillet. Cook, stirring occasionally, until browned and cooked through. Remove the chicken from the skillet.
3. To prepare the leek, you will need to trim off the root end; this is the darkest part of the leaves at the point where the color changes to light green. Cut off the dark section, leaving about 2 inches of the light green part, which is the tender portion. Cut the leek in half and put both halves in cold water. Swish the leek in the water to remove the dirt, then let it sit in the cold water so that the dirt settles to the bottom of the bowl. Remove the leek halves from the water and dry them. Slice the leek halves thinly, sideways not lengthwise.
4. Return the skillet to the heat. Add the leek slices. Cook the leeks until softened, 3 to 4 minutes. Reduce heat to medium. Put the chicken back into the skillet. Add the olives and broth. Cook for 2 to 3 minutes, until the chicken is heated through.
5. Serve the chicken mixture over the quinoa.

Nutritional information per serving: 546 calories, 35.3 g protein, 48 g carbohydrate, 24.5 g fat, 73.3 mg cholesterol, 787.6 mg sodium, 6.9 g fiber, 90 mg calcium, 5.7 mg iron

---

Cooking Quinoa

To prepare quinoa, follow these steps (if the quinoa is not prerinsed, see "Rinsing Quinoa" on page 98). Boil 2 cups water, add 1 cup quinoa, and lower the heat. Simmer until the quinoa is just cooked (little tails will pop out of each quinoa grain after about 15 to 20 minutes).

Tilapia with Artichokes and Tomatoes

Serves 4 (Serving size: 1 fish fillet and about ¼ cup topping)

So, you think you don't like fish? This dish can turn anyone into a fish lover. This recipe calls for Rice Chex—remember, Rice Chex is now gluten-free!

Gluten-free cooking spray or 2 teaspoons vegetable oil

½ cup Rice Chex cereal

2 tablespoons millet flour

1 tablespoon grated Parmesan cheese

¼ teaspoon dried thyme leaves

½ teaspoon black pepper

1 egg

1 pound tilapia fillets (4 4-ounce pieces)

1 tablespoon unsalted butter, melted

1 tablespoon olive oil

1 clove garlic, minced

1 pint grape tomatoes

1 8½-ounce can artichoke hearts, drained and chopped

1 teaspoon grated lemon zest

1. Preheat the oven to 425 degrees. Spray a baking sheet with cooking spray or lightly coat it in vegetable oil.
2. In a food processor, blend the cereal, flour, cheese, thyme, and ¼ teaspoon of the black pepper until fine crumbs are formed. Pour the crumb mixture into a shallow dish.
3. In a separate dish, beat the egg.
4. Dip the fish in the egg, then in the crumb mixture. Place the fish on the cookie sheet. Drizzle with butter, and bake it for about 15 minutes, until the fish is cooked through.
5. While the fish is cooking, heat the olive oil in a large nonstick skillet over medium heat. Add the garlic. Cook for 2 to 3 minutes, stirring constantly. Be careful not to let the garlic burn.
6. Add the grape tomatoes, artichokes, and the remaining ¼ teaspoon of the black pepper. Continue to cook for about 5 minutes, or until the tomatoes soften and the skin just starts to split. Remove from heat. Add the lemon zest.
7. Place the fish on a serving platter. Top with the tomato-artichoke mixture. Serve over your favorite gluten-free grain.

Tip: Any mild white fish such as sole or cod can be substituted for the tilapia.

Nutritional information per serving: 239 calories, 26.5 g protein, 11.5 g carbohydrate, 10.1 g fat, 118.3 mg cholesterol, 311.8 mg sodium, 2.1 g fiber, 52.2 mg calcium, 2.3 mg iron

---

Turkey Cutlets Marsala

Serves 4 (Serving size: 1 cutlet)

The sauce in this recipe is delicious over any grilled meat, such as beef, chicken, or veal.

1 tablespoon unsalted butter
1 tablespoon olive oil
½ cup brown rice flour
½ teaspoon salt
¼ teaspoon black pepper
4 4-ounce turkey cutlets
¼ cup minced shallots
1 clove garlic, minced

1 cup sliced fresh mushrooms
2 tablespoons cornstarch
½ cup Marsala wine
1 cup gluten-free, low-sodium beef stock
½ teaspoon dried thyme leaves
2 tablespoons chopped fresh parsley

1. In a large skillet, melt the butter with 1 teaspoon of the olive oil over medium heat.
2. In a medium bowl, combine the flour with the salt and pepper. Coat the turkey cutlets with flour and place in the skillet. Cook for 3 to 4 minutes on each side, until browned and cooked through. Remove the cutlets from the skillet and cover to keep warm.
3. Add the remaining 2 teaspoons of olive oil to the pan. Add the shallots, garlic, and mushrooms, and sauté until the mushrooms are tender.
4. Add the cornstarch and continue to cook, stirring constantly, for about 1 minute.
5. Remove the pan from the heat, add the Marsala wine, and return the pan to the heat. Stir to combine. Add the beef stock and thyme. Simmer for 5 to 6 more minutes or until the sauce has thickened.

6. Pour the sauce over the turkey. Sprinkle the dish with fresh parsley. Serve with steamed broccoli and quinoa noodles.

Tip: The beef stock gives the turkey a rich color and flavor, but chicken or vegetable stock will also work as a substitute.

Nutritional information per serving: 296 calories, 29.5 g protein, 25.1 g carbohydrate, 8.7 g fat, 57.6 mg cholesterol, 578.8 mg sodium, 1.3 g fiber, 11.9 mg calcium, 1.6 mg iron

Walnut-Crusted Orange Roughy with Fresh Herb Pesto

Serves 4 (Serving size: 1 fillet with 2 tablespoons pesto)

Orange roughy is a mild white fish and is exquisite paired with the flavorful pesto in this recipe.

¼ cup chopped walnuts, plus 3 tablespoons to use later (reserve 1 tablespoon for garnish)

½ cup brown rice flour

½ teaspoon salt

¼ teaspoon pepper

1 pound orange roughy fillets

1 tablespoon olive oil, plus ¼ cup olive oil to use later

1 cup fresh basil leaves

1 cup plus 1 tablespoon fresh flat-leaf parsley (reserve 1 tablespoon for garnish)

½ teaspoon minced garlic

½ cup water

1. Preheat the oven to 400 degrees.
2. In a small food processor, blend together ¼ cup walnuts and the brown rice flour, salt, and pepper until very fine. Put nut mixture in a shallow dish.
3. Coat the fish fillets with the brown rice mixture, pressing it into the fish on both sides.
4. Heat 1 tablespoon of the olive oil in a medium skillet over medium heat. Brown the fish on both sides, then transfer the fillets to a baking sheet. Bake in the oven for 10 to 15 minutes, until cooked through.

5. In a blender, make the pesto. Put the basil, parsley, 2 tablespoons walnuts, garlic, ¼ cup olive oil, and ¼ cup water. Blend, adding more water as needed, until a thick paste is formed.

6. Serve each fish fillet over brown rice or millet with 2 tablespoons pesto. Sprinkle with chopped walnuts and chopped parsley. Add a side of steamed mixed vegetables to complete your meal.

Tip: If you can't find roughy, any firm white fish may be substituted.

Nutritional information per serving: 400 calories, 22.8 g protein, 18.4 g carbohydrate, 26.7 g fat, 68 mg cholesterol, 383.6 mg sodium, 2.5 g fiber, 66.9 mg calcium, 3.3 mg iron

Chicken Fajitas with Black Beans
Serves 4 (Serving size: 2 fajitas)

Fajitas are a great party food. Put the ingredients in festive little serving dishes, and let your guests assemble the fajitas themselves. This recipe is also great with shrimp or beef instead of chicken.

1 tablespoon vegetable oil

12 ounces boneless, skinless chicken breasts, cut into thin strips

1 large onion, thinly sliced

1 green pepper, cored and thinly sliced

1 red bell pepper, cored and thinly sliced

1 teaspoon chili powder

½ teaspoon ground cumin

½ teaspoon oregano

2 tablespoons chopped fresh cilantro

1 tablespoon fresh lime juice

8 corn tortillas, warmed

1 16-ounce can gluten-free vegetarian refried black beans, warmed

1 cup prepared gluten-free salsa

½ cup reduced-fat sour cream

1. Heat the oil in a large nonstick skillet over medium-high heat.
2. Add the chicken and cook for 3 to 4 minutes until browned.
3. Add the onion, peppers, chili powder, cumin, and oregano. Cook over medium heat for 10 minutes until the vegetables are tender and the chicken is cooked through.
4. Remove from heat. Sprinkle with the cilantro and lime juice.
5. Serve the chicken with the peppers and onions rolled in the tortillas and with the beans, salsa, and sour cream on the side.

Tip: If you don't have vegetarian refried beans on hand, you can puree cooked beans in a food processor with enough water to give them a creamy dip consistency.

Nutritional information per serving: 416 calories, 30 g protein, 54 g carbohydrate, 11 g fat, 61 mg cholesterol, 546 mg sodium, 8 g fiber, 158 mg calcium, 4 mg iron

Potato-Crusted Grouper with Tarragon
Serves 4 (Serving size: 1 grouper fillet)

This grouper has a delicious potato crust made with instant mashed potato flakes. Most potato flakes should be gluten-free, but check the labels to be sure. For an alternative to potato flakes, see the tip below.

1 tablespoon olive oil

1 pound (4 fillets at 4 ounces each) grouper fillets, skinless (if you don't have grouper, you may substitute salmon or cod)

½ teaspoon salt

¼ teaspoon black pepper

½ cup instant mashed potato flakes

½ teaspoon dried parsley flakes

1 teaspoon lemon zest

¼ cup low-fat sour cream

2 teaspoons gluten-free Dijon mustard

1 teaspoon fresh chopped tarragon

1. Preheat the oven to 425 degrees.
2. Brush a 9 × 13-inch pan with 1 teaspoon of the olive oil.
3. Place the grouper in the pan, and season it with salt and pepper.
4. In a food processor, mix the potato flakes, parsley, lemon zest, and the remaining 2 teaspoons of olive oil.
5. Sprinkle the coating evenly on top of each grouper fillet.
6. Bake for 15 minutes, then turn the oven to broil and broil for 1 to 2 minutes until the crust is browned.
7. Mix the sour cream, mustard, and tarragon, and serve over the fish.

Tip: AlpineAire Foods makes gluten-free dehydrated whole potato flakes and the only ingredient is potatoes! This product can be mail ordered from alpineaire.com. As an alternative to the potato flakes, you can slice 1 medium potato and arrange the slices over the grouper; sprinkle it with parsley, lemon zest, and olive oil; and continue with the directions on page 171.

Nutritional information per serving: 175 calories, 23 g protein, 6 g carbohydrate, 5.8 g fat, 46 mg cholesterol, 426 mg sodium, less than 1 g fiber, 51 mg calcium, less than 1.2 mg iron

CREATIVE GLUTEN-FREE

Crustless Quiche Lorraine
Serves 6 (Serving size: ⅙ of the pie)

Sometimes breakfast for dinner is just what we want in the middle of a dark, cold winter. This quiche includes turkey bacon, which is usually gluten-free, but be sure to check labels carefully.

1 teaspoon olive oil	4 large eggs
4 slices gluten-free turkey bacon, diced	1 12-ounce can evaporated 2% milk
¼ cup chopped onions	¼ teaspoon salt
¾ cup shredded Swiss cheese	⅛ teaspoon black pepper
Gluten-free cooking spray or 2 teaspoons vegetable oil	¼ teaspoon paprika

1. Preheat the oven to 400 degrees.
2. Heat the olive oil in a small skillet. Add the bacon and onions, and cook over medium-high heat until the onions have softened and the bacon is crisp.
3. Put the bacon and onions in a 9-inch pie plate that has been sprayed with cooking spray or lightly coated in vegetable oil. Sprinkle with Swiss cheese.
4. Beat the eggs, milk, salt, and pepper. Pour over the bacon, onions, and cheese.

5. Bake for 30 to 35 minutes until the center is firm.

6. Sprinkle with paprika and serve.

Tip: To reduce the fat content in this recipe, substitute 3 egg whites or ¼ cup Egg Beaters for each egg. You can also substitute low-fat cheese for regular cheese.

Nutritional information per serving: 178 calories, 13.9 g protein, 7.6 g carbohydrate, 10 g fat, 162 mg cholesterol, 365 mg sodium, less than 1 g fiber, 333 mg calcium, 0.8 mg iron

Baked Polenta with Tomato Sauce and Goat Cheese

Serves 4 (Serving size: about 1 cup)

Here's another gluten-free comfort food! This dish just might become a staple in your house. To reduce the sodium content of this recipe, use a tomato product with no added salt or reduced sodium.

2½ cups water

¾ cup instant polenta

1 teaspoon olive oil

2 cloves garlic, minced

1 14.5-ounce can Italian-style tomatoes

¼ teaspoon salt

½ teaspoon sugar

¼ teaspoon black pepper

4 ounces goat cheese crumbles (or any soft cheese, if goat cheese is not available)

1. Bring the water to a boil in a medium saucepan. Add the polenta, and stir for 3 to 4 minutes until the mixture thickens. Pour into a 9 × 13-inch pan. Place the pan in the refrigerator, and let the polenta cool and harden for 30 minutes.

2. Cut the polenta into 2-inch squares.

3. Brush a 1½-quart baking dish with ½ teaspoon of the olive oil. Arrange the polenta squares in a single layer, overlapping the pieces slightly.

4. Heat the remaining ½ teaspoon olive oil in a small saucepan over medium heat. Add the garlic and sauté for 1 minute. Be careful not to burn the garlic.

5. Add the tomatoes, salt, sugar, and pepper. Simmer for 15 minutes.

6. Preheat the oven to 400 degrees.

7. Pour the tomato sauce over the polenta. Sprinkle with goat cheese.

8. Bake for 30 minutes.

Tip: You can use store-bought prepared polenta if you don't want to make it yourself. Slice the prepared polenta and continue from step # 3. Most prepared polenta should be gluten-free, but check the labels to be sure.

Nutritional information per serving: 232 calories, 8.5 g protein, 27 g carbohydrate, 10 g fat, 22 mg cholesterol, 726 mg sodium, less than 1 g fiber, 121 mg calcium, 1.7 mg iron

---

Quinoa with Roasted Garlic and Shrimp
Serves 4 (Serving size: about 1 cup)

*Garlic becomes sweeter and milder when roasted.
If you have never roasted a bulb of garlic and added it
to a dish, you are in for a treat with this recipe.*

1 medium head of garlic (or more, to taste)

½ teaspoon olive oil

1 tablespoon butter

1 cup uncooked quinoa (see box on page 166)

2 cups water or gluten-free chicken broth

½ teaspoon salt

¼ teaspoon black pepper

1 teaspoon dried gluten-free Italian seasoning (or a mixture of dried basil, dried oregano, and dried thyme)

1 tablespoon vegetable oil

12 ounces raw shrimp, peeled and deveined

¾ cup pine nuts

2 green onions, chopped

¼ cup sun-dried tomatoes in oil, drained and cut into thin strips

1. Preheat the oven to 400 degrees. Slice the top off the head of garlic and drizzle it with olive oil. Wrap it in foil and bake for 45 to 50 minutes until very soft.

2. Heat the butter in a saucepan over medium heat. Add the quinoa and stir to coat.

3. Add the water or broth, salt, pepper, and Italian seasoning, and cook the quinoa for 15 to 20 minutes until all of the liquid is absorbed and the quinoa is tender.
4. Heat the vegetable oil in a large skillet over medium-high heat. Add the shrimp and sauté for 3 to 5 minutes or until the shrimp are cooked and pink. Remove from heat.
5. Heat a small nonstick skillet over medium heat. Add the pine nuts and cook, stirring frequently, until toasted. They will be brown and fragrant.
6. Squeeze 4 to 5 cloves of the roasted garlic into the sautéed shrimp. Add the onions, pine nuts, tomatoes, and quinoa. Stir to combine.

Tip: If you roast more garlic than you use, refrigerate it for a future meal. Roasted garlic should be used within 3 to 4 days. For mouthwatering garlic bread, spread roasted garlic on gluten-free French bread, drizzle it with olive oil, and bake or grill it until crispy.

Nutritional information per serving: 333 calories, 18 g protein, 25 g carbohydrate, 18.7 g fat, 91 mg cholesterol, 346 mg sodium, 2.7 g fiber, 57 mg calcium, 5.3 mg iron

---

Turkey Chili with Cocoa
Serves 4 (Serving size: about 1 cup)

This is turkey chili with a twist—cocoa powder. Don't tell your family and see whether they can guess the secret ingredient.

2 teaspoons vegetable oil
1 pound ground turkey breast
½ cup chopped onions
½ cup diced green peppers
2 cloves garlic, minced
2 tablespoons chili powder

1 teaspoon paprika
1 tablespoon unsweetened cocoa powder
1 bay leaf
1 8-ounce can tomato sauce
Hot sauce to taste

1. Heat the oil in a medium saucepan. Add the turkey and cook until browned.
2. Add the onions, peppers, and garlic, and cook for about 5 minutes until softened.

3. Stir in the chili powder, paprika, cocoa, and bay leaf.
4. Add the tomato sauce, reduce heat, and simmer for 45 minutes to blend the flavors.
5. Remove the bay leaf before serving the chili. Add the hot sauce, as desired, to taste. Serve the chili with grated low-fat cheddar cheese and low-fat sour cream.

Tip: This chili goes well with homemade baked corn chips. To make them, cut corn tortillas into quarters, spray them with gluten-free cooking spray or toss them with small amount of olive oil, lightly salt them, and bake in a 350 degree oven until crispy.

Nutritional information per serving: 184 calories, 27 g protein, 10 g carbohydrate, 4.5 g fat, 45 mg cholesterol, 392 mg sodium, 3 g fiber, 26 mg calcium, 3 mg iron

Quinoa and Cheddar–Stuffed Eggplant

Serves 4 (Serving size: approximately ½ cup)

This is a flavorful, hearty vegetarian dish. If you would like to make it vegan, skip the cheese—it will still taste good. If you don't have quinoa on hand, cooked brown rice, cooked millet, or chickpeas can be substituted.

2 large eggplants, about 1 pound each

2 tablespoons olive oil

1 shallot, minced

2 cloves garlic, minced

2 tablespoons tomato paste

1½ cups cooked quinoa (cooked according to package instructions and rinsed,

if necessary; see box on page 166)

⅓ cup gluten-free vegetable broth

¼ teaspoon salt

¼ teaspoon black pepper

1 teaspoon red pepper flakes

½ cup shredded cheddar cheese

1 tablespoon fresh chopped parsley

1. Cut the eggplants in half lengthwise; rub the cut surface with 4 teaspoons of the olive oil and place them cut side down in a large shallow baking dish. Bake at 350 degrees for 30 minutes.

2. Scoop out the eggplant pulp, leaving the shell intact for the stuffing.

3. Heat 2 teaspoons of the olive oil in a large nonstick skillet over medium heat.

4. Add the shallot and garlic, and sauté for 5 minutes until softened.

5. Add the tomato paste and eggplant pulp, and cook for 2 to 3 more minutes

6. Add the quinoa, broth, salt, black pepper, red pepper flakes, cheese, and parsley. Stir to combine.

7. Stuff the eggplant shells with the quinoa mixture.

8. Bake the eggplant at 350 degrees for 25 to 30 minutes and serve.

Tip: When choosing an eggplant, pick one that is heavy for its size, is uniform in color, and does not have any soft spots.

Nutritional information per serving: 272 calories, 8 g protein, 32 g carbohydrate, 13.4 g fat, 10.3 g fiber, 15 mg cholesterol, 366 mg sodium, 145 mg calcium, 2.2 mg iron

Baked Quinoa Ratatouille

Serves 4 (Serving size: about 1¼ cups)

This is ratatouille with a twist: quinoa. If you love ratatouille but have never tried quinoa, this is an appetizing way to do so. If you don't have quinoa on hand, this dish is still good without it.

1 tablespoon olive oil

2 cloves garlic, minced

1 red onion, thinly sliced

1 14½-ounce can diced tomatoes with liquid

2 tablespoons tomato paste

1 teaspoon dried basil

½ teaspoon dried oregano

½ teaspoon dried thyme

1 tablespoon chopped fresh parsley

1 large eggplant (about 1 pound), cubed

1 green pepper, thinly sliced

2 zucchini squash, sliced

1 yellow summer squash, sliced

1 cup cooked quinoa (cooked according to package instructions and rinsed, if necessary; see box on page 98)

¾ cup shredded part-skim mozzarella cheese (or Italian cheese blend, if desired)

1. Preheat the oven to 375 degrees.
2. Heat the olive oil in a large nonstick skillet over medium heat. Add the minced garlic and onion slices, and sauté for 5 minutes until softened.
3. Stir in the diced tomatoes, tomato paste, basil, oregano, thyme, and parsley. Continue to cook for 1 to 2 minutes. Remove from heat.
4. Layer half of the tomato and onion mixture in the bottom of a 9 × 13-inch baking dish. Top with all of the uncooked sliced and cubed vegetables, then add the remaining tomato and onion mixture. Spread the cooked quinoa on top and sprinkle with the shredded cheese.
5. Cover with foil and bake for 40 to 45 minutes. Remove the foil for the last 5 minutes of cooking.

Tip: To reduce the amount of sodium, use low-sodium tomatoes instead of regular.

Nutritional information per serving: 234 calories, 11 g protein, 31.4 g carbohydrate, 8 g fat, 8.3 g fiber, 13.4 mg cholesterol, 380 mg sodium, 272 mg calcium, 2.7 mg iron

Amaranth-Crusted Chicken
Serves 4 (1 4-ounce breast per serving)

With its crispy crust, this baked dish is like a healthy version of fried chicken. Your kids will love it, and the sesame flavor is sophisticated enough for guests.

Gluten-free cooking spray or 1 tablespoon vegetable oil

⅓ cup amaranth flour (if you don't have amaranth flour, use amaranth grain and finely grind it in a coffee grinder)

1 tablespoon sesame seeds
½ teaspoon salt
¼ teaspoon black pepper
¼ cup tahini
4 boneless, skinless chicken breasts (about 4 ounces each)

1. Preheat the oven to 400 degrees. Line a baking sheet with aluminum foil, and spray it with cooking spray or lightly coat it with vegetable oil.

2. In a shallow dish, mix the amaranth flour, sesame seeds, salt, and pepper.

3. Pour the tahini into a separate dish.

4. Dip the chicken into the tahini, then into the flour mixture until each piece is well coated.

5. Place the chicken breasts on the prepared baking sheet. Spray the top of the chicken with cooking spray or drizzle with vegetable oil. Bake for 25 to 30 minutes, until cooked through. Turn the chicken over once when it's halfway cooked and browned on one side.

Nutritional information per serving: 256 calories, 30 g protein, 8.8 g carbohydrate, 11 g fat, 1.5 g fiber, 65.7 mg cholesterol, 370 mg sodium, 66 mg calcium, 2.5 mg iron

---

Broccoli and Cheese and Rice Pie

Serves 8 (Serving size: ⅛ pie)

This recipe is gluten-free comfort food and a great dish to eat on a cold winter's day. You can substitute any vegetable or low-fat cheese that you have on hand.

Gluten-free cooking spray or 2 teaspoons vegetable oil

2 cups cooked brown rice (cook according to package instructions)

1 cup egg whites or egg substitute such as Egg Beaters (or 12 large egg whites)

1 teaspoon garlic powder

½ teaspoon salt

¼ cup grated Parmesan cheese

½ onion, finely chopped

10 ounces frozen chopped broccoli (defrosted and drained)

¾ cup low-fat shredded cheddar cheese

½ cup skim milk

½ cup heavy cream

½ teaspoon black pepper

¼ teaspoon nutmeg

1. Preheat the oven to 350 degrees.

2. Spray a 9-inch pie pan with cooking spray or lightly coat it with vegetable oil.

3. Mix the brown rice with ¼ cup of the egg whites, garlic powder, salt, and Parmesan cheese and pour into the prepared pan.

4. Bake for about 15 to 20 minutes until set and just crisping on outside.

5. While the rice is in the oven, spray a skillet with cooking spray or lightly cover it in vegetable oil, and sauté the onions until they start to brown. Add the broccoli and continue to cook until the broccoli is cooked through.

6. Pour the broccoli and onion mixture over the rice mixture and top with the shredded cheese.

7. Mix together the skim milk, heavy cream, the rest of the egg whites, pepper, and nutmeg.

8. Pour milk mixture over the pie mixture.

9. Bake for about 40 to 55 minutes until set, and serve warm.

Nutritional information per serving: 169 calories, 9.5 g protein, 15.3 g carbohydrate, 7.7 g fat, 1 g fiber, 28 mg cholesterol, 444 mg sodium, 166 mg calcium, 0.9 mg iron

---

Shrimp Scampi over Kasha and Onions

Serves 4 (Serving size: approximately 8 shrimp)

If you don't have kasha on hand, you can serve the scampi over brown rice, gluten-free pasta, or steamed broccoli. They are all equally delicious!

For Scampi:

1 tablespoon olive oil
½ cup finely chopped shallots
2 tablespoons minced garlic (or to taste)
½ teaspoon salt
¼ teaspoon black pepper
¼ teaspoon dried oregano
¼ cup white wine

2 tablespoons lemon juice
2 tablespoons butter
1 pound medium shelled shrimp
1 tablespoon chopped fresh parsley
2 tablespoons chopped green onion (for garnish)

1. Heat the olive oil in a large skillet, add the shallots and garlic, and sauté for about 3 to 4 minutes.
2. Add the salt, pepper, oregano, white wine, lemon juice, and butter, and heat until the butter melts.
3. Add the shrimp and cook until they just turn pink.
4. Garnish the shrimp with the chopped parsley and green onions, and serve over kasha and onions.

Tip: For money-saving scampi, substitute 1 pound of boneless, skinless chicken breasts, cut into 2-inch pieces, instead of the shrimp.

Nutrition Information per serving: 233 calories, 24 g protein, 6.5 g carbohydrate, 11 g fat, 188 mg cholesterol, 503 mg sodium, less than 1 g fiber, 77 mg calcium, 3.2 mg iron

For Kasha and Onions:

¾ cup uncooked kasha (roasted buckwheat groats)

1½ cups water or gluten-free chicken broth

3 tablespoons olive oil or butter

1 tablespoon minced garlic

1 large Spanish onion, chopped

½ teaspoon salt

½ teaspoon black pepper

1. Prepare the kasha by first rinsing it in hot water. Boil the water or broth and add the kasha. Cook until all of the water or broth is absorbed. If it's too chewy, add more water.
2. While the kasha is cooking, sauté the garlic in the oil or butter for about 1 minute, add the onions, and cook until the onions start to brown. If the pan dries out, add some water, a couple of tablespoons at a time.
3. Toss the cooked onions with the kasha, salt, and pepper.

Nutritional information per serving: 227 calories, 6.7 g protein, 30.5 g carbohydrate, 10 g fat, 32 mg cholesterol, 505 mg sodium, 4.5 g fiber, 26.4 mg calcium, 0.93 mg iron

Sesame and Millet–Crusted Tuna and Pineapple Kabobs

Serves 4 (Serving size: 2 kabobs)

Millet grits make a nice crunchy topping for fish.
If desired, marinate the tuna kabobs in your
favorite gluten-free salad dressing.

8 6-inch wooden skewers

2 tablespoons sesame seeds

2 tablespoons millet grits

1 pound fresh tuna, cut into chunks (approximately 2 × 2 inches)

¼ pineapple (about 1½ cups), cut into cubes

1 red onion, cut into quarters

2 red bell peppers, cut into chunks (approximately 1½ × 2 inches)

2 tablespoons gluten-free, low-sodium soy sauce

1 teaspoon garlic powder

1 tablespoon sugar

¼ teaspoon sesame oil

1 tablespoon cider vinegar

1. Preheat the oven to 375 degrees.
2. Soak the skewers in warm water for 5 minutes (this helps prevent food from sticking to the skewer).
3. In a skillet, toast the sesame seeds and millet for 2 to 4 minutes until they start to brown.
4. Press the tuna into the millet/sesame seed mixture so that the seeds coat the tuna.
5. Make the kabobs, alternating the tuna, pineapple, red onion, and peppers, on the skewer.
6. Place the tuna kabobs on a sheet pan.
7. Mix together the gluten-free, low-sodium soy sauce, garlic powder, sugar, sesame oil, and cider vinegar.
8. Pour the dressing mixture over the kabobs.
9. Bake for about 15 minutes until the tuna, peppers, and onions are cooked. Serve with cooked quinoa or brown rice and steamed vegetables.

Nutrition Information per serving: 299 calories, 29.7 g protein, 20 g carbohydrate, 10.6 g fat, 43 mg cholesterol, 573 mg sodium, 3.7 g fiber, 68.7 mg calcium, 2.6 mg iron

Mediterranean Chicken with Sorghum, Feta, and Tomato Served over Millet

Serves 4 (Serving size: 1 chicken breast with ¼ cup millet)

This recipe calls for popped sorghum. Yes, you can pop sorghum just as you do corn.

¼ cup toasted whole sorghum, ground

1 teaspoon garlic powder

½ teaspoon onion powder

⅛ teaspoon salt

¼ teaspoon black pepper

1 egg

Gluten-free cooking spray or 1 teaspoon vegetable oil

1 pound thinly sliced, skinless, boneless chicken breasts

2 tablespoons olive oil

2 tablespoons chopped garlic

1 onion, thinly sliced

2 large tomatoes, chopped

1 teaspoon dried oregano

¼ cup white wine

1 tablespoon lemon juice

4 ounces feta cheese

½ cup chopped black olives

2 tablespoons capers

1 cup cooked hulled millet or grits

1. Preheat the oven to broil.
2. Toast the sorghum in a skillet over medium heat for a few minutes, taking care not to burn it. It will begin to pop like popcorn. Then grind it in a coffee grinder on medium grind.
3. In a large bowl, mix together the toasted sorghum, garlic powder, onion powder, salt, and pepper.
4. In a medium bowl, beat the egg.
5. Spray a baking sheet with cooking spray or lightly coat it in vegetable oil.
6. Dredge the chicken breasts in the egg and then coat them with the sorghum mixture on both sides. Place them on the baking sheet, and drizzle the olive oil over the top of the chicken before broiling.
7. Broil the chicken on both sides until just cooked.
8. In a skillet sprayed with cooking spray or coated with 2 teaspoons vegetable oil, sauté the chopped garlic and onion until they start

to brown. Add the tomato, oregano, wine, and lemon juice, and cook until the tomatoes soften. Add the feta, olives, and capers and cook for 4 minutes more.

9. Turn the oven down to 350 degrees. Pour the feta mixture over the chicken, and bake for about 10 minutes.

10. Serve the chicken over the cooked millet.

Nutritional information per serving: 463 calories, 36 g protein, 31 g carbohydrate, 20.3 g fat, 144 mg cholesterol, 738 mg sodium, 4.1 g fiber, 222 mg calcium, 3.1 mg iron

Slow-Cooker Sloppy Joes
Serves 6 (Serving size: about ¾ cup)

These Sloppy Joes are a tasty, budget-conscious, easy-to-prepare dish that will bring you back to your childhood. You can increase the amount of fiber in the recipe by adding chopped vegetables or beans.

1 pound lean ground beef (such as sirloin)

1 cup chopped onion

1 teaspoon garlic powder

¾ cup ketchup

1 teaspoon yellow mustard

1 tablespoon brown sugar

¼ teaspoon black pepper

½ cup puffed amaranth

2 cups shredded cabbage

⅔ cup water

1. Put all of the ingredients, in the order listed, into a slow cooker. Set the slow cooker on low, and cook for about 4 hours.

2. Serve on gluten-free hamburger rolls or in a baked potato.

Tip: If you don't have a slow cooker, this meal can also be prepared in a skillet on the stovetop in about 30 minutes.

Nutritional information per serving: 180.7 calories, 17 g protein, 14.6 g carbohydrate, 6 g fat, 41.6 mg cholesterol, 398 mg sodium, 1.4 g fiber, 31 mg calcium, 2 mg iron

Sage Butter Sautéed Chicken Breasts and Pancetta over Millet

Serves 4 (Serving size: 1 chicken breast over ½ cup millet)

This delicious and decadent dish is sure to please all of your guests. The recipe also works well with veal cutlets or butterflied shrimp.

4 tablespoons chopped pancetta (about ⅛ × ⅛-inch pieces)

2 tablespoons brown rice flour

¼ teaspoon salt

¼ teaspoon black pepper

1 pound boneless, skinless chicken breasts, thinly sliced

1 tablespoon butter

2 teaspoons dried sage

1 teaspoon dried minced garlic

2 tablespoons white wine

2 tablespoons heavy cream

2 tablespoons Parmesan cheese

2 cups cooked hulled millet

1. Heat a large skillet over medium heat. Add the pancetta and cook until just crispy. Remove from the skillet, leaving the drippings in the pan.
2. Meanwhile, mix together the brown rice flour, salt, and pepper.
3. Dredge the chicken breasts in the seasoned rice flour until the chicken is well coated on both sides.
4. To the pancetta drippings in the skillet, add the butter and sage and heat for about 2 minutes until the butter is melted. Add the chicken and sprinkle top with minced garlic. When the chicken is cooked on one side, turn it over and cook until just done.
5. To the skillet, add the wine and heavy cream, and cook with the chicken for about 2 minutes until the sauce starts to thicken.
6. Sprinkle the chicken with Parmesan cheese, and serve over the cooked millet.

Nutritional information per serving: 369 calories, 32.8 g protein, 33.2 g carbohydrate, 10.5 g fat, 87 mg cholesterol, 310 mg sodium, 2 g fiber, 59 mg calcium, 1.9 mg iron

Turkey Meatloaf

Serves 8 (Serving size: 1⅛-inch slices)

This meatloaf is good enough to serve to guests, partly because of the presentation: it's covered in a layer of turkey bacon.

½ cup gluten-free rolled oats (or cooked millet or quinoa)

Gluten-free cooking spray or 1 teaspoon vegetable oil

1⅓ pounds ground turkey

1 egg

½ teaspoon salt

⅛ teaspoon black pepper

1 teaspoon garlic powder

½ teaspoon onion powder

⅓ cup ketchup

½ teaspoon dried oregano

½ teaspoon dried thyme leaves

½ cup finely chopped onion

2 stalks celery, finely chopped

4 pieces turkey bacon, cut in halves

1. Preheat the oven to 350 degrees.
2. Process the oats in a coffee grinder for a few seconds to make them more finely ground, but not as fine as flour. If you're using millet or quinoa, skip this step.
3. Spray a 9 × 5-inch loaf pan with cooking spray or lightly coat it with vegetable oil.
4. In a large bowl, mix together the turkey, oats, egg, salt, pepper, garlic powder, onion powder, ketchup, oregano, thyme, onion, and celery.
5. Fill the loaf pan with the turkey mixture, and spread with a spatula.
6. Arrange the turkey bacon pieces on top of the meatloaf, placing one slice next to the other to cover the whole loaf.
7. Bake uncovered for 55 to 65 minutes until cooked through and the meatloaf reaches an internal temperature of 165 degrees.

Tip: This meatloaf also works well with ⅓ pound ground sirloin and 1 pound turkey.

Nutritional information per serving: 188 calories, 17 g protein, 8.9 g carbohydrate, 9.1 g fat, 92.9 mg cholesterol, 506 mg sodium, less than 1 g fiber, 27 mg calcium, 1.6 mg iron

Potato Lasagna

Serves 6 (Serving size: 1½ × 1½-inch square)

*This recipe is a nice twist on traditional lasagna.
As always, sour cream and potatoes are a winning
duo. You can also replace the ground chicken breast
with kidney beans for a great meatless meal.*

3 to 4 medium potatoes, unpeeled, scrubbed, and sliced ⅛-inch thick

2 tablespoons olive oil

¼ teaspoon salt

¼ teaspoon black pepper

Gluten-free cooking spray or 4 teaspoons olive oil

½ cup chopped onion

8 ounces ground chicken breast

2 tablespoons tomato paste

2 ounces provolone cheese

½ cup sour cream

1 medium zucchini, thinly sliced

1 tomato, thinly sliced

¼ cup gluten-free marinara sauce

2 tablespoons grated Parmesan cheese

1. Preheat the oven to 375 degrees. Place the potatoes on a baking sheet and brush them with 2 teaspoons of the olive oil. Sprinkle with salt and pepper, making sure to coat both sides evenly. Bake for 15 minutes, or until the potatoes just start to soften. Remove from the oven and cool slightly.
2. Spray a medium skillet with cooking spray or coat it with 2 teaspoons of olive oil. Add the onions and chicken. Cook, stirring constantly and breaking up the meat until the chicken is browned and the onions are translucent. Stir in the tomato paste.
3. To assemble the lasagna, spray a 9 × 9-inch square pan with cooking spray or coat it with the remaining 2 teaspoons olive oil. Place a layer of potatoes on the bottom, cover with the provolone cheese, and then spread with the sour cream. Arrange all of the zucchini and tomato slices on top, then another layer of potatoes, then all of the meat, and a final layer of potatoes. Spread the marinara sauce on top, and sprinkle with Parmesan cheese.

4. Cover with aluminum foil and bake for 30 minutes. Remove the foil during the last 5 minutes of cooking.

Tip: You can peel the potatoes and the zucchini first, if you prefer.

Nutritional information per serving: 276.8 calories, 13.5 g protein, 24.9 g carbohydrate, 14.4 g fat, 47.7 mg cholesterol, 335.8 mg sodium, 3.2 g fiber, 138.5 mg calcium, 1.8 mg iron

---

10

Sweet Somethings

Top off your meal with healthy and yummy desserts. Yes, it is possible! This chapter contains scrumptious recipes to satisfy every craving.

Quick and Easy Gluten-Free

Creamy Frozen Fruit Ice
Cinnamon Apple Parfait
Chocolate Banana Swirl
Soft Pumpkin Chocolate Chip Cookies
Individual Peach Cobblers
Teff Pie Crust
Coconut Almond Cookies
Chocolate Hazelnut Granola Quesadillas

Creative Gluten-Free

Chocolate Pudding Cake
Poached Pears over Ice Cream with Caramel
Creamy Dreamy Brown Rice and Quinoa Pudding
Coconut Sorbet with Papaya
Baked Pears with Vanilla Yogurt

Chocolate Buckwheat Crepes with Raspberry Ricotta Filling
Chocolate Sponge Cake with Chocolate Glaze
Strawberry Pie in Teff Crust

QUICK AND EASY
GLUTEN-FREE

Creamy Frozen Fruit Ice
Serves 4

If you are looking for a way to get your kids to eat and enjoy fruit, this is it! Bananas are the key to the creamy texture of this dessert.

4 small bananas (peeled, cut into 2-inch pieces, and frozen)

2 cups frozen berries

2 tablespoons all-fruit preserves

⅛ cup water

1. Puree the bananas, berries, and fruit preserves in a food processor.
2. Add the water until you achieve the desired creaminess.
3. Serve the fruit ice immediately with your favorite toppings (see tip).

Tip: Serve with any of the following toppings: ½ cup toasted coconut, ¼ cup chopped gluten-free dark chocolate, ¼ cup chopped nuts, or 2 tablespoons creamy peanut butter or another nut butter.

Nutritional information per serving (does not include toppings): 164.5 calories, 1.6 g protein, 41 g carbohydrate, less than 1 g fat, 0 mg cholesterol, 1.9 mg sodium, 5 g fiber, 12 mg calcium, less than 1 mg iron

---

Cinnamon Apple Parfait
Serves 4

If you are lucky enough to go apple picking this fall, plan to make this mouthwatering dessert when you return home.

3 medium apples, peeled, cored, and sliced in half

1 tablespoon lemon juice

2 tablespoons dark brown sugar

2 teaspoons cinnamon

2 cups vanilla ice cream

2 tablespoons toasted chopped pecans

1. Toss the apples with the lemon juice.
2. Grill the apples on a tabletop grill over medium heat until just cooked.
3. Cut the apples into 2-inch pieces and sprinkle with brown sugar and cinnamon.
4. In each of 4 dessert glasses, put ½ cup ice cream, ¼ of the apples, and ½ tablespoon pecans.

Tip: Many other fruits also grill well, such as pears, papayas, mangoes, pineapple, and peaches.

Nutritional information per serving: 243 calories, 3 g protein, 37 g carbohydrate, 10.5 g fat, 32 mg cholesterol, 60 mg sodium, 4 g fiber, 116 mg calcium, less than 1 mg iron

Chocolate Banana Swirl

Serves 4

If you have never eaten ricotta cheese for dessert, you are in for a treat. Some of us could eat ricotta cheese mixed with sugar by the spoonful! Add gluten-free dark chocolate pieces for a nice twist.

2 cups part-skim ricotta cheese

1 tablespoon cocoa powder

2 tablespoons confectioner's sugar

2 tablespoons brown sugar

1 medium banana, sliced

½ teaspoon cinnamon (optional)

1. Mix together the ricotta cheese, cocoa powder, confectioner's sugar, and brown sugar until blended well.
2. Taste the mixture, and add extra sweetener if desired.
3. Separate the ricotta mixture into 4 individual dessert cups.
4. Top with sliced banana slices, sprinkle with cinnamon, and serve.

Tip: The ricotta mixture can be made without adding cocoa powder.

Nutritional information per serving: 231 calories, 14.6 g protein, 22 g carbohydrate, 10 g fat, 38 mg cholesterol, 156 mg sodium, 1.4 g fiber, 344 mg calcium, less than 1 mg iron

Soft Pumpkin Chocolate Chip Cookies

Makes 24 cookies

This soft, cakelike cookie is perfect for fall!

2 tablespoons butter, softened

¾ cup brown sugar

¼ cup white sugar

1 egg

1 teaspoon vanilla extract

1 cup canned pumpkin puree

1 cup sorghum flour

½ cup tapioca flour

½ cup potato starch

2 tablespoons almond flour or meal

¼ teaspoon xanthan gum

1 teaspoon baking powder

½ teaspoon salt

½ teaspoon cinnamon

1 teaspoon pumpkin pie spice (or a combination of ground cinnamon, cloves, nutmeg, and ginger)

½ cup finely chopped dark chocolate

1. Preheat the oven to 350 degrees. Line a cookie sheet with parchment paper.
2. Cream together the butter and sugars. Add the egg, vanilla, and pumpkin, and mix until well combined.
3. Sift together all of the dry ingredients except the chocolate, from the sorghum to the pumpkin pie spice.
4. Stir the dry ingredients into the pumpkin mixture. Fold in the chocolate.
5. Drop the batter by the tablespoon onto the prepared cookie sheet. Bake for 12 to 15 minutes, until the cookies are just set.
6. Cool the cookies on a cookie sheet or a wire rack.

Nutritional information per cookie: 118 calories, 1.6 g protein, 22 g carbohydrate, 3 g fat, 11 mg cholesterol, 70.7 mg sodium, 1.1 g fiber, 5.8 mg calcium, less than 1 mg iron

Individual Peach Cobblers

Serves 6

Instead of making this cobbler in one large baking dish, you can use individual custard cups for a unique presentation.

4 cups peeled, sliced peaches (fresh or frozen)

1 tablespoon lemon juice

¼ teaspoon cinnamon

3 tablespoons plus 2 teaspoons sugar

1 tablespoon cornstarch

¼ cup brown rice flour

¼ cup sorghum flour

½ cup tapioca starch

1½ teaspoons baking powder

½ teaspoon baking soda

¼ teaspoon salt

3 tablespoons cold unsalted butter

½ cup buttermilk (or combine ½ cup milk minus ½ tablespoon with ½ tablespoon vinegar)

¼ teaspoon nutmeg

1. Preheat the oven to 400 degrees. Place 6 (7-ounce) custard cups on a cookie sheet.

2. Toss the peaches with the lemon juice, cinnamon, 2 tablespoons of the sugar, and 1 tablespoon of cornstarch. Divide the peaches evenly among the 6 cups, and bake in the preheated oven for 15 minutes.

3. In a medium bowl, combine the rice and sorghum flours, tapioca starch, 1 tablespoon of the sugar, baking powder, baking soda, and salt.

4. Using a pastry blender or 2 knives, cut in the butter until the mixture is crumbly. Add the buttermilk, and stir until the mixture is moistened.

5. Remove the peaches from the oven. Drop the topping by tablespoons on top of the peaches, dividing the batter evenly among all six cups.

6. Mix the nutmeg and 2 teaspoons of the sugar together, and sprinkle on top of each cup.

7. Return the cups to the oven and bake for an additional 20 to 25 minutes or until the topping is golden brown. Serve warm with vanilla ice cream or whipped cream.

Nutritional information per serving: 198 calories, 2.4 g protein, 34 g carbohydrate, 6.3 g fat, 16 mg cholesterol, 188 mg sodium, 1.7 g fiber, 48.9 mg calcium, less than 1 mg iron

Teff Pie Crust

Makes 1 pie crust (Serving size: ⅛ pie crust)

This is a versatile pie crust that you can use for all of your sweet pies. It can be stored in the refrigerator for two to three days before use.

1 cup teff flour

¼ cup almond meal or flour

¼ cup real maple syrup

2 tablespoons melted butter

¼ teaspoon salt

1. Preheat the oven to 375 degrees.
2. Combine all of the ingredients. Press the dough evenly into a 9-inch pie plate.
3. Bake for 10 minutes.

Nutritional information per serving: 124 calories, 3.6 g protein, 18.8 g carbohydrate, 4.1 g fat, 7.6 mg cholesterol, 96.7 mg sodium, 2 g fiber, 49.5 mg calcium, 1.6 mg iron

Coconut Almond Cookies

Makes 1½ dozen cookies

This delectable treat is a cross between a macaroon and an almond cookie. When you buy almond paste, please read the label carefully as not all almond paste is gluten-free.

1 cup gluten-free almond paste

½ cup sugar

2 tablespoons brown rice flour

1 cup sweetened coconut flakes

2 egg whites

½ teaspoon vanilla extract

1. Preheat the oven to 300 degrees. Line a baking sheet with parchment paper or a silicone baking mat.
2. Combine the almond paste, sugar, and brown rice flour, breaking up the almond paste with your hands or with a pastry blender.
3. Stir in the coconut.
4. In a small bowl, beat the egg whites with the vanilla until foamy. Stir into the coconut almond mixture.
5. Drop the batter by level tablespoons onto the prepared baking sheets.

6. Bake for 25 minutes or until the edges are browned. Remove from the baking sheet to cool on a wire rack.

Tip: For a chocolatey variation, drizzle the cookies with melted chocolate after baking. Chop up some semisweet chocolate into small pieces until you have about ¼ cup. Put them into a small glass bowl, microwave for about 30 seconds on high, and stir. If the chocolate is not completely melted, keep stirring and microwaving it for 30 seconds until it is.

Nutritional information per cookie: 103 calories, 1.9 g protein, 14.7 g carbohydrate, 4.6 g fat, 0 mg cholesterol, 18.6 mg sodium, less than 1 g fiber, 17 mg calcium, less than 1 mg iron

Chocolate Hazelnut Granola Quesadillas

Makes 4

This is a quick and easy dessert the kids will love!
Make as many quesadillas as you need.

4 corn tortillas

4 tablespoons chocolate hazelnut spread

4 tablespoons gluten-free granola

½ pear, thinly sliced

1. Spread each tortilla with 1 tablespoon of the chocolate hazelnut spread. Layer 1 tablespoon granola on one half of the tortilla, and 3 to 4 pear slices on the other.
2. Heat a nonstick skillet over medium heat. Cook the open tortilla in the pan for 1 to 2 minutes. Fold it in half and continue to cook for 1 to 2 minutes longer until lightly browned on each side.
3. Serve immediately.

Tip: Peanut butter and apples are a nice substitute for the chocolate hazelnut spread and pears.

Nutritional information per serving: 212.5 calories, 4.3 g protein, 29.5 g carbohydrate, 9.2 g fat, 0 mg cholesterol, 20 mg sodium, 3.5 g fiber, 34.1 mg calcium, less than 1 mg iron

CREATIVE GLUTEN-FREE

Chocolate Pudding Cake

Serves 6 (Serving size: ½ cup)

Many of us probably remember chocolate pudding cakes from when we were kids. How wonderful to have a gluten-free version! This may become a family favorite in your house.

½ cup brown rice flour

¼ cup finely ground almonds

¼ teaspoon xanthan gum

⅔ cup sugar

1½ teaspoons baking powder

½ cup unsweetened cocoa, divided

1 teaspoon instant coffee

½ cup skim milk

3 tablespoons vegetable oil

1 teaspoon vanilla extract

⅔ cup brown sugar

1¼ cups boiling water

1. Preheat the oven to 350 degrees.
2. Combine the rice flour and ground almonds, xanthan gum, sugar, baking powder, ¼ cup of the cocoa, and the coffee in the bottom of an 8-inch square baking pan. Stir to mix well.
3. Add the milk, oil, and vanilla. Stir until thoroughly mixed. Spread the mixture in the pan.
4. Sprinkle the brown sugar and the remaining ¼ cup of cocoa on top of the batter.
5. Pour the hot water over the top. Do not stir.
6. Bake for 30 minutes. Do not overcook. The cake is meant to be gooey inside. It will be set and cooked in the middle but bubbly around the edges.

Nutritional information per serving: 298 calories, 3.5 g protein, 56 g carbohydrate, 8 g fat, less than 1 mg cholesterol, 79 mg sodium, 3 g fiber, 70.7 mg calcium, 1.6 mg iron

Poached Pears over Ice Cream with Caramel

Serves 8

This is a nice festive dessert to serve during the holidays. You can use store-bought caramel sauce to save time, but read the label to make sure it's gluten-free.

4 cups water

1 cup red wine or red grape juice

½ cup sugar

1 teaspoon lemon zest

5 whole cloves

1 teaspoon vanilla extract

4 whole pears, peeled (leave stems in)

2 cups vanilla ice cream

½ cup homemade caramel sauce (see recipe below)

1. Combine the water, wine, sugar, lemon zest, cloves, and vanilla in a large saucepan. Bring to a boil and cook, stirring constantly, until the sugar is dissolved.
2. Reduce heat to a simmer. Add the pears. Cook, turning them occasionally, for about 10 minutes or until the pears are tender. The cooking time will vary, depending on the size, type, and ripeness of the pears used. Pears are done when they are fork tender.
3. Allow the pears to cool in the cooking liquid. When they're cool, remove them from the liquid. Cut them in half and remove the cores. Transfer the pears to a serving dish, and serve each pear half with ¼ cup of ice cream.
4. Drizzle the pear and ice cream with the caramel sauce.

CARAMEL SAUCE

½ cup light brown sugar

¼ cup water

1 tablespoon butter

2 tablespoons half-and-half

½ teaspoon vanilla extract

1. Combine the sugar, water, and butter in a small saucepan. Cook over medium heat, stirring constantly, until the sugar dissolves.
2. Bring to a boil and cook for 3 minutes, stirring constantly.
3. Remove from heat. Stir in the half-and-half and vanilla.

Nutritional information per serving: 235 calories, 2 g protein, 41 g carbohydrate, 5 g fat, 15 mg cholesterol, 38 mg sodium, 2 g fiber, 172 mg calcium, less than 1 mg iron

Creamy Dreamy Brown Rice and Quinoa Pudding

Serves 6 (Serving size: approximately ⅔ cup)

This recipe is a healthy and delicious take on traditional rice pudding.

1½ cups cooked long-grain brown rice (not instant)

½ cup cooked quinoa (see box on page 166)

½ cup raisins (or try dried cranberries or cherries)

¾ cup sugar

1 12-ounce can evaporated 2% milk

½ cup whole milk

1 teaspoon cinnamon

¼ teaspoon nutmeg (use freshly grated whole nutmeg, if available, for added flavor)

1 teaspoon vanilla extract

1. In a medium saucepan, combine the rice, quinoa, raisins, sugar, evaporated milk, and whole milk. Bring to a boil.
2. Reduce heat and simmer for 15 to 20 minutes, stirring frequently, until most of the liquid is absorbed. If the pudding is too thin, cook a little longer.
3. Remove from heat. Stir in the cinnamon, nutmeg, and vanilla.
4. Serve warm or cold. The pudding thickens as it cools. Sprinkle with extra cinnamon, if desired.

Nutritional information per serving: 187 calories, 4 g protein, 28 g carbohydrate, 2.5 g fat, 4.5 mg cholesterol, 21 mg sodium, 2 g fiber, 193 mg calcium, 1.2 mg iron

Coconut Sorbet with Papaya

Serves 4 (Serving size: ¾ cup)

We love coconut sorbet. If you can't eat ice cream but miss creamy frozen desserts, this is the one for you. In one author's opinion, there is nothing better than coconut sorbet and chopped semisweet chocolate.

1 cup water

¾ cup granulated sugar

1 cup coconut milk

1 cup chopped papaya or ⅛ cup dried papaya

1. Put the water and sugar in a medium saucepan. Bring to a boil, stirring constantly, until the sugar is dissolved. Reduce heat and simmer for about 5 minutes to make a simple sugar syrup.
2. Stir in the coconut milk.
3. Pour the mixture into a shallow container, and freeze for 2 to 3 hours.
4. Remove the container from the freezer. Scrape the mixture into a food processor, and mix until smooth.
5. Fold in the papaya and serve.

Tip: Instead of papaya, you can use toasted sweetened coconut, fresh or canned pineapple, or mangoes, or leave out that ingredient completely.

Nutritional information per serving: 298 calories, 1.5 g protein, 44.5 g carbohydrate, 14 g fat, 0 mg cholesterol, 10 mg sodium, 1.9 g fiber, 18.4 mg calcium, 1 mg iron

Baked Pears with Vanilla Yogurt
Serves 4

This is a fabulous fall dessert and a nice change from baked apples (not that they aren't delicious, too).

2 6-ounce containers nonfat vanilla yogurt

1 8-ounce container nonfat plain yogurt

2 large pears, peeled and cored

2 teaspoons cinnamon

2 tablespoons dark brown sugar

2 tablespoons chopped walnuts

1. Preheat the oven to 350 degrees
2. Mix together the plain and vanilla yogurt.
3. Cut the pears in half, and place them on a baking sheet that has been covered with aluminum foil.
4. Sprinkle the pears with the cinnamon and sugar, and bake for about 15 to 20 minutes until the pears are soft.
5. Cut the pears in quarters.
6. Pour the yogurt into four small bowls, and top with the pear quarters and chopped walnuts.

Tip: Use an apple corer to core pears. Stick the stem in the round center of the corer, then push down on the pear until the corer works its way through. Turn the corer to remove the core.

Nutritional information per serving: 189 calories, 7 g protein, 37.3 g carbohydrate, 2.5 g fat, 0 mg cholesterol, 96 mg sodium, 5 g fiber, 318 mg calcium, less than 1 mg iron

Chocolate Buckwheat Crepes with Raspberry Ricotta Filling

Serves 8 (Serving size: 1 crepe with ¼ cup filling and ¼ cup raspberries)

These crepes have a subtle chocolate flavor that lends itself well to the sweet raspberry filling. They make a special breakfast or brunch treat.

⅔ cup buckwheat flour

⅓ cup tapioca flour

1 tablespoon unsweetened cocoa powder

1 tablespoon sugar

2 eggs

1 cup 1% milk

½ teaspoon salt

2 tablespoons butter, melted

Gluten-free cooking spray or about 2 teaspoons vegetable oil

Raspberry Ricotta Filling

2 cups part-skim ricotta cheese

2 tablespoons raspberry all-fruit spread

1 tablespoon sugar

2 cups fresh or frozen red raspberries

Powdered sugar (for garnish)

1. In a large mixing bowl, whisk together the buckwheat flour, tapioca flour, cocoa, sugar, and eggs. Add the milk, and stir to combine.
2. Beat in the salt and butter. Continue to mix until smooth.
3. Heat a medium nonstick skillet over medium-high heat. Spray it with cooking spray or coat it with vegetable oil.
4. Pour ¼ cup of the batter onto the skillet. Tilt the skillet so that the batter coats the surface evenly.
5. Cook for about 1 minute, until the bottom starts to brown. Flip the crepe with the spatula, and cook the other side for about 30 seconds.

6. Remove the crepe to a platter, and cover to keep warm.

7. Continue cooking until all the crepes are done.

8. Meanwhile, make the raspberry filling by mixing the ricotta cheese with the fruit spread and sugar.

9. Place ¼ cup of the cheese mixture and ¼ cup of the raspberries on each crepe.

10. Roll each crepe over the filling, and sprinkle it with powdered sugar.

Tip: For a stronger chocolate flavor, add more cocoa. Leave the cocoa out entirely for a savory variation.

Nutritional information per serving: 182.6 calories, 4 g protein, 30.8 g carbohydrate, 5.4 g fat, 11 mg cholesterol, 191 mg sodium, 2.4 g fiber, 54.5 mg calcium, 1.2 mg iron

Chocolate Sponge Cake with Chocolate Glaze

Serves 10 (Serving size: 1 2½–3-inch piece)

Make this rich, elegant cake for special occasions, and your guests will rave!

Gluten-free cooking spray or 2 teaspoons vegetable oil

4 eggs, separated

1 cup sugar

4 tablespoons water

1 teaspoon vanilla extract

½ cup tapioca flour

½ cup sorghum flour

1 teaspoon baking powder

½ teaspoon xanthan gum

½ teaspoon salt

¼ teaspoon cream of tartar

2 ounces bittersweet chocolate, finely grated

1. Preheat the oven to 325 degrees. Spray a bundt pan with cooking spray or coat it with vegetable oil.

2. Beat the egg yolks with the sugar until the mixture is very light yellow. Add the water and vanilla.

3. Sift the tapioca and sorghum flours, baking powder, xanthan gum, and salt together. Beat into the egg yolks.

4. In a separate bowl, beat the egg whites with cream of tartar until stiff peaks form.

5. Fold the chocolate into the egg whites.

6. Fold the egg whites and the grated chocolate into the batter. Pour into the prepared pan, and bake for 40 to 45 minutes, until a toothpick inserted in the center comes out clean.

7. Invert the cake onto a wire rack, and let it cool for about 10 minutes. Using a knife, loosen sides from the pan and invert the cake onto a serving plate.

CHOCOLATE GLAZE

2 ounces bittersweet chocolate, melted

2 tablespoons half-and-half

½ cup powdered sugar

2 to 3 tablespoons warm water

Whisk all of the ingredients together until smooth. Drizzle over the cooled cake.

Tip: If you prefer your desserts a little less rich, sprinkle the cake with powdered sugar and skip the glaze.

Nutritional information per serving: 242.8 calories, 4.3 g protein, 44 g carbohydrate, 7 g fat, 86 mg cholesterol, 174 mg sodium, 1.7 g fiber, 35 mg calcium, 1.6 mg iron

Strawberry Pie in Teff Crust
Serves 8

1 quart fresh strawberries (or another berry, if desired)

¾ cup sugar

3 tablespoons cornstarch

½ cup water

1 prepared Teff Pie Crust (page 194)

1. Slice half of the strawberries and layer them in the pie crust. (You may also choose not to slice them and lay them in the pie crust whole.)

2. Mash the remaining strawberries, and combine them with the sugar in a medium saucepan. Bring to a boil over medium heat, stirring frequently.

3. In a small bowl, stir together the cornstarch and water. Stir into the strawberry and sugar mixture. Reduce the heat and simmer until the liquid has thickened, about 10 minutes.

4. Pour the cooked strawberry mixture over the strawberries in the pie crust. Place the pie in the refrigerator, and chill for 6 hours before serving.

Nutritional information per serving: 232 calories, 4 g protein, 46 g carbohydrate, 4.3 g fat, 7.6 mg cholesterol, 98 mg sodium, 3.5 g fiber, 36 mg calcium, 1.4 mg iron

---

11

Gluten-Free Meal Plans

Are you looking for a quick and easy way to plan your meals? Here are twenty-eight days of gluten-free menu suggestions that incorporate some of the terrific recipes found in this book. (Adjust the number of daily snacks according to your personal requirements.)

Recipes featured in this book are marked with an asterisk.

Day 1

Breakfast: Instant quinoa cereal, with 1% milk and fresh fruit
Snack: Fresh fruit salad
Lunch: Grilled chicken over mixed greens, with gluten-free brown rice crackers
Snack: Low-fat plain or flavored yogurt
Dinner: Pork Kabobs over Apple Millet* with green beans
Snack: Veggie sticks with gluten-free ranch dressing

Day 2

Breakfast: Gluten-free whole-grain bread with almond butter and fruit preserves
Snack: Gluten-free trail mix
Lunch: Baked potato stuffed with broccoli and melted shredded cheddar cheese, with mixed green salad

Snack: Hummus and veggie sticks

Dinner: Baked Salmon with Mustard Sauce* with grilled asparagus over millet

Snack: Dried fruit with almonds

Day 3

Breakfast: Egg white omelet served with warmed corn tortillas

Snack: Peanut butter and banana

Lunch: Layered Eggplant and Goat Cheese Tower*

Snack: Corn chips and gluten-free salsa

Dinner: Chicken Fajitas with Black Beans*

Snack: String cheese with raisins

Day 4

Breakfast: Plain yogurt and berries with ground flaxseed

Snack: Gluten-free brown rice crackers with low-fat cream cheese and all-fruit preserves

Lunch: Walnut-Crusted Orange Roughy with Fresh Herb Pesto* and a side salad

Snack: Fruit sorbet

Dinner: Grilled steak with baked potato and salad

Snack: Gluten-free low-fat pudding with chopped walnuts

Day 5

Breakfast: Cottage cheese and fresh fruit

Snack: Edamame beans

Lunch: Turkey Chili with Cocoa* with a mixed salad

Snack: Small bowl of gluten-free cereal with low-fat milk

Dinner: Roasted chicken with baby potatoes and green beans

Snack: All-fruit ice pop

Day 6

Breakfast: Gluten-free yogurt layered with corn Chex in a parfait glass

Snack: Gluten-free quinoa cookies

Lunch: Gazpacho with White Beans*

Snack: Dried apricots and cream cheese on gluten-free brown rice crackers

Dinner: Grilled turkey burger with a mixed salad
Snack: Peanut Butter Oatmeal Granola Bar*

Day 7

Breakfast: Corn tortilla filled with scrambled eggs, cheese, and chopped tomato
Snack: Gluten-free brown rice cake with almond butter
Lunch: Chili Lime Shrimp Salad Bowls*
Snack: Three-bean salad
Dinner: Grilled chicken burger with sautéed onions and mushrooms over brown rice
Snack: Low-fat cheese cubes and gluten-free brown rice crackers

Day 8

Breakfast: Chocolate Chip Banana Bread*
Snack: Corn chips with gluten-free salsa
Lunch: Homemade Hummus with Spicy Salsa* with mixed raw veggies and gluten-free brown rice crackers
Snack: Applesauce mixed with raisins and cinnamon
Dinner: Pork kabobs with cherry tomatoes, pineapple, and onions over quinoa
Snack: Fruit sorbet

Day 9

Breakfast: Cheddar and Bacon Drop Biscuits*
Snack: Gluten-free fruit and nut bar
Lunch: Amaranth-Stuffed Peppers*
Snack: Gluten-free, low-fat strawberry milkshake
Dinner: Taco Pizza*
Snack: 100% vegetable chips

Day 10

Breakfast: Poached eggs over grits
Snack: Guacamole with white corn tortilla chips
Lunch: Blue Cheese Turkey Salad with Sliced Apples*
Snack: Baked sweet potato fries
Dinner: Brown rice pasta with shrimp and broccoli in garlic and oil
Snack: Plain popcorn

Day 11

Breakfast: Buckwheat Banana Pancakes*
Snack: Pumpkin and sunflower seed mix
Lunch: Grilled Romaine Salad*
Snack: Creamy Dreamy Brown Rice and Quinoa Pudding*
Dinner: Tilapia with Artichokes and Tomatoes*
Snack: Baby carrots and sun-dried tomato dip

Day 12

Breakfast: Egg and Cheese Tostadas*
Snack: Celery sticks stuffed with peanut butter
Lunch: Waldorf Quinoa Salad*
Snack: Gluten-free whole grain cereal and low-fat milk
Dinner: Turkey Cutlets Marsala*
Snack: Fruit kabobs

Day 13

Breakfast: Lemon Poppy Seed Mini Muffins*
Snack: Gluten-free flaxseed pretzels with hummus
Lunch: Chopped Salad*
Snack: Apple with a cube of low-fat cheese
Dinner: Baked cod with lemon butter and garlic, over millet and
    steamed spinach
Snack: Gluten-free chocolate soy milk

Day 14

Breakfast: Hot Mixed-Grain Cereal with Berries*
Snack: Gluten-free brown rice cakes with cream cheese and dried
    cranberries
Lunch: Scallop and Arugula Salad*
Snack: Gluten-free pumpkin soup
Dinner: Grilled Chicken Cordon Bleu* with broccoli rabe
Snack: Mango sorbet

Day 15

Breakfast: Gluten-free oatmeal with applesauce and cinnamon
Snack: Plantain Chips*

Lunch: Grilled chicken over mixed vegetables
Snack: Gluten-free yogurt with ground flaxseed
Dinner: Homemade chili in a baked potato with a salad
Snack: Gluten-free low-fat pudding

Day 16

Breakfast: Blueberry Yogurt Belgian Waffles*
Snack: Melon balls
Lunch: Turkey burger with a sweet potato and mixed greens
Snack: Sliced pears with almond silvers
Dinner: Chicken salad with grapes and gluten-free brown rice crackers
Snack: Soft Pumpkin Chocolate Chip Cookies*

Day 17

Breakfast: Grits with butter and poached eggs
Snack: Toasted corn tortillas with apple butter
Lunch: Macaroni and Cheese with Fire-Roasted Red Peppers*
Snack: Bean salad
Dinner: Turkey Meatloaf* with mashed potatoes and mixed vegetables
Snack: Raisins with string cheese

Day 18

Breakfast: Gluten-free whole grain cereal and low-fat milk
Snack: Gluten-free brown rice crackers with peanut butter
Lunch: Broccoli and Cheese and Rice Pie*
Snack: Gluten-free rice cakes with all-fruit spread
Dinner: Steamed seafood with mussels in garlic butter with Teff Flatbread*
Snack: Blueberries over skim ricotta with honey and cinnamon

Day 19

Breakfast: Carrot Raisin Pineapple Muffins*
Snack: Air-popped popcorn
Lunch: Sliced turkey breast in corn tortillas with coleslaw and mustard
Snack: Olives with roasted peppers

Dinner: Grilled salmon with asparagus and baked potato
Snack: Chocolate Pudding Cake*

Day 20

Breakfast: Scrambled eggs in a gluten-free teff wrap
Snack: Baby carrots and hummus
Lunch: Tuna salad over mixed greens with chick peas
Snack: Gluten-free salsa and corn chips
Dinner: Baked Polenta with Tomato Sauce and Goat Cheese*
Snack: Fresh fruit salad

Day 21

Breakfast: Blueberry Yogurt Belgian Waffles*
Snack: Dried apricots and sliced mozzarella cheese
Lunch: Tomato Vegetable Soup with Quinoa*
Snack: Celery sticks with hummus
Dinner: Grilled cheeseburger served with baked homemade sweet
    potato fries
Snack: Fruit ice

Day 22

Breakfast: Sautéed veggies and tofu scrambled and served with a
    corn tortilla
Snack: Gluten-free trail mix
Lunch: Steamed veggies and black beans with a garlic sauce over
    millet
Snack: Plain yogurt with mixed berries and flaxseed
Dinner: Baked chicken with quinoa and asparagus
Snack: Individual Peach Cobbler*

Day 23

Breakfast: Polenta with Cinnamon Sugar*
Snack: Gluten-free fruit and nut bar
Lunch: Fruit and cheese platter with gluten-free brown rice cakes
Snack: Jell-O
Dinner: Chickpeas and mixed veggies over millet
Snack: Fruit kabobs

Day 24

Breakfast: Spiced Quinoa Cereal*

Snack: Sliced banana with almond butter

Lunch: Shredded beet and carrot salad with tuna and quinoa

Snack: Bean salad

Dinner: Grilled skirt steak and roasted tomatoes with baked
potato

Snack: All-fruit ice pop

Day 25

Breakfast: Feta, tomato, and scrambled eggs with toasted corn tortillas

Snack: Dried plums

Lunch: Turkey and Swiss with shredded lettuce and tomatoes in a
gluten-free teff wrap with yellow mustard

Snack: Arepas with White Bean Pimento Spread*

Dinner: Broiled chicken breast and gluten-free honey mustard sauce
with corn and a mixed green salad

Snack: Low-fat pudding

Day 26

Breakfast: Egg white, broccoli, and cheese omelet with potatoes

Snack: Berries over skim ricotta with cinnamon and honey

Lunch: Toasted Amaranth–Crusted Chicken Salad*

Snack: Gluten-free chocolate soy milk

Dinner: Filet mignon with garlic mashed potatoes and green beans

Snack: Gluten-free ice cream with chopped walnuts

Day 27

Breakfast: French Toast*

Snack: Mixed fruit salad

Lunch: Mixed greens and chopped veggies with shredded cheese,
black beans, and gluten-free dressing

Snack: Baked apple with cinnamon and brown sugar

Dinner: Brown rice pasta with tomato sauce with shrimp and
broccoli

Snack: All-fruit ice pop

Day 28

Breakfast: Citrus Millet Muffin*

Snack: Yogurt with berries

Lunch: Poached salmon over mixed greens with gluten-free dressing

Snack: Gluten-free brown rice crackers with goat cheese and cran-raisins

Dinner: Sage Butter Sautéed Chicken Breasts and Pancetta over Millet* with a mixed green salad

Snack: Poached Pears over Ice Cream with Caramel*

Part Three

Resources

In the following pages, you will find resources for many of the ingredients used in this book's recipes, including whole grains, enriched grains, and other ingredients that sometimes are not gluten-free. To help you simplify your gluten-free lifestyle, additional sources of information are provided, such as useful Web sites, recommended books, and contact information for celiac disease organizations and celiac disease medical centers.

Where to Buy Gluten-Free Whole Grains

Gluten-free grains and flours are widely available in natural food stores, especially large chains such as Whole Foods and Trader Joe's. They are also increasingly being sold in grocery stores. If you are unable to find a particular grain or flour in a local store, you can buy it through a mail-order company. The following companies sell gluten-free grains and flours. Note: This is not an exhaustive list.

Arrowhead Mills

Arrowhead Mills Consumer Relations
The Hain Celestial Group
4600 Sleepytime Drive
Boulder, CO 80301
800-434-4246
www.arrowheadmills.com

> Gluten-free flours and grains from Arrowhead Mills include blue cornmeal (whole grain), buckwheat flour, millet flour, yellow cornmeal (whole grain), amaranth, buckwheat groats, hulled millet, quinoa, long-grain brown rice (whole grain), and brown basmati rice (whole grain).

Authentic Foods

1850 W. 169th Street, Suite B
Gardena, CA 90247
800-806-4737
www.authenticfoods.com

> This company's gluten-free flours include sorghum flour.

Bob's Red Mill Whole Grain Store

5000 S.E. International Way
Milwaukie, OR 97222
800-349-2173
www.bobsredmill.com

Bob's gluten-free flours and grains include buckwheat groats, kasha, hulled millet, millet flour, amaranth flour, amaranth grain, brown rice flour, quinoa flour, quinoa grain, sorghum flour, teff flour, teff grain, rolled oats, steel-cut oats, masa harina, cornmeal, corn flour, and corn grits.

Cream Hill Estates

9633 rue Clement
LaSalle, Quebec
H8R 4B4 Canada
866-727-3628
www.creamhillestates.com

This company's gluten-free flours and grains include rolled oats, oat groats, and oat flour.

Gifts of Nature

810 7th Street E., #17
Polson, MT 59860
888-275-0003
www.giftsofnature.net

The gluten-free grains and flour sold by Gifts of Nature include oats, whole-oat groats, and brown rice flour.

Gluten-Free Oats

578 Lane 9
Powell, WY 82435
307-754-2058
www.glutenfreeoats.com

This company's gluten-free flours and grains include rolled oats.

Lundberg Family Farms

5370 Church Street

P.O. Box 369

Richvale, CA 95974

530-882-4551

Lundberg's gluten-free grains and flours include wild rice, brown rice, and brown rice flour.

Northern Quinoa Corporation

P.O. Box 519

428 3rd Street

Kamsack, Saskatchewan

S0A 1S0 Canada

866-368-9304

www.quinoa.com

The gluten-free grains and flours available from this company include quinoa seeds, quinoa flakes, quinoa flour, rolled quinoa, and black quinoa.

Nu-World Amaranth

P.O. Box 2202

Naperville, IL 60567

630-369-6819

www.nuworldamaranth.com

This company's gluten-free grains and flours include amaranth seeds, amaranth flour, and puffed amaranth.

Only Oats

FarmPure Foods

316 1st Avenue East

Regina, Saskatchewan

S4N 5H2 Canada

866-461-3663

www.onlyoats.com

The gluten-free flours and grains sold by this company include whole oats, steel-cut oats, oat flakes (regular and quick), oat bran, and oat flour.

Shiloh Farms

191 Commerce Drive
New Holland, PA 17557
800-362-6832
www.shilohfarms.com

The gluten-free flours and grains available from Shiloh Farms include whole sorghum grain.

Sunwest Foods

1550 Drew Avenue, Suite 150
Davis, CA 95616
530-758-8550
www.sunwestfoods.com

This company's gluten-free grains include wild rice.

The Birkett Mills

163 Main Street
Penn Yan, NY 14527
315-536-3311
www.thebirkettmills.com

Gluten-free flours and grains sold by the Birkett Mills include whole buckwheat groats, whole buckwheat flour, and kasha.

The Teff Company

P.O. Box A
Caldwell, ID 83606
888-822-2221
www.teffco.com

The Teff Company's gluten-free grains and flours include teff grain and teff flour.

The Quinoa Corporation

P.O. Box 279
Gardena, CA 90248
310-217-8125
www.gluten.net

Gluten-free grains and flours available from the Quinoa Corporation include quinoa grain, quinoa flakes, and quinoa flour.

Twin Valley Mills

RR 1, Box 45
Ruskin, NE 68974
402-279-3965
www.twinvalleymills.com

This company's gluten-free grains and flours include sorghum flour.

Where to Buy Enriched and Fortified Gluten-Free Foods

Only a small number of manufacturers of gluten-free foods enrich their products. Those products that *are* enriched, however, are frequently available in natural food stores and supermarkets that have a natural food section. If you are not able to find these products in your local store, you can mail-order most of them. Note: This is not an exhaustive list.

Astoria Mills

540 Old Harwood Ave.
Ajax, Ontario
L1T 3L1 Canada
905-686-4631
www.astoriamills.ca

Astoria Mills enriches and fortifies its gluten-free flour blends and baking mixes.

Duinkerken Foods Incorporated

57 Watts Avenue
Charlottetown, Prince Edward Island
C1E 2B7 Canada
902-569-3604
www.duinkerkenfoods.com

This company's mixes for bread, cookies, pizza crust, biscuits, waffles, and muffins are enriched.

Ener-G Foods

5960 First Avenue South
Seattle, WA 98124
800-331-5222
www.ener-g.com

Many of the ready-to-eat bread products made by this company are enriched.

Enjoy Life Natural Brands

3810 River Road
Schiller Park, IL 60176
888-503-6569
www.enjoylifefoods.com

The granolas, snack bars, and bagels made by this company are enriched or fortified.

General Mills

P.O. Box 9452
Minneapolis, MN 55440
800-248-7310
www.generalmills.com

Many varieties of Chex ready-to-eat breakfast cereal made by this company are fortified (and gluten-free!). General Mills has unveiled gluten-free Chex cereals in many parts of the country, so keep an eye out for these products when you shop.

Gluten-Free Creations Bakery

2940-b E. Thomas Road
Phoenix, AZ 85016
602-522-0659
www.glutenfreecreations.com

The baked goods made by this company are enriched.

Glutino

P.O. Box 840
Glastonbury, CT 06033
www.glutenfree.com/Glutino

Many Glutino brand ready-to-eat bread products are enriched.

Kinnikinnick Foods

10940-120 Street
Edmonton, Alberta
T5H 3P7 Canada
877-503-4466
www.kinnikinnick.com

Many of the ready-to-eat bread products made by this company are enriched.

Maplegrove Gluten-Free Foods

13112 Santa Ana Avenue, Unit A2-A3
Fontana, CA 92337
909-823-8230
www.maplegrovefoods.com

The Pastato brand potato elbows, potato spaghetti, and potato penne made by this company are fortified.

Perky's Natural Foods

3810 River Road
Schiller Park, IL 60176
888-473-7597
www.perkysnaturalfoods.com

PerkyO's ready-to-eat breakfast cereals, made by this company, are fortified.

Schar, USA

1050 Wall Street West
Suite 203
Lyndhurst, NJ 07071
www.schar.com

Schar enriches some of its gluten-free breads. Watch for enriched pasta products coming soon.

Sources of Other Gluten-Free Ingredients and Products

In addition to gluten-free grains and flours, a few other ingredients, such as almond flour, flaxseed meal, gluten-free pastas, potato starch, and xanthan gum, which are called for in certain recipes in this book, may not be readily available in your local grocery store, although you can find most of them in your natural food store. In addition, some products, such as soy sauce, broths, and Worcestershire sauce, often contain gluten, although gluten-free varieties are available. Sources of these ingredients are provided in this section. Contact information for gluten-free convenience-food items mentioned in this book is listed here as well.

Note: This is not an exhaustive list of all gluten-free brands that are on the market. The product listing was accurate at the time this book went to press; however, manufacturers can change their product formulations at any time. It is very important to read the product labels each time you shop.

Almond Flour/Meal

Authentic Foods

1850 W. 169th Street, Suite B
Gardena, CA 90247
310-366-7612
www.authenticfoods.com

Almond flour may be mail-ordered.

Bob's Red Mill Whole Grain Store

5000 S.E. International Way
Milwaukie, OR 97222
800-349-2173
www.bobsredmill.com

Almond flour may be mail-ordered

Almond Paste

Love n' Bake

www.lovenbake.com

According to the company's Web site, Love n' Bake almond paste is gluten-free. Products may be ordered online.

Solo

800-328-7656
www.solofoods.com

Solo almond paste is free of gluten-containing ingredients. The product can be ordered through amazon.com.

Bars

Andi

www.autismndi.com

According to the firm's Web site, all varieties of Andi bars are gluten-free. Products may be ordered online.

Kind Snacks

www.kindsnacks.com

According to the company's Web site, all Kind bars are gluten-free. Products may be ordered online.

Larabar

www.larabar.com

According to Larabar's Web site, all varieties of Larabars are gluten-free. Products may be ordered online.

Bean Flour

Authentic Foods

1850 W. 169th Street, Suite B
Gardena, CA 90247
800-806-4737
www.authenticfoods.com

Products may be mail-ordered.

Bob's Red Mill Whole Grain Store

5000 S.E. International Way
Milwaukie, OR 97222
800-349-2173
www.bobsredmill.com

Products may be mail-ordered.

Broth/Stock

Imagine Foods

Imagine Consumer Relations
The Hain Celestial Group
4600 Sleepytime Drive
Boulder, CO 80301
800-434-4246
www.imaginefoods.com

Most Imagine Foods broths are gluten-free.

Kitchen Basics

P.O. Box 41022
Brecksville, OH 44141
440-838-1344
www.kitchenbasics.net

According to the company's Web site, all Kitchen Basics broths are gluten-free.

Pacific Foods

19480 SW 97th Avenue
Tualatin, OR 97062
503-692-9666
www.pacificfoods.com

According to the Pacific Foods Web site, all Pacific Foods brand broths are gluten-free.

Progresso

General Mills, Inc.
P.O. Box 9452
Minneapolis, MN 55440
800-446-1898
www.bettycrocker.com/products/progresso-broth/Progresso-broth-products.htm

According to Progresso's Web site, all Progresso broths are gluten-free.

Brown Rice Crackers

Edward & Sons Baked Brown Rice Snaps

Edward & Sons Trading Company, Inc.
P.O. Box 1326
Carpinteria, CA 93014
805-684-8500
www.edwardandsons.com

According to the firm's Web site, all Edward & Sons brown rice snaps are gluten-free. Products may be mail-ordered.

Hol-Grain brown rice crackers

Conrad Rice Mill
P.O. Box 10640
New Iberia, LA 70562
800-551-3245
www.conradricemill.com

Crackers may be mail-ordered.

Mary's Gone Crackers

P.O. Box 965
Gridley, CA 95948
888-258-1250
www.marysgonecrackers.com

Crackers and cracker "crumbs" may be mail-ordered.

Cooking Spray

Pam Cooking Spray

ConAgra Foods, Inc.
P.O. Box 3768, Dept. PAM
Omaha, NE 68103-0768
800-726-4968
www.pam4you.com

According to the company's Web site, Original Pam, Butter Flavor Pam, and Olive Oil Pam are free of ingredients derived from wheat (barley and rye are not mentioned). Pam Baking is not gluten-free—it contains flour.

Some brands of Wegman's cooking sprays are labeled gluten-free. Many other brands appear to be gluten-free, based on their ingredients, such as varieties of Smart Balance, Nature's Promise, and Mazola.

Contact the manufacturers for more information. The source of this ingredient information is Zeer Select (www.zeer.com).

Cornflakes

Barbara's Bakery

3900 Cypress Drive
Petaluma, CA 94954
800-343-0590 x1032
www.barbarasbakery.com

Barbara's products are widely available in natural food stores and may be mail-ordered.

Nature's Path

9100 Van Horne Way
Richmond, British Columbia
V6X 1W3 Canada
888-808-9505
www.naturespath.com

This company's products are widely available in natural food stores.

U.S. Mills

200 Reservoir Street
Needham, MA 02494
781-444-0440
www.usmillsllc.com

U.S. Mills produces gluten-free Erewhon-brand cornflakes. Its products are widely available in natural food stores.

Curry Paste

A Taste of Thai

www.tasteofthai.com

According to this company's Web site, all Taste of Thai products manufactured after October 1, 2008, are gluten-free and carry a gluten-free symbol. The products are widely available in grocery stores and also may be mail-ordered.

Thai Kitchen

www.thaikitchen.com

According to the company's Web site, all Thai Kitchen curry pastes are gluten-free. Thai Kitchen products are widely available in grocery stores.

Dry Mustard

Coleman's dry mustard powder

World Finer Foods, Inc.
300 Broadacres Drive
Bloomfield, NJ 07003
973-338-0300
www.colemansmustard.com

Coleman's dry mustard powder has no gluten-containing ingredients.

McCormick ground mustard

800-474-7742
www.mccormickgourmet.com

McCormick ground mustard has no gluten-containing ingredients. Ground mustard may be mail-ordered.

Flaxseed Meal (Ground Flaxseed)

Bob's Red Mill Whole Grain Store

5000 S.E. International Way
Milwaukie, OR 97222
800-349-2173
www.bobsredmill.com

Flaxseed meal may be mail-ordered.

Frozen Foods

Amy's Kitchen

www.amys.com

Many of Amy's frozen entrees are labeled gluten-free. Amy's products are generally available in grocery stores.

Ian's Natural Foods

www.iansnaturalfoods.com

Ian's makes several gluten-free frozen food products, including chicken nuggets, chicken patties, fish sticks, and pizza. Not all products are gluten-free, so read the labels carefully. Ian's products are available in natural food stores and grocery stores.

My Gluten-Free Café (Hain Celestial)

www.glutenfreechoices.com

This company's entrees include fettuccine Alfredo and pasta primavera. Its products are available in grocery stores.

Nature's Path

www.naturespath.com

This company makes gluten-free frozen waffles. Nature's Path products are available in natural food stores.

Van's Natural Foods

www.vansfoods.com

Van's makes frozen gluten-free waffles, pancakes, and French toast. Not all products are gluten-free, so read the labels carefully. Van's products are available in natural food stores and grocery stores.

Granola

Bakery on Main

2836 Main Street
Glastonbury, CT 06033

860-895-6622
www.bakeryonmain.com

Bakery on Main granola may be mail-ordered.

Enjoy Life Natural Brands

3810 River Road
Schiller Park, IL 60176
888-503-6569
www.enjoylifefoods.com

Enjoy Life Foods Granola generally is available in natural food stores and also may be mail-ordered.

Jessica's Natural Foods

P.O. Box 145
Birmingham, MI 48012
248-723-7118
www.jessicasnaturalfoods.com

Jessica's granola may be mail-ordered.

Masa Harina

Bob's Red Mill Whole Grain Store

5000 S.E. International Way
Milwaukie, OR 97222
800-349-2173
www.bobsredmill.com

Masa harina may be mail-ordered.

Pasta

Note: **Eden Foods** (www.edenfoods.com) does not include its 100% buckwheat noodles among its gluten-free products, although the product does not have any gluten-containing ingredients. Contact the company for more information about this product.

Food Directions, Inc. (Tinkyada)

120 Melford Drive, Unit 8
Scarborough, Ontario
M1B 2X5 Canada
www.tinkyada.com

This company manufactures Tinkyada brown rice pastas, which are widely available in natural food stores.

Glutino Food Group

2055 Boulevard Dagenais, Ouest
Laval, QC
H7L 5V1 Canada
800-363-3438
www.glutino.com

This company manufactures Glutino-brand brown rice pastas, which may be mail-ordered.

King Soba Noodles

www.kingsoba.com

King Soba's 100% buckwheat noodles are labeled gluten-free. These noodles are manufactured in the United Kingdom. Currently, there is limited distribution in the United States, but there are plans to increase availability. For retail sources in your area, e-mail the company through the contact page on its Web site.

Lundberg Family Farms

5370 Church Street
P.O. Box 369
Richvale, CA 95974
530-882-4551

This company manufactures Lundberg Farms–brand brown rice pastas.

Orgran

www.orgran.com

This company makes pastas from amaranth and quinoa. Its products may be ordered online.

Quinoa Corporation (Ancient Harvest)

P.O. Box 279
Gardena, CA 90248
310-217-8125
www.quinoa.net

This company manufactures Ancient Harvest–brand quinoa/corn pastas, which are widely available in natural food stores.

Potato Starch

Bob's Red Mill Whole Grain Store

5000 S.E. International Way
Milwaukie, OR 97222
800-349-2173
www.bobsredmill.com

Potato starch may be mail-ordered.

Gifts of Nature

810 7th Street E., #17
Polson, MT 59860
888-275-0003
www.giftsofnature.net

Potato starch may be mail-ordered.

Soups

Kettle Cuisine

www.kettlecuisine.com

All Kettle Cuisine single-serving frozen soups are gluten-free. Find them in the freezer section of your natural food store or grocery store.

Simply Asia

www.simplyasia.com

Simply Asia makes a few gluten-free rice noodle soup bowls. Many products are not gluten-free, so read the labels carefully. Its products may be ordered online.

Thai Kitchen

www.thaikitchen.com

Many, but not all, of Thai Kitchen's soups and noodle bowls are labeled gluten-free, so read the labels carefully. Thai Kitchen products are widely available in natural food stores and grocery stores.

Soy/Tamari sauce

Eden Foods, Inc.

701 Tecumseh Road
Clinton, MI 49236
888-424-3336
www.edenfoods.com

According to the company's Web site, Eden Foods brand organic tamari soy sauce, brewed in the United States, is gluten-free. Its products may be ordered online.

San-J International, Inc.

2880 Sprouse Drive
Richmond, VA 23231
800-446-5500
www.san-j.com

According to the company's Web site, both the organic wheat-free tamari and the organic wheat-free, reduced-sodium tamari are gluten-free. Its products may be ordered online.

Note: There are other soy and tamari sauces that appear to be gluten-free, based on their listed ingredients. These products include

La Choy soy sauce, IGA soy sauce, Hy-Vee soy sauce, Roundy's soy sauce, Market Pantry lite soy sauce, and Spartan soy sauce. Contact the manufacturers for more information. The source of the ingredient information is Zeer Select (www.zeer.com).

Tapioca Flour/Starch

Bob's Red Mill Whole Grain Store

5000 S.E. International Way
Milwaukie, OR 97222
800-349-2173
www.bobsredmill.com

> Bob's Red Mill calls this tapioca flour—it is the same thing as tapioca starch. It may be mail-ordered.

Gifts of Nature

810 7th Street E., #17
Polson, MT 59860
888-275-0003
www.giftsofnature.net

> Gifts of Nature refers to tapioca starch as tapioca flour—they are the same thing. It may be mail-ordered.

Tortillas

La Tortilla Factory

www.latortillafactory.com

> This company makes two gluten-free tortilla wraps, from teff and millet. Its products are widely available in grocery stores.

Mission Foods

www.missionfoods.com

> Mission-brand corn tortillas are labeled gluten-free. These tortillas are widely available in grocery stores.

Worcestershire Sauce

Lea and Perrins

www.leaperrins.com

According to the company's Web site, Lea and Perrins Worcestershire sauce is gluten-free.

Note: There are other Worcestershire sauces that appear to be gluten-free, based on their listed ingredients, such as French's, Safeway, Meijer, Bulliard's, and Hy-Vee brands. Contact the manufacturers for more information. The source of the ingredient information is Zeer Select (www.zeer.com).

Xanthan Gum

Authentic Foods

1850 W. 169th Street, Suite B
Gardena, CA 90247
310-366-7612
www.authenticfoods.com

Xanthan gum may be mail-ordered.

Bob's Red Mill Whole Grain Store

5000 S.E. International Way
Milwaukie, OR 97222
800-349-2173
www.bobsredmill.com

Xanthan gum may be mail-ordered.

Helpful Web Sites

Following are some Web sites that contain helpful information about celiac disease, the gluten-free diet, food labeling, and healthful eating.

FDA Food Labeling

Food Allergen Labeling and Consumer Protection Act of 2004

www.fda.gov/Food/LabelingNutrition/FoodAllergensLabeling/
GuidanceComplianceRegulatoryInformation/ucm106187.htm

**Federal Register Proposed Rule—72 FR 2795, January 23, 2007:
Food Labeling; Gluten-Free Labeling of Foods**

www.fda.gov/Food/LabelingNutrition/FoodAllergensLabeling/
GuidanceComplianceRegulatoryInformation/ucm077926.htm

**Questions and Answers on the Gluten-Free Labeling Proposed
Rule**

www.fda.gov/Food/LabelingNutrition/FoodAllergensLabeling/
GuidanceComplianceRegulatoryInformation/ucm111487.htm

USDA Food Labeling

**Questions and Answers Related to Ingredients of Public Health
Concern**

www.fsis.usda.gov/regulations_&_policies/FAQs_for_Notice_45-
05/index.asp

Labeling of USDA-Regulated Foods

www.diet.com/dietblogs/read_blog.php?title=Labeling+of+USD
A-Regulated+Foods&blid=17330&sh=1

Interview with USDA on allergen labeling.

Alcohol Labeling

**Major food allergen labeling for wines, distilled spirits, and malt
beverages: proposed rule**

http://edocket.access.gpo.gov/2006/pdf/06-6467.pdf

Gluten-Free Living

Authors' Web Sites

www.glutenfreedietitian.com
www.glutenfreeeasy.com

"Celiac Disease vs. Gluten Sensitivity"

www.diet.com/dietblogs/read_blog.php?blid=11838&title=Celiac+
Disease+vs.+Gluten+Sensitivity

An interview with Dr. Alessio Fasano, the medical director of the University of Maryland Center for Celiac Research.

"The Celiac Disease Lactose Intolerant Connection"

www.diet.com/dietblogs/read_blog.php?title=The+Celiac+
Disease-Lactose+Intolerant+Connection&blid+12641

This Web page from diet.com includes an interview with Dr. Stefano Guandalini, the director of the University of Chicago Celiac Disease Center.

Dermatitis Herpetiformis

www.gluten.net/downloads/print/DHflat.pdf

This is a Web page from the Gluten Intolerance Group on Dermatitis Herpetiformis.

Dietary Guidelines for Americans

www.health.gov/DietaryGuidelines

This is a Web page of the U.S. Department of Health and Human Services. The Dietary Guidelines for Americans, 2005, as well as other educational materials, can be accessed from this site.

European Food Safety Authority

www.aaf-eu.org/PDF/Statement_on_permanent_exemption_
obtained_for_allergen_labelling_11-2007.pdf

This is a Web page of the European Starch Association. It contains information regarding the permanent exemption from allergen labeling of wheat-based maltodextrins, glucose syrups, and dextrose.

"Gluten-Free Allergen Advisory Labeling"
www.diet.com/dietblogs/read_blog.php?title=Gluten-Free%3A+Allergen+Advisory+Labeling&blid=12433

Living Gluten-Free
www.diet.com/dietblogs/read_blog_expert.php?uid=926693

National Institutes of Health
http://consensus.nih.gov/2004/2004CeliacDisease118html.htm

This link contains the National Institutes of Health Consensus Development Conference Statement on Celiac Disease.

http://digestive.niddk.nih.gov/ddiseases/pubs/celiac/

This is a Web page of the National Institutes of Health on celiac disease.

Whole Grains Council
www.wholegrainscouncil.org

This site contains an abundance of information, including a section on gluten-free whole grains.

Celiac Disease Organizations

All of the following organizations contain helpful information on their Web sites.

American Celiac Disease Alliance (ACDA)
http://americanceliac.org

The ACDA is an advocacy group for the celiac disease community.

Celiac Disease Foundation (CDF)
www.celiac.org

The CDF is a national support group for people with celiac disease and dermatitis herpetiformis and their families.

Celiac Sprue Association (CSA)

www.csaceliacs.org

The CSA is a national support group for people with celiac disease and dermatitis herpetiformis.

Gluten Intolerance Group (GIG)

www.gluten.net

GIG is a national support group for people with celiac disease, dermatitis herpetiformis, and other gluten sensitivities.

Gluten-Free Certification Organization (GFCO)

www.gfco.org

The GFCO is a gluten-free food certification program. It is run by the Gluten Intolerance Group.

Gluten-Free Restaurant Awareness Program (GFRAP)

www.glutenfreerestaurants.org

The GFRAP works with restaurants to create gluten-free meals for patrons. It is a run by the Gluten Intolerance Group.

National Foundation for Celiac Disease Awareness

www.celiaccentral.org.

The NFCA was founded to help increase awareness of celiac disease.

Celiac Disease Medical Centers

Celiac Disease Center at Columbia University

www.celiacdiseasecenter.columbia.edu

University of Maryland Center for Celiac Research

www.celiaccenter.org

Celiac Disease Center: Beth Israel Deaconess Medical Center

http://www.bidmc.org/CentersandDepartments/Departments/
DigestiveDiseaseCenter/CeliacDiseaseCenter.aspx

University of Chicago Celiac Disease Center

www.celiacdisease.net

Wm. K. Warren Medical Research Center for Celiac Disease

http://celiaccenter.ucsd.edu

Kogan Celiac Center of the Saint Barnabas Health Care System

www.saintbarnabas.com/SERVICES/celiac/index.html

Additional Reading

There is an abundance of books dealing with the gluten-free diet and celiac disease, including general information books and cookbooks. Listed in this section is only a sampling of the available books. For a more complete listing, go to amazon.com and, under "Books," type "gluten-free" in the search engine.

Adamson, Eve, and Tricia Thompson. *The Complete Idiot's Guide to Gluten-Free Eating.* New York: Penguin, 2007.

Ahern, Shauna James. *Gluten-Free Girl: How I Found the Food That Loves Me Back . . . And How You Can, Too.* Hoboken, NJ: Wiley, 2007.

Bower, Sylvia Llewelyn, Mary Kay Sharrett, and Steve Plogsted. *Celiac Disease: A Guide to Living with Gluten Intolerance.* New York: Demos Medical Publishing, 2006.

Brown, Marlisa. *Gluten-Free, Hassle Free: A Simple, Sane, Dietitian-Approved Program for Eating Your Way Back to Health.* New York: Demos, 2009.

Case, Shelley. *Gluten-Free Diet: A Comprehensive Resource Guide—Expanded and Revised Edition.* Case Nutrition Consulting, 2008.

Coppedge Jr., Richard J., and George Chookazian. *Gluten-Free Baking with the Culinary Institute of America: 150 Flavorful Recipes from the World's Premier Culinary College.* Avon, MA: Adams Media, 2008.

Dennis, Melinda and Daniel A. Leffler. *Real Life with Celiac Disease: Troubleshooting and Thriving Gluten Free*. Bethesda, MD: AGA Press, 2010.

Falini, Nancy. *Gluten-Free Friends: An Activity Book for Kids*. Centennial, CO: Savory Palate, Inc., 2003.

Fenster, Carol. *1,000 Gluten-Free Recipes*. Hoboken, NJ: Wiley, 2008.

Green, Peter H. R., and Rory Jones. *Celiac Disease (Revised and Updated Edition): A Hidden Epidemic*. New York: HarperCollins, 2010.

Klein, Donna. *The Gluten-Free Vegetarian Kitchen: Delicious and Nutritious Gluten-Free Dishes*. New York: HP Trade, 2007.

Mallorca, Jacqueline. *The Wheat-Free Cook: Gluten-Free Recipes for Everyone*. New York: William Morrow Cookbooks, 2007.

O'Brien, Susan. *The Gluten-Free Vegan: 150 Delicious Gluten-Free, Animal-Free Recipes*. Cambridge, MA: Da Capo Press, 2007.

The Essential Gluten-Free Grocery Guide, 2nd ed. Arlington, VA: Triumph Dining Gluten Free, 2008.

The Essential Gluten-Free Restaurant Guide, 2nd ed. Arlington, VA: Triumph Dining Gluten Free, 2007.

Thompson, Tricia. *Celiac Disease Nutrition Guide*, 2nd ed. Chicago, IL: American Dietetic Association, 2006.

————. *The Gluten-Free Nutrition Guide*. New York: McGraw-Hill, 2008.

Glossary

Alcohol and Tobacco Tax Trade Bureau
A governmental agency that, among many other things, regulates the labeling of malt beverages, wine, and distilled spirits.

allergen advisory statements
A voluntary statement you may see on food labels that concerns the manufacturing process. Examples include "made in a facility that also manufactures products containing soy and gluten" and "produced in a facility that uses wheat, milk, soy, almonds, pecans, and hazelnuts." These statements are not related to the Food Allergen Labeling and Consumer Protection Act and currently are not regulated by the Food and Drug Administration.

amaranth
A gluten-free seed that is often called a pseudocereal because it is used like a true grain.

autoimmune disease
A condition in which the immune system attacks itself, causing damage to the body, when it comes in contact with something it perceives to be harmful.

blue cheese

A type of cheese containing blue mold spores of a type that sometimes may be grown on gluten-containing media. These are purified mold spores in blue cheese, however, and the likelihood that they contain intact gluten protein is low. In our opinion, blue cheese is safe for you to eat unless the label contains the words "wheat," "barley," "rye," "oats," or "malt," or the company states that its product is not gluten-free. For a more complete discussion of blue cheese, see http://glutenfreedietitian.com/newsletter/?page_id=25.

brewer's yeast

A type of yeast that may be a by-product of beer brewing and as a result may be contaminated with malt and grain. At this time, it is recommended that you avoid products containing brewer's yeast.

buckwheat

A gluten-free seed that is often called a pseudocereal because it is used like a true grain.

caramel

A color additive made from the heat treatment of dextrose, invert sugar, lactose, malt syrup, molasses, starch hydrolysates, or sucrose. If caramel is an ingredient in an FDA-regulated food and it contains protein from wheat, the word "wheat" must be included on the food label. In USDA-regulated foods, caramel may contain wheat protein and the word "wheat" may not be included on the food label. Nonetheless, even if caramel is derived from wheat or barley, it is unlikely to contain much (if any) gluten protein. In our opinion, you do not need to worry about the ingredient caramel.

celiac disease

A genetically based autoimmune reaction to gluten. The only treatment for celiac disease is a lifelong gluten-free diet.

cross-contact

The contamination of one product with ingredients from another product.

current good manufacturing practice

A quality control system used by manufacturers to ensure that food has been prepared under safe and sanitary conditions.

dermatitis herpetiformis (DH)

The skin form of celiac disease. The treatment for DH includes a lifelong gluten-free diet.

dextrin

An incompletely hydrolyzed starch that may be made from corn, waxy maize, waxy milo, potato, arrowroot, wheat, rice, tapioca, or sago starches. If dextrin is used as an ingredient in an FDA-regulated food product and it contains wheat protein, the word "wheat" will be included on the food label. In USDA-regulated foods, dextrin may contain wheat protein and the word "wheat" may not be included on the food label.

durum

A type of wheat.

einkorn

A type of wheat.

emmer

A type of wheat.

enriched

In terms of grain foods, "enriched" means that vitamins and minerals that were removed along with the bran and the germ when the grain was refined are later added back to the food.

FALCPA

Food Allergen Labeling and Consumer Protection Act. This act took effect on January 1, 2006 and stipulates how major food allergens must be identified on the labels of packaged food products regulated by the Food and Drug Administration.

fatty acid

Fats are composed of three groups of fatty acids—saturated, polyunsaturated, and monounsaturated—and are classified as one or the other based on the predominant fatty acid they contain.

flavorings

According to the Code of Federal Regulations, natural flavoring may be derived from a spice, a fruit, a vegetable, an edible yeast, an herb, a bark, a bud, a root, a leaf or similar plant material, a meat, a seafood, poultry, eggs, or dairy products. If natural flavoring is an ingredient in an FDA-regulated food product and it contains protein from wheat, the word "wheat" will be included on the food label. In a USDA-regulated food product, if a flavoring contains protein, the protein source must be listed in the ingredient list by its common or usual name.

flaxseed (also known as linseed)

The seed of the herb flax. Flaxseed is increasingly being added to gluten-free foods as a source of fiber, as well as omega-3 fatty acids.

Food and Drug Administration

A government agency that, among many other things, regulates the labeling of all packaged food products, with the exception of egg products, meat products, and poultry products.

fortified

In terms of food products, "fortified" means that one or more vitamins or minerals have been added to the product. The particular nutrient(s) may or may not have been found in the food naturally.

glucose syrup

Partially hydrolyzed corn starch. Other starches, such as wheat starch, may also be used to make glucose syrup. If glucose syrup is an ingredient in an FDA-regulated food and it contains wheat protein, the word "wheat" will be included on the food label. In USDA-regulated foods, glucose syrup may contain wheat protein, and the word "wheat" may not be included on the food label. Nonetheless, glucose syrup is unlikely to contain significant amounts of gluten protein. In our opinion, you do not need to worry about the ingredient glucose syrup.

gluten

In the context of celiac disease and non-celiac gluten sensitivity, gluten is a protein found in wheat, barley, and rye.

gluten-free

In the United States (under the FDA's proposed labeling rules), "gluten-free" means that a product does not contain any wheat, barley, or rye and that any ingredients derived from these grains have been processed to remove gluten and the final food product contains less than 20 parts per million of gluten.

gluten-free oats

Oats that have been grown, harvested, and processed under carefully controlled conditions to decrease or eliminate cross-contact with wheat, barley, and rye. By definition (under the FDA's proposed labeling rules), gluten-free oats must contain less than 20 parts per million of gluten.

kasha

Roasted buckwheat groats.

lactose intolerance

A reduced ability to digest the milk sugar lactose, due to a decrease in the enzyme lactase. Individuals with celiac disease often have a temporary form of lactose intolerance caused by shortening of the intestinal villi (lactase is found on the tips of the villi). Once the intestines have healed, this form of lactose intolerance generally resolves.

low nutrient density

If a food is calorie-rich and nutrient-poor, it is said to have a low nutrient density. For example, a 100-calorie serving of Pepsi has a much lower nutrient density than a 100-calorie serving of cooked squash.

low density lipoprotein cholesterol (LDL)

A type of cholesterol that is often produced by diets that are high in saturated fat. A high level of LDL cholesterol in the blood is associated with an increased risk of heart disease. Diets that consist primarily of polyunsaturated and monounsaturated fats may contribute to low levels of LDL cholesterol in the blood.

malt

A liquid or a powder made from barley.

maltodextrin

Partially hydrolyzed corn starch, rice starch, or potato starch. Wheat starch also may be used to make maltodextrin. If maltodextrin is an ingredient in an FDA-regulated food and it contains protein from wheat, the word "wheat" must be included on the food label. In USDA-regulated foods, maltodextrin may contain wheat protein and the word "wheat" may not be included on the food label. Regardless, maltodextrin is unlikely to contain significant amounts of gluten protein. In our opinion, you do not need to worry about the ingredient maltodextrin.

millet

A gluten-free grain.

modified food starch

A food additive that is modified through treatment with acids, bleaching agents, oxidizing agents, esterifying agents, or enzymes. Modified food starch may be made from wheat starch. If modified food starch is an ingredient in an FDA-regulated food and it contains wheat protein, the word "wheat" will be included on the food label. In USDA-regulated foods, modified food starch may contain wheat protein and the word "wheat" may not be included on the food label.

non-celiac gluten sensitivity

Currently considered a nonautoimmune, nonallergic immune reaction to gluten. The treatment for non-celiac gluten sensitivity is a gluten-free diet.

organic

Foods may carry voluntary USDA "organic" labels if they are made from at least 95 percent organic ingredients. If they are made from all organic ingredients, they may carry a "100% organic" label. To qualify for organic, ingredients must meet standards established by the USDA.

parts per million

A proportion that measures how many milligrams out of a kilogram contain a contaminant such as gluten. If a food contains 20 parts per million of gluten, it contains 20 milligrams of gluten in 1 kilogram of food. This is the same as 0.002 percent gluten.

potato starch

A gluten-free starch made from potatoes. This is not the same as potato flour which is ground from whole potatoes.

plant taxonomy

A system for classifying plants that illustrates how closely various plants are related.

pseudocereals

The term that is sometimes used to describe amaranth, buckwheat, and quinoa. These foods are not true cereal grains but are frequently referred to as grains because their seeds are used in baking and cooking in a manner similar to grains.

quinoa
A gluten-free seed that is often called a pseudocereal because it is used like a true grain.

refined grain
A grain food that has had the germ and the bran removed and that contains only the endosperm.

sorghum
A gluten-free grain.

soy sauce
An Asian sauce that typically contains wheat, although gluten-free varieties are available.

spelt
A type of wheat. For a more in-depth discussion of spelt, see www.diet.com/dietblogs/read_blog.php?title=Gluten-Free%3F+Spelt+Is+Wheat . . . +Don%92t+Eat%21&blid=14473.

starch hydrolysate
Starch that has been partially broken down into smaller chains of molecules.

stock (vegetable, chicken, beef)
This ingredient sometimes contains wheat or barley, so check labels carefully.

tamari
An Asian sauce that sometimes contains wheat, so check labels carefully.

tapioca starch
A gluten-free starch from the cassava plant.

teff
A gluten-free grain.

triticale
A hybrid grain that is a cross between wheat and rye.

United States Department of Agriculture

A government agency that, among many other things, regulates the labeling of egg products, meat products, and poultry products.

vegan diet

A diet that does not include any animal products, including eggs, milk, and any ingredients derived from animal products, such as honey and gelatin.

vegetarian diet

A diet that does not include meat, poultry, and fish.

wheat-free

If a product is labeled "wheat-free," it means that none of the ingredients used to make the product, including incidental additives, contain wheat protein.

wheat starch

The starch portion of wheat grain. Although most of the protein has been removed, a small amount remains. Under proposed gluten-free labeling rules, a food labeled "gluten-free" may contain wheat starch as long as the final food product has less than 20 parts per million of gluten.

whole grain

A grain food that consists of all three parts of the grain seed, namely, the germ, the bran, and the endosperm.

wild rice

A gluten-free grain. Despite its name, it is not "true" rice, although it is used like rice.

Worcestershire sauce

This condiment may contain soy sauce, which typically is made with some wheat. There are gluten-free Worcestershire sauces available.

xanthan gum

An additive that is frequently added to gluten-free foods to improve the texture and the mouth-feel and to act as a thickener.

Bibliography

Alcohol and Tobacco Tax Trade Bureau, U.S. Department of the Treasury. "Classification of Brewed Products as 'Beer' under the Internal Revenue Code of 1986 and 'Malt Beverages' under the Federal Alcohol Administration Act," TTB ruling number 2008-3, July 7, 2008, www.ttb.gov/rulings/2008.3.pdf.

————. Code of Federal Regulations Title 27 (Alcohol, Tobacco Products, and Firearms), Parts 4, 5, and 7, www.access.gpo.gov/nara/cfr/waisdix_03/27cfrvl_03.html.

————. "Major Food Allergen Labeling for Wines, Distilled Spirits, and Malt Beverages (Notice of Proposed Rulemaking)," 27 CFR Parts 4, 5, and 7 (Notice No. 62), http://edocket.access.gpo.gov/2006/pdf/06-6467.pdf.

————. "The Beverage Alcohol Manual: A Practical Guide: Basic Mandatory Labeling Information for Distilled Spirits," vol. 2, www.ttb.gov/spirits/bam.shtml.

American Academy of Pediatrics. "Children's Health Topics: Vitamin D," www.aap.org/healthtopics/vitamind.cfm.

American Dietetic Association. "Celiac Disease: Evidence Based Nutrition Practice Guideline," www.adaevidencelibrary.com/topic.cfm?cat=3677&library=EBG.

Bardella MT, Fredella C, Prampolini L, Molteni N, Giunta AM, and Bianchi PA. "Body composition and dietary intakes in adult celiac disease patients consuming a strict gluten-free diet," *Am J Clin Nutr* 72 (2000): 937–939.

Catassi C, Fabiani E, Iacono G, D'Agate C, Francavilla R, Biagi F, Volta U, Accomando S, Picarelli A, De Vitis I, Pianelli G, Gesuita R, Carle F, Mandolesi A, Bearzi I, and Fasano A. "A prospective, double-blind, placebo-controlled trial to establish a safe gluten threshold for patients with celiac disease," *Am J Clin Nutr* 85 (2007): 1660–1666.

Center for Food Safety and Applied Nutrition, Food and Drug Administration. Food Allergen Labeling and Consumer Protection Act of 2004 (Title II of Public Law 108-282), www.cfsan.fda.gov/~dms/alrgact.html.

European Food Safety Authority. "Permanent exemption obtained for 'allergen labelling' of wheat-based maltodextrin, glucose syrups, dextrose," www.aaf-eu.org/PDF/Statement_on_permanent_exemption_obtained_for_allergen_labelling_11-2007.pdf.

Food and Drug Administration. Code of Federal Regulations, www.gpoaccess.gov/cfr/retrieve.html.

———. "Food Labeling: Nutrient Content Claims, Definition of Term: Healthy," Code of Federal Regulations (21 CFR Part 101) [Docket Nos. 91N–384H and 95P–0241], RIN 0910–AA19, www.fda.gov/ohrms/dockets/98fr/032598c.pdf.

———. "Report to the US Senate and the US House of Representatives. July 2006" (discussion of cross-contact with food allergens), Food Allergen Labeling and Consumer Protection Act of 2004 (Title II of Public Law 108-282), www.cfsan.fda.gov/~acrobat/alrgrep.pdf.

———. "Food Labeling: Gluten-Free Labeling of Food, Proposed Rule," 21 CFR Part 101, Docket No. 2005N-0279, Federal Register 72(14) (January 23, 2007), www.cfsan.fda.gov/~lrd/fr070123.html.

Hopman EGD, le Cessie S, von Blomberg BME, and Mearin MC. "Nutritional management of the gluten-free diet in young people with celiac disease in the Netherlands," *J Pediatr Gastroenterol Nutr* 43 (2006): 102–108.

Kasarda DD. "Toxic cereal grains in coeliac disease," in Feighery C and O'Farrelly C, editors, "Gastrointestinal Immunology and Gluten-Sensitive

Disease (Proceedings of the Sixth International Symposium on Coeliac Disease)," Dublin, Ireland: Oak Tree Press, 1994, pp. 203–220.

———. "Gluten and gliadin (precipitating factors in coeliac disease)," in Maki M, Collin P, and Visakorpi JK, editors, "Coeliac Disease (Proceedings of the Seventh International Symposium on Coeliac Disease)," Tampere, Finland: Coeliac Disease Study Group, 1997, pp. 195–212.

Lichtenstein AH, Appel LJ, Brands M, Carnethon M, et al. "Diet and lifestyle recommendations revision 2006: A scientific statement from the American Heart Association Nutrition Committee," *Circulation* 114 (2006): 82–96, http://circ.ahajournals.org/cgi/reprint/CIRCULATIONAHA.106.176158.

Mariani P, Viti MG, Montuori M, La Vecchia A, Cipolletta E, Calvani L, and Bonamico M. "The gluten-free diet: A nutritional risk factor for adolescents with celiac disease?" *JPGN* 27 (1998): 519–523.

National Academy of Sciences. *Lost Crops of Africa: Volume 1: Grains* (1996), chapter 4, "Pearl Millet," http:nap.edu/openbook/0309049903/html/127/html.

———. *Lost Crops of Africa: Volume 1: Grains* (1996), chapter 7, "Sorghum," http:nap.edu/openbook/0309049903/html/77/html.

———. *Lost Crops of Africa: Volume 1: Grains* (1996), chapter 12, "Tef," http:nap.edu/openbook/0309049903/html/215/html.

National Institutes of Health Consensus Development Program. "Consensus Development Conference Statement," NIH Consensus Development Conference on Celiac Disease, June 28–30, 2004, http://consensus.nih.gov/2004/2004CeliacDisease118html.htm.

National Osteoporosis Foundation. "Prevention: Vitamin D," www.nof.org/prevention/vitaminD.htm.

"Position of the American Dietetic Association: Vegetarian Diets," *J Am Diet Assoc* 109 (2009): 1266–1282.

Tatham AS, et al. "Characterization of the major prolamins of tef and finger millet," *Journal of Cereal Science* 24 (1996): 65–71.

Thompson T. "Folate, iron, and fiber contents of the gluten-free diet," *J Am Diet Assoc* 100 (2000): 1389–1396.

———. "Gluten contamination of commercial oat products in the United States," *N Engl J Med* 351 (2004): 2021–2022.

———, Dennis M, Higgins LA, Lee AR, and Sharrett MK. "Gluten-free diet survey: Are Americans with coeliac disease consuming recommended amounts of fibre, iron, calcium and grain foods?" *J Hum Nutr Diet* 18 (2005): 163–169.

———. "Thiamin, riboflavin, and niacin contents of the gluten-free diet: Is there cause for concern?" *J Am Diet Assoc* 99 (1999): 858–862.

———. "Questionable foods and the gluten-free diet: Survey of current recommendations," *J Am Diet Assoc* 100 (2000): 463–465.

Thompson, Tricia. "Celiac Disease vs Gluten Sensitivity," Diet.com, www .diet.com/dietblogs/read_blog.php?blid=11838&title=Celiac+Disease +vs.+Gluten+Sensitivity.

Agricultural Research Service, U.S. Department of Agriculture. "National Nutrient Database for Standard Reference, Release 19 (2006)," www.nal .usda.gov/fnic/foodcomp/search/.

Food Safety and Inspection Service, United States Department of Agriculture. "Food Safety: Natural Flavorings on Meat and Poultry Labels. Help: Common Questions," www.fsis.usda.gov/Help/FAQs_Flavorings/index .asp.

———. "Questions and Answers Related to Ingredients of Public Health Concern," www.fsis.usda.gov/regulations_&_policies/FAQs_for_ Notice_45-05/index.asp.

———. "Verification of Activities Related to an Establishment's Controls for the Use of Ingredients of Public Health Concern," FSIS Notice 45-05, www.fsis.usda.gov/regulations_&_policies/Notice_45-05/index.asp.

University of Missouri Extension. "Buckwheat: A multi-purpose short-season alternative," http://extension.missouri.edu/xplor/agguides/crops/g04306 .htm.

University of Wisconsin Extension and the University of Minnesota. *Alternative Field Crop Manual*, "Amaranth," www.hort.purdue.edu/new crop/afcm/amaranth.html.

———. *Alternative Field Crop Manual*, "Buckwheat," www.hort.purdue. edu/newcrop/afcm/buckwheat.html.

———. *Alternative Field Crop Manual,* "Quinoa," www.hort.purdue.edu/newcrop/afcm/quinoa.html.

———. *Alternative Field Crop Manual,* "Wild Rice," www.hort.purdue.edu/newcrop/afcm/wildrice.html.

U.S. Department of Health and Human Services. "Dietary Guidelines for Americans, 2005," www.health.gov/dietaryguidelines/dga2005/document/.

Whole Grains Council. "Definition of whole grains," www.wholegrainscouncil.org/whole-grains-101/definition-of-whole-grains.

Recipe Index

Subject Index